THE MIDDLE LEVEL TEACHERS' HANDBOOK

ABOUT THE AUTHORS

Gilbert Harrison Hunt holds Ph.D. and M.A. degrees from the University of North Carolina (1975, 1971) and the B.S. degree from Campbell University (1969). He is Professor and Chair of the Professional Program in Teacher Education at Coastal Carolina University, Conway, South Carolina. Dr. Hunt taught at the middle level with the Harnet County, North Carolina, public school system. He is co-author of *Effective Teaching: Preparation and Implementation*, author of numerous articles in professional journals, and is a member of Phi Delta Kappa, Kappa Delta Pi, National Middle School and Association, and Association of Teacher Educators.

Dennis Gene Wiseman holds Ph.D. and M.A. degrees from the University of Illinois (1974, 1970) and the B.A. degree from the University of Indianapolis (1969). He is Professor and Dean of the School of Education and Graduate Studies at Coastal Carolina University, Conway, South Carolina. His teaching specialization areas are curriculum and instruction, social studies education, and educational psychology. Dr. Wiseman has taught with both the Champaign, Illinois, and Indianapolis, Indiana, public school systems. He is co-author of *Effective Teaching: Preparation and Implementation,* author of numerous articles in professional journals, and actively involved in collaboration activities between K-12 and higher education.

Sandra Pope Bowden holds a Ph.D. degree in Secondary Education and M.A. and B.A. degrees in English from the University of South Carolina (1979, 1973, 1966) and is a graduate of the Harvard Institute for School Leadership (1995). She is Associate Professor and Associate Dean of the School of Education and Graduate Studies at Coastal Carolina University, Conway, South Carolina. Dr. Bowden taught in grades seven through twelve in Lexington District 1 and in Lexington/Richland District 5 in Columbia, South Carolina, and taught English and speech methods and multicultural education courses at Louisiana State University in Baton Rouge. Dr. Bowden directs the Center for Middle Level Initiatives at Coastal Carolina University.

THE MIDDLE LEVEL TEACHERS' HANDBOOK

Becoming A Reflective Practitioner

By

GILBERT HUNT, PH.D.

DENNIS WISEMAN, PH.D.

SANDRA BOWDEN, PH.D.

Coastal Carolina University
Conway, South Carolina

CHARLES C THOMAS • PUBLISHER, LTD.
Springfield • Illinois • U.S.A.

Published and Distributed Throughout the World by
CHARLES C THOMAS • PUBLISHER, LTD.
2600 South First Street
Springfield, Illinois 62794-9265

©1998 by CHARLES C THOMAS • PUBLISHER, LTD.
ISBN 0-398-06831-3 (cloth)
ISBN 0-398-06832-1 (paper)

Library of Congress Catalog Card Number: 97-37556

With THOMAS BOOKS *careful attention is given to all details of manufacturing
and design. It is the Publisher's desire to present books that are satisfactory as to their
physical qualities and artistic possibilities and appropriate for their particular use.*
THOMAS BOOKS *will be true to those laws of quality that assure a good name
and good will.*

Printed in the United States of America
SM-R-3

Library of Congress Cataloging-in-Publication Data

Hunt, Gilbert
    The middle level teachers' handbook : becoming a reflective practi-
tioner/by Gilbert Hunt, Dennis Wiseman, Sandra Bowden
  p.   cm.
    Includes bibliographical references and index
    ISBN 0-398-06831-3 (cloth)   ISBN 0-398-06832-1 (pbk.)
    1. Middle school teachers--United States--Handbooks, manuals, etc.
    2. Middle school --United States--Handbooks, manuals, etc.
    3. Middle school teaching--United States--Handbooks, manuals,etc.
    I. Wiseman, Dennis. II. Bowden, Sandra. III. Title
LB1776.5.H85 1998
372. 1102--dc21   97-37556
                                     CIP

PREFACE

For the last few years, the state of South Carolina, as has been the case with many other states, has wrestled with numerous policy initiatives aimed at the licensing of teachers specifically to teach ten-to-fourteen-year-olds at the middle level. As teacher educators who have worked in partnerships with middle schools in the South Carolina Center for Middle Level Initiatives at this university, we have sought to incorporate the best practice of an elementary school and a secondary school teacher education program into a specialized middle level teacher preparation program for undergraduate students who are preparing to teach and for graduate students who are currently teaching. The perceptive observation by C. K. McEwin in Judith L. Irvin's, *Transforming Middle Level Education: Perspectives and Possibilities* (Allyn and Bacon, 1992) concerning the lack of teacher preparation at the middle level was a call to action for us.

> A perennial roadblock to excellence in middle level education is the practice of staffing middle level schools with teachers and other professional personnel who have no special preparation for teaching or working in other ways with young adolescents. Teacher preparation institutions, state departments of education, and the profession itself have largely failed to recognize the importance of designing specific preparation programs for middle level teachers and other professionals who are responsible for the education and welfare of these youth. (p. 369)

As professionals who have been middle school practitioners, who now are teacher educators, and who have evolved as teachers during a climate of change in public education and society in the last twenty years, we prepared this textbook to meet the need of future and current middle level teachers.

Much has been written in recent years regarding what constitutes quality middle level schooling. The temptation for the authors to offer a prescriptive textbook was great; however, we believe that such a prescriptive focus would not serve to define the unique and widely varied characteristics of middle level students. Rather than a prescriptive approach, we have developed this book around the essential features of a middle level school as identified by the National Middle School Association in their landmark publication *This We Believe* (National Middle School Association, 1992). Using the essential elements identified in this work as a guide, this textbook is intended to aid readers in the development of the teaching philosophies, behaviors, and skills relevant to effective instruction in the unique middle school situation. This emphasis reflects our basic philosophy that the teacher ultimately determines the quality of schooling and that the learning environment should be student-centered while maintaining a strong academic foundation.

This study begins with an overview of the origins and essential elements of middle level schools; proceeds through discussions of middle level teachers, students, schooling structures, and teaching strategies; and concludes with a view of the future. Specifically, chapters offer suggestions for teaching and learning in the middle level environment, for planning the curriculum, for providing developmentally appropriate instruction, and for assessing and reporting student progress.

This textbook is designed with the beginning middle level teacher in mind and is meant to be used as an introduction to middle level education. As such, we hope that it provides a comprehensive introduction to the middle level student, middle level curriculum, and middle level schooling in general.

Gilbert H. Hunt
Dennis G. Wiseman
Sandra P. Bowden

ACKNOWLEDGMENTS

The authors thank our colleagues in the Horry County School District for their special contributions to the completion of this text: Mr. Zeb Pack, Executive Director of Middle Grades Education; Mr. Mike Blanton, Principal, North Myrtle Beach Middle School; Mr. Wendell Shealy, Principal, Carolina Forest Middle School; Ms. Cindy Thibideau, Assistant Principal, Carolina Forest Middle School; and Ms. Linda Johnson and her instructional team at Whittemore Park Middle School.

We also acknowledge the support provided by our colleagues at the School of Education and Graduate Studies at Coastal Carolina University. Special thanks go to Ms. Lynne Brock for her technical assistance during the entire project. Finally, we thank the editorial staff at Charles C. Thomas Publishers for their assistance in the publication of this book.

CONTENTS

THE MIDDLE LEVEL TEACHERS' HANDBOOK

Chapter 1

ORIGINS AND ESSENTIAL ELEMENTS OF MIDDLE LEVEL SCHOOLS

RATIONALE FOR MIDDLE LEVEL

It is difficult to imagine a time of greater change in one's life than that which occurs roughly between the ages of ten to fourteen. This is a time of transition for all individuals regardless of culture. As such, some cultures facilitate this change very well while others less so. In the changing tide of education in the United States, much attention has been given in recent years to providing a better environment to facilitate adjustment and learning in this age range. The result has been the national middle school movement.

The modern middle school is an institution designed to be responsive to the developmental needs of those students most typically 10-14 years of age. In 1966, Donald Eichhorn wrote *The Middle School* which became the philosophical foundation of the modern middle school movement. Eichhorn established that the social and psychological development of middle level students was unique and that these students have needs that set them apart from both elementary and high school students. In its evolution, the middle school has become distinctive in that it offers unique experiences designed for those students that Eichhorn called students in "transescence" which refers to that period in human development ranging from late childhood and ending in the early stages of adolescence. Although 1966 is a watermark date for substantial development of the middle school concept, many educators realized long before that time that a separate school for early adolescent students was needed. In fact, there is evidence that some educators felt that the traditional elementary-high school structure was not serving the needs of all students as early as the late nineteenth century (Clark and Clark, 1994). Today's middle school has evolved from a series of educational structures affecting school organization, scope and sequence, and instruction. All of these structures were developed, of course, to serve these special "students in transesence" according to the needs of society and to knowledge concerning human development common to this age group.

Establishment of Junior High Schools

In 1888, Charles Eliot, then president of Harvard University, proposed that school programs should be shortened and enriched in order to prepare students better for college. The resulting "economy of time" movement led to a restructuring of school organization which added the seventh and eighth grades to the secondary program, thus changing the traditional school structure from grades one through eight and nine through twelve to a structure of grade one through six and seven through twelve. Many educators also decided, however, that college preparation should not become the main purpose of the new organization. The "raison d'être" for the new seventh and eighth grades should be attuned to the needs of students' development rather than just to prepare them for college (Lounsbury, 1992).

G. Stanley Hall (1905) greatly added to the then sparse knowledge base concerning human development with his landmark two-volume work, *Adolescence.* Hall's position was that the quality of education received during adolescence was a critical factor in the overall future development of the individuals involved. As a result, the junior high school movement found support in the early twentieth century. A movement that began as an expansion of high school for the purposes of better college preparation ultimately took on an identity that became more student centered (Lounsbury, 1992).

The first junior high schools opened during the 1909-1910 school year in Columbus, Ohio, and Berkeley, California. Within a decade, the movement was well underway. Thomas Briggs (1920) and Leonard Koos (1920) were two of the early leaders of the movement. Koos issued what is usually considered the first statement of purposes for the junior high school (Kellough and Kellough, 1996). Koos (1920) maintained that the junior high would make more economical use of instructional time, provide for students' developmental differences, offer vocational education, begin departmentalized instruction, and enhance the development of educational and social skills through physical education.

The junior high school grew rapidly in the early twentieth century. By 1925 there were 880 junior high schools in the United States; that number increased to 1,950 in 1934 and to 5,000 by 1960. There were approximately 8,000 junior high schools by the year 1970, the zenith of the movement (Lounsbury, 1992).

The structural organization of junior high schools varied somewhat from the beginning. The junior high school was frequently composed of grades 7-9; however, the 7-8 pattern was always popular as were the 6-8, 8-9, and 7-10 patterns (Lounsbury, 1992). The junior high school should be seen, historically, as an important advancement in education which represented a needed "bridge" between elementary and high school. The junior high school was born at a time when there was much concern about student dropouts and failures. Many students were failing and dropping out of school, never reaching the high school setting. The development and growth of the junior high school model, with methods and materials designed specifically for the young adolescent, was intended to help in the transition from elementary to high school and decrease dropouts and failures (Van Til, Vars, and Lounsbury, 1961; Briggs, 1920; Koos, 1920).

Although it provided a significant advancement in the education of early adolescents, the junior high school eventually was typically seen as part of the secondary school movement as opposed to a movement entirely separate from both the elementary and secondary schools. For example, teachers in the junior high school most often were content specialists trained initially to be high school teachers. Though many junior high school leaders understood the importance of specialized training for junior high school teachers, this training did not become a reality. Early leaders such as Briggs (1920) and Koos (1920) stressed the need for this specialized training. Noar (1961), a progressive junior high school educator from the 1940s through the 1960s, included a chapter on teacher training in her book on this subject, yet high school methodology and materials were too frequently the norm in junior high schools. Lounsbury (1992) noted that often junior high schools were housed in former high school buildings, organized around the traditional departmentalization structure common to high schools, and used the high school as a model for clubs, teams and other activities. Kellough and Kellough (1996) observed that the junior high school seemed to be an institution that was trying hard to be the high school.

During the post-World War II period, educators began to criticize the junior high school because of its seeming lack of innovation. By the 1960s, the new middle school movement was underway. However, some educators (Lounsbury, 1992) are quick to note that the junior high and middle school movements are not separate but are one in the same. The middle school, it is argued, grew as a normal extension from the junior high school. Many junior high school leaders held the same beliefs in student-centeredness, correlation of curriculum, guidance orientation, and exploratory study that is so common to the modern middle school movement in spite of the fact that these school characteristics were not consistently a part of the junior high school curriculum and organization. For example, in the 1940s, Skokie Junior High School, located in traditionally progressive Winnetka, Illinois, had a 6-8 organization with an interdisciplinary curriculum and a flexible scheduling plan (Lounsbury, 1992). Other junior highs of the same time period, for example, Gillespie Junior High School in Philadelphia, were noted for having student-centered, affective educational programs that had goals similar to those of the modern middle school (Noar, 1961).

Often when educators talk about types of schools, they are discussing ideal models more so than observed realities. In spite of differences from school to school, junior high schools had a common set of characteristics (Clark and Clark, 1994; Kellough and Kellough, 1996). Table 1.1 provides a listing of characteristics many educators would attribute to the classical junior high school.

The Emerging Middle School

As more and more educators became disenchanted with the lack of dramatic difference between the functioning of the junior high school and the traditional high school, the birth of a new school in the middle took place in the early 1960s. In truth, the middle school was founded on many of the same principles and the same philosophy of the classical junior high school. The middle school movement, however, gave new, needed energy to the notion that students between elementary and high school needed greater attention given to their special academic, social, and psychological needs. Many important leaders in the junior high school movement, such as Gordon Vars and John Lounsbury, added their knowledge of teaching this age group to the new movement.

Table 1.1
CHARACTERISTICS OF JUNIOR HIGH SCHOOLS

Trait	Description
Grade Levels	The most common grade configurations were grades 7 - 9 and grades 7 - 8.
Content Organization	The content was generally presented in the single subject format common to high schools in a presentation format best described as subject - centered.
Faculty Organization and Scheduling	The faculty was most commonly organized by departments, and students moved from subject matter to subject matter during each period or time block.
Grouping	Students were grouped homogeneously for the most part and moved from classroom to classroom staying with the same homeroom unit all day.
Instruction	Instruction was typically offered in a format common to the traditional high school of the day; whole group instruction using lecture, skills practice, and drill was the common practice.
Extracurricular Opportunities	Interscholastic sports were usually offered. Students had to try out for teams as in high school.

As vital as any contribution to the new middle school movement was D.H. Eichhorn's *The Middle School* in 1966. Eichhorn built the case for the new middle school movement on a better understanding of those students who are past elementary-school age yet who are pre-high-school age. Eichhorn coined the term "transescence" to describe the period in human development spanning the time from late childhood through the time of early adolescence. Educators were encouraged to focus on a school that was typically grades 6-8 (sometimes 5-8) with a student-centered, developmentally appropriate curriculum. After the Soviet Union took the lead in technology with the launching of *Sputnik* in 1957, James Conant (1960), Harvard University president, spurred the middle school movement on with his call for public school reform. Conant's suggestion to institute *new math* and *new science* in the middle grades and to expand study in secondary schools by returning grade nine to the high schools was well received (Lounsbury, 1992).

A further boost to the middle school movement came from the

work of developmentalist J.M. Tanner (1972). Tanner reported that children were maturing earlier and that the sixth grade student of that day was like the seventh or eighth grade student of the pre-World War II era. Tanner's data added support to the movement to add the sixth and even the fifth grade to seventh and eighth grades of the middle school. Finally, changes in school structure caused by the racial desegregation of schools, by the consolidation of schools, and by the establishment of new attendance areas also aided the middle school movement. Shifts in school populations often resulted in empty buildings which became, in many instances, new middle schools (Lounsbury, 1992).

Under the leadership of many enthusiastic middle school educators such as William Alexander (1968), many schools were designated as middle schools in the 1960s and 1970s. While this was the case, there was evidence that the middle schools of the 1960s and 1970s were not really offering major reforms. Surveys by Brooks (1978) and Gatewood (1973) indicated that little difference actually existed between the middle schools of the 1970s and the previous junior high schools. Lounsbury (1992) reported that by the mid-1980s the 5-3-4 grade organizational structure was the most common one used in the United States. In fact, a number of the "new" middle schools were created by merely changing the names of previous junior high schools. In too many cases the name change from junior high to middle school was virtually the only real change that took place at these sites. That is, there were and still are schools named "middle school" that have many, if not all, of the characteristics that were previously used to describe the classical junior high school. In spite of these observations, the number of middle schools continued to increase throughout the 1970s and 1980s (Alexander and McEwin, 1989).

The development of the middle school movement was greatly influenced by research on human development in the late 1970s and early 1980s as the number of middle schools was increasing. The brain growth periodization research of H.T. Epstein and C.F. Toepfer (1978) supported the position that the human brain experiences growth spurts at specific stages of development. Epstein and Toepfer proposed that middle school was a time period when students experienced a minimal brain growth. The 12-14-year-old was, according to Epstein and Toepfer, at a cognitive plateau. It was further hypothesized that a predominantly cognitive curriculum was detrimental to the middle school student. This research encouraged the development of a curriculum for middle school students characterized by review and reinforcement of previously learned material and that avoided incorporating complex cognitive processes (Hester and Hester, 1983). Although brain periodization research influenced the direction of the middle school curriculum in many areas, a number of educators questioned the theory that middle school students should avoid strenuous cognitive tasks (Brooks, 1984; McQueen, 1984). Tom Erb (1995) in a *Middle School Journal* editorial observed that the notion that middle school students were unable to handle academically rigorous content actually contributed to the image of the middle school curriculum as being "watered-down" and concerned more with improving student self-esteem than with developing their academic abilities.

The Modern Middle Level School

The middle school movement was invigorated by several important policy statements made in the 1980s. These policy statements impacted the amount of attention focused on middle level education by both the educational community and the public in general. As a result of this renewal of focus, educators began to spend less time arguing about the advantages of middle schools over junior high schools and more time discussing the qualities of the most appropriate, effective middle level programs.

In 1982, the National Middle School Association commissioned a task force to identify the elements of an ideal middle level school (National Middle School Association, 1982, 1992). The resulting document, which was updated in 1992, has become a benchmark in the growth of the middle level movement. Most educators turn to *This We Believe* as a guide to the essential elements of the emerging, modern middle level school. The task force commissioned was composed of an elite group of nationally recognized and respected middle school leaders: William Alexander, Alfred A. Arth, Charles Cherry, Donald Eichhorn, Conrad Toepfer, and Gordan Vars. Moreover, the monograph itself was edited for the National Middle School Association by John H. Lounsbury. It is little wonder the document became a defining statement of middle level education. In brief, *This We Believe* identified ten elements characteristic of a quality middle school which can be seen in Figure 1.1.

1. Educators knowledgeable about and committed to young adolescents.

2. A balanced curriculum based on the needs of young adolescents.

3. A range of organizational arrangements.

4. Varied instructional strategies.

5. A full exploratory program.

6. Comprehensive advising and counseling.

7. Continuous progress for students.

8. Evaluation procedures compatible with the nature of young adolescents.

9. Cooperative planning.

10. Positive school climate.

Figure 1.1. Essential elements characteristic of effective middle level schools (National Middle School Association, 1982).

This We Believe lists ten specific characteristics that quality middle level schools should have.

- A quality school for early adolescents must have as its foundation highly qualified teachers and administrators trained for and committed to providing developmentally appropriate learning experiences for middle level students.
- The curriculum must be designed specifically based on the needs and characteristics of middle level students. However, the curriculum also must be balanced providing an integration of both academic and affective goals.
- Due to the wide range of differences among the students, middle level schools should exhibit a variety of organization structures. The middle level school should be flexible in its organization including such structures as graded and multi-aged classes, homogeneous and heterogeneous grouping, and block and alternative scheduling may all be employed.
- A variety of teaching methods should be used to provide instruction to students who possess such a wide variety of needs and diverse

ranges of ability and motivation. It was emphasized that most middle level students are capable of learning without a teacher being present.

- Due to the developmental characteristics of the students, a full menu of exploratory courses (high-interest, short-term experiences characterized by providing ample opportunity for hands-on learning) are needed.
- A comprehensive advisor-advisee program should be developed to allow all students an opportunity to interact with a small group of peers and an adult prepared to give caring attention to the needs of individual students.
- All students must be given the opportunity to realize success in an environment where students progress at their own rate in accordance with their own learning styles toward goals they help to set.
- Since middle level students are progressing through a special period of self-concept development, the evaluation system used for these students should be helpful in allowing them to clarify their strengths and weaknesses in a supportive fashion.
- Team or cooperative planning is necessary to provide middle level students with the type of learning experiences that will address their varied needs. The curriculum should be developed cooperatively by teachers, administrators, and parental and community members in order to be most effective and appropriate for the developmental group.
- The climate of a true middle school must reflect a family atmosphere that will communicate a feeling of belonging and caring to all students. No middle level student should feel alienated from the school community where a respect for all students is promoted.

In 1985, the National Association of Secondary School Principals' Council on Middle Level Education developed an important statement concerning middle level education: *An Agenda for Excellence at the Middle Level.* Figure 1.2 displays the twelve essential elements the NASSP identified as being critical in order to have an effective middle level school.

Clark and Clark (1994) in their discussion of *An Agenda for Excellence at the Middle Level* noted that a strength of the NASSP document was that it focused on school climate, school-community connections, and client-centeredness, not on program elements such as "whole language" instruction that appear to be effective. The essence of client centeredness, as defined by the Council on Middle Level Education, is an educational program that is developmentally appropriate (National Association of Secondary School Principals, 1985).

---

1. A guiding set of values.

2. A supportive school climate.

3. A foundation that is developmentally appropriate.

4. A balanced curriculum.

5. Appropriate instructional strategies.

6. An organizational structure that maximizes the learning environment.

7. A curriculum that requires students to become technologically literate.

8. A faculty that is trained and certified specifically to teach young adolescents.

9. A program that allows students to make a smooth transition from elementary school to high school.

10. A strong, supportive administrative leader.

11. A support and communication system connecting the school and the community.

12. A student-centered environment responsive to the special developmental needs of young adolescents.

Figure 1.2. Essential elements of effective middle level schools adapted from NASSP Council on Middle Level Education (1985).

In 1989, a task force of the Carnegie Council on Adolescent Development published a report that had further significant impact on the modern middle level education movement. Entitled *Turning Points: Preparing American Youth for the 21st Century,* the report was supportive of the middle school movement, but, at the same time, was critical of the fact that many middle schools at that time were not developmentally appropriate given the special emotional and interpersonal needs of the young adolescent (Shepherd and Ragan, 1992).

The report, often referred to as simply *Turning Points,* recommended eight principles essential to the restructuring of middle level school programs which are listed in Figure 1.3.

---

1. Divide large middle level schools into smaller communities or subunits of students and teachers.

2. A core curriculum should be developed to emphasize critical thinking, health practices, and community service.

3. Organize the middle level school to insure opportunity for success while eliminating tracking by ability.

4. Give the major authority for organizational and curricular change to the local teachers and principals.

5. Middle level teachers should be trained in preservice programs designed specifically for the certification of such teachers.

6. Middle level schools should have environments that promote good health practices.

7. A network of communication must link the school staff and the community.

8. Middle level schools should form partnerships with the community.

Figure 1.3. Essential elements to guide the restructuring of middle level schools adopted from *Turning Points: Preparing American Youth for the 21st Century* (Carnegie Council on Adolescent Development, 1989).

The Carnegie Council's report has served as a major document guiding middle level educators since its publication. More recently the council produced an updated report entitled *Great Transitions: Preparing Youth for a New Century* which provided new data to support the need for developmentally appropriate middle level schools (Carnegie Council on Adolescent Development, 1995). As important as middle level educators have claimed the recommendations of *Turning Points: Preparing American Youth for the 21st Century* to be, there remains a great deal of evidence that those recommendations were not readily adhered to by school districts across the nation at that time (MacIver, 1990; Alexander and McEwin, 1989).

In 1990, the National Association of Secondary School Principals produced another important middle level report (Lounsbury and Clark, 1990). Entitled *Inside Grade Eight: From Apathy to Excitement,* this document offers eleven recommendations under three specific headings as seen in Figure 1.4.

School Organization

1. Interdisciplinary instruction must be used within the context of content integration and team teaching.

2. Advisor-advisee programs must be implemented.

3. Tracking (i.e., homogeneous ability grouping) must be terminated.

Developmental Responsiveness

4. Students must realize immediate success in developmentally responsive programs.

5. Curriculum and programs must respond to the needs of early adolescents by avoiding developmentally inappropriate requirements.

6. Educators musts recognize and respond to the social needs of middle level students.

7. Students must be provided ample opportunity to become involved in learning processes.

8. Learning activities must focus on higher levels of intellectual behavior and analytical thinking.

9. The curriculum content must be relevant to the life of early adolescent students.

10. Middle level educators must raise the expectations and level of excitement students have about school.

Personnel

11. Teacher quality is the most important ingredient in the development of effective middle level schools.

Figure 1.4. Essential elements of effective middle level schools adopted from *Inside Grade Eight: From Apathy to Excitement* (Lounsbury and Clark, 1990).

Curriculum and Instruction

1. *Core curriculum* of a comprehensive academic orientation should be provided for all students.

2. *Knowledge* to empower students is offered through a study of the core, electives, and exploratory curriculum.

3. *Thinking and communication* will be enhanced in all students.

4. *Character development* should be enhanced through giving students the opportunity to make reasoned moral and ethical choices.

5. *Learning to learn* will be developed through learning strategies and study skills emphasizing reflective thinking and moving toward independent learning.

6. *Instructional practice* should be consistent with the goals of the core curriculum and appropriate for the developmental characteristics of young adolescents.

Student Potential

7. *Academic counseling* should provide students with the necessary academic information to assure future success.

8. *Equal access* to the most advanced levels of curricula are open to all students.

9. *Student diversity and underrepresented minority* status should lead to encouragement and incentive to pursue educational and occupational goals.

10. *At-risk students* should have access to programs emphasizing personal commitment to academic success.

11. *Physical and emotional development* through access to specific primary health services and guidance/counseling programs are necessary paths to academic success for some students.

Organization and Structure

12. *School culture* should reflect a student-centered educational philosophy.

Figure 1.5. Recommendations for restructuring middle level education in the state of California adapted from *Caught in the Middle: Educational Reform for Young Adolescents in California Public Schools* (California State Department of Education, 1987).

13. *Extracurricular and intramural activities* should be easily accessible and promote a sense of connectedness to the school through participation, interaction, and service.

14. *Student accountability* for their social behavior and academic excellence should characterize the middle level environment.

15. *Transition* from elementary to middle school and from middle to high school should be successful and positive for the students.

16. *Structure* of school organization should identify the middle level as grades six, seven, and eight.

17. *Scheduling should be an expression of middle grade philosophy* and should allow students to access a full range of instructional programs and support services.

18. *Assessment* should be comprehensive and, most importantly, should be used to gather data leading to improved academic programs and more effective support services.

Teaching and Administration

19. *Professional preparation* for teachers and administrators should be specialized for grades six, seven, and eight, focusing on content, instruction, and developmental characteristics.

20. *Staff development* for both principals and teachers should be comprehensive, well-planned and long-ranged in nature while emphasizing professional collegiality.

Leadership and Partnership

21. *Parents, communities, and school boards* should share in the accountability for middle grade educational reform.

22. *State-of-the-art middle grade schools* should be developed in one hundred sites to serve as a catalyst for middle grade educational reform in California.

Figure 1.5 *(continued)*. Recommendations for restructuring middle level education in the state of California adapted from *Caught in the Middle: Educational Reform for Young Adolescents in California Public Schools* (California State Department of Education, 1987).

The essential characteristics of the modern middle school certainly emerged from exhaustive reports such as the ones referenced here: *This We Believe: An Agenda for Excellence at the Middle Level; Turning Points: Preparing American Youth for the 21st Century;* and *Inside Grade Eight: From Apathy to Excitement.* Moreover, as the middle level education movement began to build more and more momentum, several states issued important statements of their own on the proper education of early adolescents. Between 1984 and 1989 a number of states issued reform documents that served as models for other states across the nation (Allen, Splittgerber, and Manning, 1993). *Caught in the Middle: Educational Reform for Young Adolescents in California Public Schools,* a task force report published by the California State Department of Education (1987), stressed concerns with curriculum, instruction, faculty, students, school organization, and leadership and partnerships. *Restructuring Education in the Middle School Grades,* produced by the Virginia State Department of Education (1989), focused on creating goals to guide middle level education and identified state-of-the-art middle level schools. The New York State Department of Education (1989) identified ten goals for middle level education in the document *Regents Challenge for Excellence in Middle Level Education Programs.* Also, as in Virginia, the state of New York identified schools in the state to implement important, innovative middle level practices. By 1996, twenty-one states had produced documents on the status of middle level education (Rosenzweig, 1997).

Two of the most often quoted state documents are *Caught in the Middle: Educational Reform for Young Adolescents in California Public Schools and Regents Challenge For Excellence in Middle Level Education Programs.* See Figure 1.5 for a complete listing of recommendations from the California State Department of Education; note that there are twenty-two components listed under five major headings.

Finally, Figure 1.6 lists the thirteen key elements of an effective middle level school as identified by the New York State Department of Education (1989) in *Regents Challenge for Excellence in Middle Level Education Programs.* Much like the earlier statement by the California State Department of Education (1987), this document influenced many middle level programs across the nation.

1. Middle level schools should be composed of at least three grade levels.

2. Middle level schools should be characterized by small enrollments.

3. Middle level schools should be organized into small subunits to lessen the feeling of isolation among students.

4. Professional staff should receive multiyear assignments.

5. Students should be grouped in heterogeneous classrooms with specific short-term regrouping for certain learning experiences.

6. Teaching terms should be formed to share responsibilities for a common group of students.

7. Teaching team members should be provided with a common planning time.

8. Interdisciplinary curriculum endeavors should be supported through a system of flexible scheduling.

9. The transition from elementary to high school should be gradual.

10. The educational program should support co-curricular and extracurricular activities.

11. The co-curricular and extracurricular components should be easily accessible to students with special needs.

12. The regular programs of the middle level school should be readily accessible to students with special needs.

13. Guidance, counseling, and health-related support services should be easily accessed by all students.

Figure 1.6. Essential elements of effective middle level schools adapted from *Regents Challenge for Excellence in Middle Level Education* (New York State Department of Education, 1989).

Of the many significant documents and reports that have helped to shape the philosophy of the emerging middle level school, several important strands seem to emerge. The following characteristics run through most of the current reform movements:

• Middle level schools should contain at least grades six, seven, and eight.

- Schools should be divided into subunits referred to as "teams" or "houses" which will allow teachers to relate with a smaller number of students.
- The curriculum should be structured in an interdisciplinary fashion by interdisciplinary teaching teams.
- Middle level educators should be professionals with specialized preparation to teach early adolescent students.
- The curriculum should be exploratory in nature allowing choices from a wide range of special-interest activities, service opportunities, clubs, intramurals, and elective mini-courses among others.
- An advisor-advisee program to ensure that each student has a bonding relationship with at least one caring adult should be provided.
- Space and time should be organized with flexible block scheduling to address the needs of young adolescents.
- Schools should provide a safe, healthy student-centered environment based on participation, not competition.
- Schools should serve as a "bridge" facilitating a smooth transition from elementary to high school.
- Middle level educators should promote and reinforce active parent involvement in educational programs.
- Middle level educators should promote strong school-community ties through educational and service components.
- Schools should give priority to a complete and challenging intellectual program where all students will have an opportunity to realize success.

These twelve characteristics are not intended to form an exhaustive list of all essential qualities of middle level schools. Such a list is an impossibility since all communities have special needs and society, in general, is always experiencing change. However, they are basic to what most middle level educators feel are the essential components for effective teaching and learning.

Developing a Knowledge Base

Becoming an effective middle level teacher requires a knowledge of the research on best practice and a knowledge of the developmental characteristics of middle level students. Cohen (1994) has noted that a number of important locations on the Internet may help the middle level educator. Some of Cohen's suggestions are the following:

- *Classroom Connect* (http://www.classroom.net/) – A guide printed each month for educators that outlines opportunities to be available on the Internet and commercial on-line services.
- *K12* Net (http://www.vivanet.com/freenet/k/K12Net/intro_to.html) – A bulletin board network developed for teachers, students, and parents.
- *TERC* (http://www.terc.edu/) – A network of programs that fo-cuses on the areas of math and science.
- *International Society for Technology and Education* (http://isteonline.uoregon.edu/) – A network of educators encouraging the use of technology in the schools.
- *National Middle School Association* (http://www.nmsa.org/) – A network providing a resource center on NMSA conferences as well as professional development web links.
- *National Association of Secondary School Principals* (http //www.nassp.org/) – A network for educators interested in both the education of middle and high school students.

A number of important books and articles also have been written about middle level education, and many are currently being produced. Figure 1.7 represents a selection of important readings covering various topics significant in middle level education. This list, along with many of the references noted in this chapter, is a source of additional information concerning middle level education.

Additionally, a source of the most current research and information available concerning middle level education is generated at middle level education research centers across the country. For example, the National Middle School Resource Center housed at the University of South Florida has not only been responsible for generating research in the area of middle level education but also acts as a clearinghouse for dissemination of middle level innovations. The Center for Early Adolescents at the University of North Carolina at Chapel Hill conducted and disseminated vast amounts of research by such scholars as Gayle Dorman and Joan Lipsitz. The Center for Research on Elementary and Middle Schools at Johns Hopkins University is well known for conducting vital research and disseminating it nationally through periodic research monographs including data collection by J. Epstein and D. MacIver. The Center for Prevention Research and Training at the University of Illinois and, more recently, The National Center for Public Education at the University of Rhode Island have

- Alexander W., and McEwin, C.K. (1989). *Schools in the middle: Status and progress*. Columbus, Ohio: National Middle School Association.

- Beane, J. (1990). *A middle school curriculum: From rhetoric to reality*. Columbus, Ohio: National Middle School Association.

- Bergmann, S. (1989). *Discipline and guidance: A thin line in the middle level school*. Reston, Virginia: National Association of Secondary School Principals.

- Doda, N. (1981). *Teacher to teacher*. Columbus, Ohio: National Middle School Association.

- Epstein, J., and McIver, D. (1990). *Education in the middle grades: Overview of national practices and trends*. Columbus, Ohio: National Middle School Association.

- Erb, T., and Doda, N. (1989). *Team organization: Promise, practice and possibilities*. Washington, D.C.: National Education Association.

- Feldman, S., and Elliott, G. (Eds.). (1990). *At the threshold: The developing adolescent*. Cambridge, MA: Harvard University Press.

- George, P., and Oldaker, L.L. (1985). *Evidence for the middle school*. Columbus, Ohio: National Middle School Association.

- George, P., Stevenson, C., Thomason, J., and Beane, J. (1992). *The middle school: And beyond*. Alexandria, Virginia: Association for Supervision and Curriculum Development.

- Irvin, J. (1990). *Coming of age: The impact of PRIME legislation on middle level schools in Florida*. Tallahassee: Florida Department of Education.

- James, M. (1986). *Advisor-advisee programs: Why, what, and how*. Columbus, Ohio: National Middle School Association.

- Lounsbury, J., and Vars, G. (1978). *A curriculum for the middle school years*. New York: Harper and Row.

- McEwin, C.K., and Alexander, W. (1990). *Middle level programs and practices in elementary schools*. Columbus, Ohio: National Middle School Association.

- Van Hoose, J. and Strahan, D. (1988). *Adolescent development and school practices: Promoting harmony*. Columbus, Ohio: National Middle School Association.

Figure 1.7. A list of key resources in middle level education.

- Vars, G.F. (1987). *Interdisciplinary teaching in the middle grades.* Columbus, Ohio: National Middle School Association.

- Wiles, J., and Bondi, J. (1993). *The essential middle school.* Englewood Cliffs, N.J.: Merrill/Macmillan.

Figure 1.7. *(continued).* A list of key resources in middle level education.

conducted research and disseminated information to help school districts provide better middle level education in our nation's schools.

Summary

This chapter has served to define the emerging middle level school by discussing its salient characteristics. The middle level school is, above all else, a student-centered institution dedicated to the intellectual, social, and emotional growth and well-being of early adolescent students.

The chapter examines the early junior high school movement which grew from a desire for better college preparation of public school students. The junior high school was soon driven philosophically by educators seeking to create a learning environment more suitable for young adolescents, one based primarily on the developmental needs of the age group, not simply on preparation for high school. The junior high school, however, evolved into an institution with many of the characteristics of the classical high school.

The chapter then traces the middle school movement of the 1960s when the junior high school began its evolution into the middle school based on a more sophisticated knowledge of the uniqueness of early adolescent students. Through the 1960s to the 1980s, middle schools grew in numbers, although real change from the junior high school was often difficult to detect. Since the late 1980s, arguments concerning the quality of middle schools versus junior high schools have waned and have been replaced with efforts to define the best possible learning environment for middle level students. The chapter concludes with an analysis of the common characteristics of the current reform movement and recommendations for reading for educators who want to develop a broader knowledge base for middle level teaching.

REFERENCES

Alexander, W.M. (1968). *A survey of organizational patterns of reorganized middle schools.* Final report, USDOE Project 7-D-026. Gainesville, Florida: University of Florida.

Alexander, W.M., & McEwin, C.K. (1989). *Schools in the middle: Status and progress.* Columbus, Ohio: National Middle School Association.

Allen, H., Splittgerber, F., & Manning, M.L. (1993). *Teaching and learning in the middle level school.* New York: Merrill/Macmillan.

Briggs, T.H. (1920). *The junior high school.* Boston: Houghton Mifflin Company.

Brooks, K. (1978). "The middle school – A national survey." *Middle School Journal,* 1X(2), 6-7.

Brooks, M.G. (1984). "We are not testing Epstein's ideas: A response to Richard McQueen." *Educational Leadership,* 41(5), 72.

Carnegie Council on Adolescent Development (1995). *Great transitions: Preparing adolescents for a new century.* New York: Carnegie Corporation of New York.

Carnegie Council on Adolescent Development (1989). *Turning points: Preparing American youth for the 21st century.* Washington, D.C.: Author.

Caught in the middle: Educational reform for young adolescents in California public schools. (1987). Sacramento: California State Department of Education, Middle Grades Task Force.

Clark, S., & Clark D. (1994). *Restructuring the middle level school: Implications for school leaders.* Albany, N.Y.: State University of New York Press.

Cohen, P. (1994). "The online classroom." *ASCD Update,* 36(10)1-6.

Conant, J.B. (1960). *Education in the junior high school years.* Princeton, New Jersey: Educational Testing Service.

Eichhorn, D.H. (1966). *The middle school.* New York: The Center for Applied Research in Education, Inc.

Epstein, H.T., & Toepfer, C.F. (1978). "A neuroscience basis for reorganizing middle grades education." *Educational Leadership,* 35(8), 656-660.

Erb, T. (1995). "Its academics, stupid! If you care enough." *Middle School Journal,* 27, 1, 2.

Gatewood, T.E. (1973). "What research says about the middle school." *Educational Leadership,* 31(3), 221-224.

Hall, G.S. (1905). *Adolescence Vol. 1.* New York: D. Appleton Century.

Hester, J.P., & Hester, P.J. (1983). Brain research and the middle school curriculum." *Middle School Journal,* 15, 407.

Kellough, R.D., & Kellough, N.G. (1996). *Middle school teaching: A guide to methods* and resources. Englewood Cliffs, New Jersey: Prentice-Hall, Inc.

Koos, L.V. (1920). The *junior high school.* New York: Harcourt, Brace and Howe.

Lounsbury, J.H. (1992). "Perspectives on the middle school movement." In J.L. Irvin (Ed.), *Transforming middle level education: Perspectives and possibilities.* Boston: Allyn and Bacon Co.

Lounsbury, J.H., & Clark, D.C. (1990). *Inside grade eight: From apathy to excitement.* Reston, VA: National Association of Secondary School Principals.

MacIver, D.J. (1990). "Meeting the needs of young adolescents: Advising groups, interdisciplinary teaching teams, and school transition programs." *Phi Delta Kappan,* 71(6), 458-464.

McQueen, R. (1984). "Spurts and plateaus in brain growth: A critique of the claims of Herman Epstein." *Educational Leadership,* 41(5), 67-71.

National Association of Secondary School Principals' Council on Middle Level Education. (1985). *An agenda for excellence at the middle level.* Reston, VA.: National Association of Secondary School Principals.

National Middle School Association. (1982). *This we believe.* Columbus, Ohio: National Middle School Association.

National Middle School Association. (1992). *This we believe.* Columbus, Ohio: National Middle School Association.

Noar, G. (1961). *The junior high school: Today and tomorrow.* Englewood Cliffs, New Jersey: Prentice-Hall, Inc.

Regents challenge for excellence in middle level education programs. (1989). Albany, N.Y.: New York State Department of Education.

Restructuring education in the middle school grades. (1989). Richmond, VA Virginia State Department of Education.

Rosenzweig, S. (1997). "The five-foot bookshelf: Readings on middle-level education and reform." *Kappan,* 78(7), 551-556.

Shepherd, G.D. & Ragan, W.B. (1992). *Modern elementary curriculum.* New York: Harcourt Brace Jovanovich College Publishers.

Tanner, J.M. (1972). "Sequence, tempo, and individual variation in growth and development of boys and girls aged twelve to sixteen." In J. Kagan and R.C. Coles (Eds.), *Twelve to sixteen: Early adolescence.* New York: Norton.

Van Til, W., Vars, G.F., & Lounsbury, J.H. (1961). *Modern education for the junior high school years.* Indianapolis: Bobbs-Merrill Company, Inc.

Chapter 2

ESSENTIAL CHARACTERISTICS OF MIDDLE LEVEL TEACHERS

A teacher at any level must possess many important characteristics and skills in order to be successful. Teachers function in an ever-changing society with many complex personal and professional demands as they strive to offer the best possible instruction to their students. Students today come to school with many different backgrounds, learning styles and goals making the teacher's role even more challenging. Middle schools exist in challenging and exciting multicultural environments ripe with cultural diversity. This complex environment is in constant change which dictates that teachers must themselves be lifelong learners within their profession. Further, the impact of technology on teaching has changed the concepts of both academic content and of the appropriate methods for communicating such concepts. For example, middle level students not only need to learn how to use microcomputers and gain access to the boundless advantages of the Internet for communication, they also must consider the ethical considerations involved in such empowerment in today's society. The effective middle school teacher has the moral responsibility to be a leader, a communicator and a problem solver in the classroom, the profession, and the community. Effective middle school teachers must be able to relate to students, to other teachers both within and outside of their immediate instructional team, and to parents and other community members. As a result, an effective teacher, a reflective practitioner, must possess the following attributes:

1. leadership skills,
2. scholarship and reflective thinking skills,
3. communications skills,
4. understanding of cultural diversity,
5. technological competency, and
6. the ability to self-evaluate.

Leadership Skills

Waller (1932), in his classic work on teaching, describes schools as social institutions. The middle school is a well-defined social environment with well-defined roles for both students and teachers. As Waller so clearly noted, a basic role of the teacher is that of "leader." A leader is a person who is able to influence the behavior of others; certainly a major role of the middle level teacher is to influence the behavior of students.

Many adults, both educators and parents included, have long held the view that many middle school students are especially challenging to manage. Though much of what has been said about the unique behavior of middle school students has certainly been exaggerated, middle level students are clearly going through a period of powerful developmental change and self-definition (see Chapter 3). Often the middle level years are not easily navigated and, because of this, middle level teachers need to have especially well-developed skills in relating to and leading their students. A clear understanding of student developmental traits, patience, and self-confidence are all personal traits common to effective middle school teachers.

Within the teaching profession, teachers are placed in many difficult leadership roles. The fact that they are teachers gives them leadership responsibility; the foundation of their leadership is initially based on the respect or prestige given to members of the profession. However, all leaders must rely ultimately on personal traits for their effectiveness as they interact socially with those they are to lead. This is especially true for middle level teachers.

Because middle level students are searching for their identity and autonomy as these relate to society's expectations for their behavior, they may have trouble adjusting to institutional leaders, such as parents and teachers. These students, who so often seem caught between childhood and adulthood, are not always likely to follow the lead of an adult figure simply because the school says they should. Middle school students respond much better to authority figures if a personal relationship has been developed between them.

If a middle school teacher is to influence the behavior of a group of students, or any individual student for that matter, that teacher must possess certain professional and personal traits. For example, middle level teachers (1) must have a knowledge of the developmental characteristics of their students and (2) be able to relate to them in such a way that they will conform to the teachers' desires. Middle school students, for the most part, attempt to analyze their relationships with other people in order to understand themselves better. As a result, considering this, the average middle school student is apt to be more preoccupied with personal issues rather than academic goals when at school. At school, surrounded by peers, the average middle school student often is more concerned with socializing than academics. What better way for students to "find themselves" than to experiment socially with friends?

Principles of Leadership

There are, of course, many effective middle school teachers with a vast array of professional and personal traits; obviously all effective teachers are not alike in every way. There are, however, a number of leadership traits of teachers that lead middle level students toward desired academic and social goals. Successful teachers establish classroom routines and environments while they consistently:

- focus on the behavior of the student,
- avoid overreacting to situations,
- resolve their own problems,
- avoid retreating by following through on established directives, and, generally,
- structure the environment in such a way that they can do the first four.

1. *Focus on the Behavior of the Student:* Middle level teachers focus on the behavior, not the student, when correcting undesirable behaviors. Often cited as an axiom for classroom management, this trait may well be of greatest importance for middle level teachers. As a developmental group, middle school students are somewhat fragile psychologically and emotionally. They often struggle to please their peers, their parents, and their teachers. Frequently there are conflicts between the expectations of the adult world, and the peer group as middle level students are characterized by a desire to be accepted and respected by both. Essentially, middle level students want to break off with their childhood and enter the adult world but are uncertain as how best to do so. This identity struggle may cause great confusion.

A teacher or parent who directs criticism personally to such a student is likely to find that the student becomes very defensive and hurt or even rebellious. Because of this, it is important for middle school teachers to communicate to their students that they may not care for the student's behavior, but that they still respect and care for the student. For example, if a student is failing to complete homework assignments, the teacher should talk to the student privately about the problem behavior while avoiding personal public attacks. There is absolutely no place for public embarrassment. As Gordon (1981) has noted in his Teacher Effectiveness Training model, it is critical not to attack the student with comments such as "You are lazy," "You lack responsibility," or "You are wasting my time." Such comments only serve to undermine the self-concept of middle school students, alienate the students, and lead to even more unwanted behavior.

2. *Avoid Overreacting:* Successful middle level teachers must strive to avoid overreacting to certain student behavior. Due to social pressures and a desire to experiment with new behaviors, middle school students occasionally may exhibit behavior that seems somewhat outrageous. When confronted with such behavior, the teacher must remain both poised and patient, listening first and reacting thoughtfully. A verbal confrontation, especially in front of the offending student's peers, only will increase a problem. Teachers should not ignore or accept inappropriate behavior on the part of students, but also should not allow themselves to be pulled into personal conflicts that will be detrimental to their ability to lead the students in the future. Teachers will be able to respond appropriately to students when they have established a classroom environment of trust. Both teacher and students in such an environment will have established mutual respect for each other. Some teachers, especially inexperienced ones, may overreact to many disturbances and, soon, themselves are manipulated by the students.

3. *Resolve Their Own Problems:* Effective middle level teachers must learn to resolve behavior problems themselves. Though teachers should seek advice and help from other teachers both inside and outside their team and from administrators, they cannot manage students or resolve problems without constantly requiring such assistance. If this is the case they will be seen by both students and colleagues as ineffective. Part of being a good leader in the classroom involves conducting classroom procedures in a confident manner; it will be diffi-

cult to manage students if they perceive the teacher to be uncertain and uncomfortable as a leader.

4. *Avoid Retreating:* Middle level teachers must avoid retreating when managing student behavior. Retreating by a teacher, or not following through on established directions, is a behavior described by Schlechty (1976) and later discussed by Hunt and Bedwell (1982) and Bedwell, Hunt, Touzel and Wiseman (1991). Retreating is a social behavior common to many classrooms where the teacher's leadership is undermined by one or more students. If a teacher gives a directive intended to manage student behavior which is ignored by one or more students, the teacher who does nothing about the students' non-compliance is, in fact, retreating. For example, when the rules for procedures in a classroom have been agreed upon and, after an activity, a student does not clean up his work area when it is understood that this should be done, and the teacher continues with the next activity without addressing the student behavior, the teacher is retreating. Simply put, when a teacher tells students to change their behavior, the teacher must be certain the student complies before continuing with normal duties.

The period of time immediately following a teacher directive is most critical in a management sequence. Teachers should stop and calmly wait for students to comply. They should never argue with students nor beg them to comply but should have an established procedure if students do not comply.

The difference in the classroom atmosphere between teachers who rarely retreat and those who often retreat is easily noticed. A series of retreating patterns by the teacher usually leads to a total loss of authority in the classroom. Thus, it can be said that retreating is a behavior that separates effective from ineffective classroom managers. A pattern of behavior in a middle school classroom where a teacher does not respond when students repeatedly fail to comply to directives spells disaster for the teacher.

When a student does not follow the established procedure in front of other classmates there is apt to be a negative ripple effect if the teacher does not address the behavior. That is, when students see that another classmate can break rules without being corrected, it is likely that several students will think they too do not have to comply to the teacher's requests. If the students see early in the year that some students do not follow classroom procedure, that teacher's leadership ability will be lessened.

The classroom should not be a combative environment with the teacher at odds against the students. However, in a firm and supportive fashion, teachers must demonstrate that when they ask students to do something the students are expected to comply. Otherwise, the teacher is frustrated and students will have their learning interrupted. The teacher who structures a learning environment to avoid retreating is preventing behavior problems before they occur.

5. *Structure the Environment:* Middle level teachers must structure their classroom environment for optimal learning to take place. One of the most misunderstood concepts in classroom management is "structure." Structure does not lessen student freedom or movement; it should not be thought of as restrictive. Structure is organization, and a classroom without structure is likely to be chaotic. Too many restrictions can be bad because they can overly confine students. Classrooms where students must stay seated in straight rows without being allowed to speak, as an example, are probably too restrictive. Structured classrooms provide the avenues and boundaries for movement and talking. Structure allows students to explore and enjoy learning without losing focus on acceptable procedures for expression. For example, structure allows students to know that only four students can work in a certain center at one time while eight may work in some other center at once. Structure, then, allows students to know how activities take place and assignments are completed. Middle school students both need and appreciate such structure; they are comfortable with it and often uneasy without it. If the learning environment is properly structured, all students know what is expected of them at all times. Properly developed structure actually allows freedom as opposed to denying it. Students are free in a structured environment to explore and inquire because they understand the boundaries. Teachers also are free to move around the room and work with different groups because they do not have to police the students' behavior. In fact, in a well-organized environment, the students will control themselves and each other much of the time. A well-structured environment is central to the concept of leadership in the classroom.

Due to the nature and developmental characteristics of typical middle level students, these particular five principles are the most essential to middle level teachers who desire to be effective leaders. Refer to Figure 2.1 for a review of these essential principles.

1. Focus on behavior	When students exhibit unwanted behavior, the teacher should make it clear that it is the behavior, not the students, that is inappropriate.
2. Avoid Overreacting	Teachers must remain poised and calm when dealing with inappropriate behavior. Be patient and avoid getting drawn into arguments and confrontations that result in "no win" situations.
3. Revolve Your Own Problems	Teachers should not weaken their leadership position by relying on others to control their students' behavior.
4. Avoid Retreating	When teachers ask students to do something, they must be certain the students comply before moving on to something else.
5. Structure the Environment	Teachers must structure the classroom environment so that students will understand acceptable boundaries of behavior.

Figure 2.1. Essential principles of leadership in middle level classrooms.

Styles of Leadership

Researchers have known for decades that the image a teacher projects to students has an effect on the teachers' ability to function as an instructional leader. Three styles of leadership have been popularly recognized: authoritarian, laissez-faire, and authoritative (White and Lippitt, 1960; Baumrind, 1971).

Authoritarian teachers dictate that the teacher be the center of all decision making. Such teachers ask for little student input when planning lessons or assessments. They basically see students as passive receivers of information, not as active agents of their own learning. Authoritarian teachers may be capable of following a schedule, covering material, and maintaining order in a quiet classroom; but, they may not be effective teachers in a modern middle school. The notion that students are passive receivers of information from a teacher who tells them what they should know is an idea that simply is not viable in the middle level classroom. Such authoritarian teachers were truly ineffective even in the junior high schools of the past. Authoritarian teachers in the modern middle school are unacceptable given our knowledge of best practice research.

Laissez-faire teachers, on the other hand, are somewhat the opposite of authoritarian teachers. These teachers do not even become involved in the decision-making process in the classroom. The laissez-faire teacher usually is guilty of not giving students enough direction; in fact, these teachers often do not lead at all. Such teachers often plan poorly and lack organizational skills. Their students frequently have nothing to do or are seeking guidance from any source available. Laissez-faire teachers or administrators will not be effective in a modern middle school.

The authoritative teacher, as compared to the authoritarian and laissez-faire teachers, works with the students to guide their inquiries. This teacher is the person in charge of the classroom as the instructional leader while seeking student input in planning learning activities and establishing class procedures. In this type of environment students become active participants in their own learning. The authoritative teacher has a leadership style that is the foundation for effective teaching in today's middle school.

Authoritative teachers are able to create a student-centered learning environment and, at the same time, insure that proper decisions are made to allow for the most advantageous teaching and learning to take place. Tworek (1994) pointed out that it is the role of the middle school teacher to deal with the details that are necessary to provide a complete learning experience without attempting to control everything. The authoritative teacher is able to change approaches, choose different techniques, and modify methodology based on feedback from students, parents, and other professionals.

As a result of a collaborative leadership style, the authoritative teacher builds a student-centered learning environment. Given the impact of current research by cognitive scientists which has led to our understanding of how important it is for students to construct their own knowledge and to use multiple intelligences in their learning (Bruer, 1994; Gardner, 1993; Armstrong, 1994), it is of paramount importance that students become active participants in a student-centered learning environment.

As middle level students move through a distinct developmental period, they seek independence and want to stress their individuality;

yet, middle school students also worry about fitting in with their peers. They are caught between maturity and childhood; their confidence and self-concepts are frequently threatened and vulnerable. As a result, they need teachers who are willing to listen and consider their desires when structuring the classroom environment (Gutheinz-Pierce and Whoolery, 1995). Middle level students need authoritative teachers, not authoritarian or laissez-faire leaders.

Leadership and Teamwork

An important aspect of leadership in the modern middle school focuses on the professional responsibilities of teamwork. Collaborative planning, teaching, and assessing students by more than one teacher (or teaming) has become an important characteristic of the modern middle school. Whether it is a dyadic team of two members or a team of four or five members there is an important professional responsibility associated with working collaboratively with other educators. Teachers sometimes are in leadership roles and at other times are followers.

Barth (1990), in his classic discussion of the constitution of a "good school", noted the importance of everyone in the school community having an opportunity to lead. Barth defined leadership as "making happen what you believe in." This definition has important professional ramifications. All teachers must have a set of beliefs and educational philosophy that guides them professionally. Without such beliefs there will be no vision; without vision teachers become simply people doing a job. Each teacher, the most experienced as well as the novice, must have a vision of middle level schooling and work to make that vision become reality. All team members, though, may not have a common vision. Communication and compromise are necessary characteristics of leadership if a common vision is to be realized. For this reason, it is so very important that the style of leadership be authoritative. Authoritarian and laissez-faire styles of leadership do not lend themselves to the collaborative processes needed in the teaming atmosphere of a modern middle school. Teachers today function collaboratively to make decisions about budget, hiring new faculty, evaluation, schedules, and other important governance and instructional concerns. If middle schools are to be governed in a site-based fashion, teachers must be willing to function in teams to make critical, high level decisions. Each teacher must be a leader, leading toward a vision, if the benefits of such empowerment are to be realized. It becomes the job of the curriculum leaders in the school if individual team members are to focus their vision on a single mission. For example, Goodlad (1994) notes the importance of a common mission if schools are to be effective. When all teachers share a vision that focuses on the mission statement of the school, the educational program should more consistently meet the academic and social needs of the students.

The middle level teacher as a leader in the school community must be capable of controlling undesirable student behavior while allowing students the freedom to inquire and explore in the learning environment. Leadership skills are needed to allow teachers to work collaboratively with other professionals in instructional teams and site-based management arrangements. The same leadership qualities come into play as teachers relate to parents and other community members. Teachers who successfully lead in the complex social arenas of the school and community have an authoritative style of leadership. This style of leadership allows teachers to strive for the realization of their professional vision while working collaboratively with other members of the school and community to allow necessary input.

Scholarship and Reflective Thinking Skills

Scholarship and reflective thinking skills also are essential characteristics of effective middle school teachers. Teachers must be studious and embrace the value of life-long learning and make it a valued professional and personal trait. A school, as Barth (1990) notes, should not be a place where young people come to learn from older people who have already completed their learning. School is a place where teachers, administrators and students learn together: a true community of scholars. Perhaps the most important behavior a teacher can exhibit to foster academic growth in students is to truly model learning. Teachers who learn in front of and with students and take pride in the fact that they do so gain the respect of their students. Students follow the lead of a teacher who seeks information and reflects on the findings.

Perrone (1991), in his work A *Letter to Teachers,* points to the connection between scholarship and teacher empowerment. He believes that teachers' authority status emerges from a knowledge of student developmental characteristics, systematic reflection, and a grounding in historical, philosophical, and best practice in teaching literature. From Perrone's perspective, scholarship goes beyond the content areas. Teachers must be students of teaching. Dewey (1897, 1902, 1916) often referred to the concept of a teacher as a student of teaching; this notion was basic to his philosophy of teaching. Dewey wanted teachers to be able to analyze their classrooms by asking themselves reflective questions to help them make judgments about the quality of their own teaching and the learning of their students. This type of reflective thinking would help a teacher communicate with both students and their parents. Moreover, reflective thought is popularly considered as the basis of self-assessment.

The effective middle level teacher, as described here, is a teacher capable of making independent decisions and acting without depending on others. How can a teacher possibly have reached that stage feel in control unless that teacher has reflected upon important questions about teaching and learning? In applying this concept, an effective middle school teacher should reflect upon such concerns as why some strategies were effective and others were not, what built group unity and what did not, how each student's individuality is being supported, where a given set of learning experiences is leading the class, how will learning be measured, and other such important concerns (Perrone, 1991). This type of reflection should lead teachers to finding their own answers through some type of action research in their own classrooms. Teachers who constantly reflect, read, and empirically examine their own problems will be teachers who can act to solve their own problems with conviction. They will be professional leaders.

Some teachers reject the notion that middle school teachers must be scholars as insignificant or even inaccurate. Some teachers mistakenly believe that in order to be a scholar one must complete a terminal graduate degree, write for professional journals, and spend considerable time reading the great books of the profession. Granted, there is value to each of these activities; however, a true description of teacher as a scholar goes beyond this traditional and narrow view. Professional reading, writing, and advanced study are all worthy pursuits that any middle school teacher would benefit from exploring. The teacher as scholar denotes a person who is a student of the content area and who takes joy in learning along with the students. Such a teacher has an inquiring mind and an exploring personality. Moreover, this teacher is a student of teaching who reads professional literature and discusses ideas with colleagues while analyzing and reflecting upon the immediate classroom environment with the open-mindedness of a researcher. Teachers who write about their teaching experiences make an important and very valuable contribution to the existing professional literature and to the value of the experience for themselves.

One of the most important teaching strategies used by effective middle level teachers is the modeling of desirable behaviors. What more important behaviors could be modeled in the classroom than reflective thinking and the love of learning? The modern middle school should be an exciting, student-centered learning environment where teachers dare to try new ideas based on the input and diversity of their students. It is what has been classically described as a progressive setting. The progressive position that is common to many current trends in middle school philosophy can be traced historically to giants in the field of education such as Johann Heinrich Pestalozzi who, perhaps more than anyone else, laid the foundation for modern practice in elementary education which has, in turn, greatly influenced current school reform (Knight, 1969). His progressive thought continued to blossom through the works of other great European reformers such as Friedrich Wilhelm August Froebel and, in turn, influenced early American educators such as Francis Parker, John Dewey, and William Heard Kilpatrick. These progressive educators believed in student-centered classrooms characterized by students who enjoyed their learning. The position is taken that students are to be actively involved in their own learning and teachers are to be responsive to the individuality and diversity of their students. Central to Dewey's notion of a democratic classroom is a reflective teacher who is a student of teaching: teacher as scholar and reflective thinker.

Communication Skills

Whether it is Socrates talking with Plato or a kindergarten teacher talking with a five-year-old, communication is a critical attribute of effective teaching. Communication requires sending and receiving messages through some type of language. Usually in the classroom setting such communication transpires through verbal language. Nonverbal communication, however, also is a powerful avenue for sending messages between and among teachers and students.

Some of the most significant communication in the middle level classroom will not focus on teachers talking and students listening. Valuable classroom dialogue should be structured so that students talk to one another. Gentile and McMillan (1994) found that dialogue between at-risk students in a middle school setting was very beneficial to their learning. These authors state that high-risk students learn much more from talking and listening to each other than from sitting passively and being talked to by a teacher. Teachers play an essential role in these student dialogues; teachers must act as a stimulus that motivates and models for the students. Teachers also must develop and guide the dialogue in such a fashion that a connection is built between the students' personal, real-life experiences and the school's curriculum (Gentile and McMillan, 1994). This is especially important for at-risk students who frequently have problems relating to the curriculum but actually for all students whether considered at risk or not. The importance of this type of bridging for all students should not be underestimated. When students use their own language to discuss the content and structure of the material being taught, they will find it easier to analyze and develop the ideas being presented. They are then better able to reflect at higher cognitive levels which should be apparent in their writing and problem-solving activities.

As presented here, a major communication skill for middle level teachers is the ability to stimulate and facilitate dialogue among students. Moffett and Wagner (1976) in their classic discussion of communication processes delineated guidelines that will provide middle level teachers with important background information as they prepare to facilitate student-to-student interaction. If middle school teachers follow these simple guidelines they will create a more enjoyable learning environment that will encourage students to reflect and function at higher cognitive levels.

1. *Group size for optimal discussion should be relatively small.* Group size will vary due to the task, although five students is often the best size for discussion purposes. When the teacher tries to facilitate discussion in a large group, it is usually difficult to maintain the attention and participation of all students at the same time. In fact, in large group settings the teacher usually talks much too often to a series of individual students one after the other.

2. *Groups must be provided with certain conditions which foster interaction.* If dialogue is to take place among students, each student must be able to hear what is said with as little distraction as possible. Ideally, though often not always possible, each group would have its own separate meeting place for the discussion. When having separate space is not possible, having students seated in a circle in a quiet corner of the classroom will be adequate. The teacher must see that the groups stay focused and do not distract each other and must move from group to group saying as little as necessary to keep students on task. Many teachers post on the wall a list of rules for conducting group discussions which help keep the students organized and focused.

3. *Especially in the beginning stages, discussions should be structured to help the students function.* Activity directions provide students with a sequence to follow that will help the discussion stay focused and become meaningful. Students, for example, may be asked to first read a poem, write what they feel the poem means, take turns reading aloud what the meaning might be, and finally choose a best meaning or collectively arrive at a new one the group feels is best. This type of "brainstorming" activity will help the group discussion be more relevant especially when the students are less familiar with discussion processes. Moffett and Wagner (1976) note that discussion is most productive when the questions generated have no single factually correct answer. The purpose of discussion, the authors continue, should not be to convey information which should already have been gained but to make learned information more meaningful, provide for higher levels of thought, and encourage problem solving.

4. *The role of the teacher during class discussion sessions is to facilitate the process, not to convey content.* Of major importance is that the facilitator often finds it necessary actually to teach the group discussion process to the students early in the year. The teacher then monitors the groups and gives the students feedback concerning their progress since students sometimes fail to listen to their peers because they may feel student comments are less significant than those from the teacher. The teacher's first step in teaching the process is to model good discussion techniques with the students. This will show the students that peer interaction is significant to the teacher. Obviously, a major concern with discussion groups is the tendency for some students to be inattentive, even in small groups. The practice of asking a student to summarize another students' statement will encourage students to listen.

A statement from the teacher is sometimes required in order to get everyone focused. The teacher must, however, be non-threatening in the process.

In summary, communication with students in the instructional setting should focus on the teacher's ability to facilitate student interaction. Although there are many times when teachers must talk and students must passively listen, the skillful middle level teacher stimulates and guides students so that they learn from one another while creating a personal knowledge base through reflection, higher-order thinking and problem solving.

Communicating with Parents

Today's middle school teachers should make every attempt to involve parents in the education process. Taking this view, it is essential that channels of communication stay open and active between teachers and parents. George, Stevenson, Thomason, and Beane (1992) noted that the most effective middle schools have teachers who work together with joint ownership of the school's programs and purposes. In these schools teachers are able to communicate with parents in order that the parents both understand and accept the mission of the school. In fact, they have helped develop the mission. McCaleb (1994) notes that teachers must take the responsibility for such communication if it is to take place effectively because it is the teacher who is most able to develop and nurture the desired relationship between home and school. McCaleb (1994) stresses the importance of having parents visit the classroom and notes that teachers should not be apprehensive about these visits since most parents are simply interested in seeing that their children are treated with respect and have the opportunity to learn. Yet in the diverse, multicultural settings of our schools, many parents feel disenfranchised and are apprehensive about visiting their children's schools (Finders and Lewis 1994). Many parents who grew up as disadvantaged children had very negative school experience themselves. They are not quick to trust teachers and schools. This mistrust hinders such parents from taking part in their children's education. Many parents also have both economic and time constraints which make a school visitation difficult. People who work hourly jobs often find it next to impossible to arrange meetings during normal school hours. Another concern many parents from diverse backgrounds often have is related to their unique linguistic and cultural characteristics. Some parents feel so different from the typical, middle-class school teacher that they have inhibitions about coming to the school. These parents often fear that the teacher will make them seem inferior which is most disheartening especially if their child is present. The teacher must establish an atmosphere in the classroom to insure that parents connect with the school for the benefit of the student.

Finders and Lewis (1994) provide five suggestions to establish better dialogue with parents. Following these suggestions will help middle level teachers open necessary channels of communication between home and school.

1. *Develop a trusting relationship with the parents.* Create a lasting personal relationship with each family. Teachers must have an awareness of the culture that exists in the home, and bridge that culture and the school culture in order that a trusting relationship can be established and maintained.

2. *Build upon the positive aspects of the home environment.* Some students live in home environments that cannot offer them the advantages that other students are fortunate enough to have. However, it is a dreadful mistake to start a relationship based upon the supposition that these students have a "bad home life." Too often, teachers do not look for the positive aspects in the student's environment. If all the parent can offer the student is love and the desire to improve, that is a sound beginning.

3. *Help parents understand how best they can help their student progress and to realize that they are a critical factor in their student's education.* Teachers must carefully explain to parents how they can aid their children while, at the same time, listening to suggestions and concerns the parent might voice. Remember that some parents are less skilled and have less confidence than others. Very few parents will not help their children. Guidance and collaborative support will build the parents' confidence and self-worth in cases where the parents are unsure of themselves.

4. *Build on the parents' abilities and skills.* Many parents are excellent story-tellers or have the ability to add much to the class through their personal life experiences. Some parents may be able to take part in volunteer tutoring projects while others can share information about jobs and professions. The classroom that involves parents at

such a level is truly reaching out into the community to expand the boundaries of the school.

5. *Encourage parents to express and assert their ideas and feelings.* Parents need to feel the freedom to be honest with the teacher about their children's education. Parents who are empowered to do so, discuss their feelings with the teacher in an intellectually honest fashion. Parents who feel their children are not being served well by the school need an environment where they can express these concerns and discuss the issues with teachers and administrators.

Parents and teachers together can form a collaborative team which can greatly benefit the learning of a middle level student. Teachers who encourage and promote dialogue with parents are building a learning community that should be beneficial to all concerned.

One of the most important aspects of parent-teacher communication focuses on the reporting of student progress. This is normally accomplished through the use of report cards which are discussed in Chapter 7. However, experienced teachers know that often other, less formal, communication is necessary between teachers and parents. A conversation with a parent early in the grading period often can prevent poor results later on. Many schools are now restructuring their reporting systems with performance-based report cards. If new forms of reporting progress are going to be used, it is essential that communication take place so that parents understand and appreciate the new process (Clarridge and Whitaker, 1994).

Renihan and Renihan (1995) have listed the primary expectations parents have for a middle school. Parents identified the following characteristics:

1. Clear, consistent communication,
2. Fairness in dealing with students,
3. Attention to the student's individual needs,
4. Safe environments,
5. Good teachers,
6. A welcoming atmosphere for parents, and
7. A program consistent with the developmental characteristics of middle school students.

Middle school parents are very concerned about their children and want to be involved in their school lives. The school will gain the support of a very powerful and important group through successful communication with parents. New programs and strategies often succeed or fail based on the strength of the relationship existing between parents and teachers.

Communicating with the Community

Perrone (1991) noted that one of the most important aspects of education is the use of the community as an extension of the classroom. If students are to develop a civic responsibility and the social skills necessary to work with other people, learning experiences in the community are a necessity. Middle schools that have effectively built bridges between the community and the school often have developed service learning programs for their students. Some of these schools actually have a requirement for each student to complete a number of service hours in the community, while other schools have organized a service component that weaves through the entire curriculum. Regardless of the type of program the school develops, no program can be successful without communication between the school and community. That communication must begin with interaction between teachers and parents, then spread out far beyond the school grades and across the entire community. This can be accomplished by opening the school up to parents. Chapter 4 will discuss in more detail the structure and value of such school-community programs.

Bunting (1994) pointed out that important relationships can be developed between teachers and community members that not only enrich the instructional program but also help the personal and professional growth of teachers. Through relationships with community members, teachers are able to bring limitless resources into the school that provide rich experiences and information that students are unlikely to access without the efforts of teachers to bridge the gap between the classroom and the community. The reflective practitioner should be always searching for new ways to enrich the students' learning. By creating bonds with significant community members, teachers will be able to offer middle school students a richer, fuller understanding of the world around them. Sherman and Banks (1995) and Downs (1993) have suggested that teachers can play an important role in developing communication between students and the community and have noted the importance of student surveys in developing such communication. As students develop and use surveys and interviews in the community, they will gain much knowledge about the local people and their contributions to community life. Using such techniques will help the teacher increase communication while making the school more visible and viable in the community.

Awareness and Understanding of Cultural Diversity

Awareness and understanding of cultural diversity is one of the most important aspects of teaching in middle level classrooms today. As Jasmine (1995) observed, classrooms in this country have always been diverse in their makeup; however, there is even more diversity today than in the past. Jasmine goes on to comment that teachers often find cultural diversity confusing since the variations of culture are often extreme and contradictory. Some people, for example, prefer to have their race celebrated, while others do not want race to become a prominent feature of the classroom environment. Some parents argue to get special classes for their children with exceptionalities, while others want full inclusion regardless of the handicap. Some parents fight for the right to observe special religious holidays, while others insist that all religious symbolism be rejected. This, of course, creates a strain on the teacher who wishes to establish the best environment for all students. Understanding cultural diversity and functioning in a multicultural environment are keys to relating to students, parents, and colleagues in today's school community.

Teaching in a Multicultural Environment

Teaching in a multicultural environment must begin with the attitude that it is the teachers' responsibility to adjust instruction to the needs of all students. Since the middle of the twentieth century, humanistic educators have stressed the importance of teachers addressing the needs of students and acting as facilitators of learning. It is essential that this attitude characterize teachers in today's culturally diverse society.

Teachers who are being prepared to teach in public schools must be able to assess the following areas of their professional growth: (1) beliefs about students, (2) content and materials, (3) instructional approaches, (4) educational settings, and (5) professional training (Ladson-Billings, 1994). One of the primary goals educators must strive to achieve in multicultural education is total inclusiveness in the curriculum. James Banks (1994) has argued the importance of weaving all cultures throughout the curriculum. Banks admits that Black History Month or Martin Luther King, Jr. Week can be good beginning points. However, teachers need to strive toward a more total transformation of the curriculum where all cultures are recognized. In order to reach total transformation, Banks (1994) has suggested that schools begin with special events to recognize various cultures (i.e., Jewish Cultural Day or American Indian Week) until cultural awareness characterizes the entire curriculum.

Research (Winfield, 1986; Apple, 1990; Lipman, 1993) has indicated that teacher beliefs about students do have an effect on student achievement. Some teachers clearly expect more from non-minority students and middle-class students than they expect from minority students and lower socioeconomic students. This, of course, leads to a situation where teachers fail to fully examine teaching practices when minority or lower socioeconomic students fail. Moreover, when these students are treated as though they will fail, there is often a self-fulfilling prophesy and they do indeed fail. That is, students will act like they are treated (Lipman, 1993).

Subject matter content and materials used should include all cultures interwoven in a yearlong curriculum. Subunits only on various cultures will lead students to see these cultures as less than mainstream. Most importantly, the materials must reflect the importance of all cultures, not just a few. Multicultural education is not just about African-Americans or Native Americans or Chinese-Americans; all cultures should be explored through the content of the instructional materials. Of major importance, materials must not in any way support stereotypes. Women, people of color, and low socioeconomic groups frequently have been maligned in educational literature. Swartz (1992) found that a number of textbooks have attempted to deal with diversity but at times have done so in superficial, incorrect ways.

Adjusting instructional approaches to insure the success of all children is a necessary ingredient of the modern middle school. This becomes extremely important in a culturally diverse environment. Jasmine (1995) observed that cooperative learning techniques are profitable in multicultural settings and that the use of multicultural literature is a necessary component of the school curriculum. If language differences exist among students, teachers should attempt to bridge this gap in instruction by learning or at least becoming familiar with the students' language. A teacher obviously cannot be expected to become fluent in all languages. However, learning how to ask and answer basic questions in a language common to the students will help the teacher create a more psychologically satisfying classroom environment.

The overall educational setting of the school as well as the specific setting of a given classroom must promote cultural understanding and be based on a foundation of cultural awareness. The atmosphere of the middle school must model and promote a tolerance for diversity while encouraging students and teachers alike to work collaboratively. The middle school should avoid separating students based on cultural, ethnic, or other such characteristics if the optimum in quality education is to be provided to all students.

Finally, research suggests that teachers benefit from training in cultural awareness (Zeichner 1992). Most teacher preparation programs acknowledge the importance of preparing teachers to function in a culturally diverse society. It is still doubtful, however, that the vast majority of these programs prepare teachers to insightfully address the complexities of a multicultural world. Teachers need to continue to read and take part in training sessions at every opportunity if all students are to succeed and prosper from middle level education.

Haberman (1995) has enumerated the following seven teacher characteristics that seem to be common to effective teachers in culturally diverse classrooms:

1. teachers are *persistent* in trying to find ways to engage all students in learning activities.
2. teachers use *special interests that they love to learn about* and stimulate their students to share in these interests.
3. teachers grow professionally because they can *apply the important generalizations* they have learned about teaching. For example, such teachers not only know that assessment should be continuous, they also can name specific ways to apply this generalization in their classrooms.
4. teachers *understand that teachers can be a cause for failure or success with at-risk students.* They do not blame society for all of an at-risk student's problems, they also site such concerns as poor teaching and irrelevant curriculum.

5. teachers *maintain a professional attitude* and do not take failures and misconduct on the part of students personally. They know that they have a professional responsibility to facilitate the learning of all students.

6. teachers *avoid burnout.* They know how to work within the system to get emotional support from similar-minded teachers in their school and teaching teams.

7. teachers *understand that students are fallible.* Children from diverse cultures will sometimes make mistakes in the middle-class oriented society of the public middle school. Effective teachers understand this and see it as normal.

A teacher who adapts Haberman's seven teaching functions to working with a culturally diverse student population will be well on the way to developing a multicultural awareness that will be a profit to all students. Without doubt, such teachers will be good models for all middle level students to follow in a culturally diverse society.

One important and popular technique for teaching multicultural awareness is the use of multicultural literature. Often students can use trade books to enrich their learning in ways that many textbooks simply cannot approach. Reflective teachers need to familiarize themselves with such books in order to facilitate student learning. There is a wealth of good multicultural literature which grows each year. Figure 2.2 provides a listing of a few such quality books for students.

In any middle school, it will be easy to detect diversity. One of the most obvious differences among students, yet often overlooked, is the difference in gender. As Masucci (1995) has noted, gender discrimination in the education of middle level females is a fact that has long been documented. It has been noted, for example, that boys are more apt to call out answers in class than are girls. Moreover, boys are likely to be reinforced for aggressive intellectual behavior while girls are likely to be corrected or reprimanded (Eggen and Kauchak, 1994). Gender bias is slowly being addressed. Title IX of the Education Amendment Act (passed by the federal government in 1972) made racial and gender discrimination illegal in any institution or program receiving federal funding. However, history has shown that it is very difficult to control bias through legislation. Society itself must change before discrimination is entirely removed from the educational system. Laws can provide opportunity, but young girls must make the most of those opportunities and middle school teachers must encour-

1. Baillie, A. (1992). *Little brother.* Viking Press.

2. Dooley, N. (1991). *Everybody cooks rice.* Carolrhoda Books.

3. Kranz, R. (1992). *The biographical dictionary of black americans.* Facts on File.

4. Leigh, N. (1993). *Learning to swim in Swaziland.* New York: Scholastic.

5. Luenn, N. (1993). *Song for the ancient forest* (J. Kstner, Illus). New York: Atheneum.

6. Martin, R. (1992). *The rough-face girl* (D. Shannon, Illus). New York: Putnam.

7. Paek, M. (1988). *Aekyung's dream.* Children's Book Press.

8. Pinckney, G. (1992). *Back home* (J. Pinckney, Illus). New York: Dial.

9. Stanley, F. (1991). *The last princess: The story of Princess Ka'iulani of Hawaii.* (D. Stanley, Illus). New York: Four Winds Press.

10. Steptoe, J. (1987). *Mufaro's beautiful daughters: An African folktale.* New York: Lothrop.

11. Turner, A. (1987). *Nettie's trip south* (R. Himler, Illus). New York: Macmillan.

12. Young, E. (1993). *Red thread.* New York: Philomel.

Figure 2.2. A sample of multicultural literature for middle level students.

age female students to break away from binding stereotypes.

In summary, middle school teachers must have an awareness of student differences in order to make certain that all students have an opportunity to succeed to the fullest. Teachers must help their students develop the cultural awareness they need in order to function as positive, productive citizens in our modern society. The most important and significant trait any teacher can have is to model the behavior of a culturally aware and sensitive adult. If teachers are positive and nurture caring attitudes with and among their students, the students most likely will respond by cooperating with the teacher and fellow students.

Technological Competency

It is very difficult to discuss technological competency in any normal time frame because knowledge in the area of educational technology is constantly changing. For years educators have been told to prepare for the growth of technology in classroom instruction. What the future holds in this area of teaching and learning as accessibility to technological advancements becomes easier for both teachers and students remains an open question. The 1980s saw schools caught in the technological explosion of the Information Age. It was difficult to find a book or journal in the education field that did not predict vast and hurried changes in the ways our teachers teach and the learning processes of our students. In truth, these changes were not as vast nor as hurried as many predicted. By the latter 1980s most schools had some computers and many students came to the middle school with an ability to use simple software and, in many cases, word processing. However, too frequently, schools had outdated equipment and failed to merge technology with existing curriculum in a meaningful way. Though growth has occurred, educators continue to ask important questions concerning how technology can be used to improve students' learning. As teachers begin to reflect upon the possibilities of technology and experiment with student learning with such aids as the Internet and interactive laserdisc, advances in middle school teaching and learning will become a reality.

Why Use Technology?

In reality, many teachers feel as though their middle school students are much more competent with technological devices than they are themselves. After all, many teachers live in a world where they rely on their own children to set the VCR clock and timer on their television at home. Given this uncertainty about technology and the advantages of its use, some teachers are anxious to believe that they can teach and their students can learn just as well without the use of such aids to learning. This resistance is probably understandable to an extent; however, teachers also must understand that computers and other technology open up avenues for learning that will be impossible for students to access in any other format.

Peck and Dorricott (1994) have suggested ten reasons why teachers should incorporate technological advances in their teaching.

1. *Technology can be used to provide individualized instruction.* There are a number of computer networks referred to as learning systems that allow for self-pacing while providing learning alternatives to those students who are having learning difficulty. Also, there is considerable software on the market designed to be self-instructional. Much of this material is skill-oriented. Many teachers who are oriented toward holistic, problem-solving type techniques may find this material is not what they are seeking.

2. *Technology can develop and promote higher-order thinking and inquiry learning.* Many learning programs have been developed for those teachers who are not seeking skill-oriented materials. Problem solving, communication of ideas, question asking, and critical thinking can all be developed and evaluated. Students are able to use systems which require data collection, formation of generalizations, and the reporting of findings. Students truly learn through the scientific process.

3. *Technology fosters an increase in the amount and quality of student writing.* Word processing is the area of computer technology which has had the most obvious impact. Although teachers go far beyond the use of computers as a substitute for typewriters, word processing has motivated students to increase written output. Moreover, the nature of word processing encourages students to proofread, rewrite, and work collaboratively with other students in a writing workshop format.

4. *Technology can facilitate high level processing skills in ways teachers cannot.* Students need to develop certain abilities for themselves with appropriate instruction. They need to reflect and solve open-ended problems they, themselves, originally posed. Students at the middle school level can learn to use computer-based presentations, data bases, spreadsheets, graphics and other techniques to help them think through their accomplishments, analyze their results, and communicate their findings.

5. *Technology can influence and facilitate creative, artistic expression.* Video production and computer-based animation, for example, are presentation techniques which students can use to express their ideas in a meaningful and creative fashion. Given the importance of authentic learning and assessment, the use of such creative modes of expression cannot be overstated. Not only will such techniques be motivational in the middle level classroom, many students will be presented

with ways to communicate ideas effectively while, in the past, they might have been hampered by a lack of facility in more traditional communication formats.

6. *Technology provides an avenue to global awareness.* Technology expands the walls of the school to include virtually the entire world. The Internet provides an avenue for collaborative learning with students from all parts of the world. Teachers and students alike can communicate around the world with other middle schools for shared experiences. Up-to-date geographical and demographical data can be accessed with ease. Even computer-based news services can bring current events into the classroom. Computers, in essence, link students to the world community.

7. *Technology provides opportunities for students to do more meaningful work.* Students feel their work is more meaningful when it can be shared outside of the school. Student projects can relate to community, regional, and world problems and be shared with a vast audience. Such sharing and the type of feedback it can produce can motivate students to levels of accomplishment unexpected up to this time.

8. *Technology provides access to courses of study that could not have been accessed otherwise.* Distance education making use of television and computers can bring important experiences to remote school settings. The opportunity for middle school students from all over the country to share experiences with the same team of teachers is exciting to say the least. Many students in the past were unable to have certain instruction due to the size and location of their schools and school districts; because of technology, this is much less a problem.

9. *Technology provides students with the tools necessary to function in today's society.* Technology is an important force in our students' world. They must have confidence and skills in the use of technology to become productive citizens. Students in today's middle school are creating knowledge and those who do not know how to take advantage of technological advancements will certainly become disadvantaged. The middle level teacher must facilitate computer competence among students in order to provide the opportunity for those students to succeed.

10. *Technology allows teachers to become more effective educators.* As teachers begin seeking ways to help students learn more effectively through technology, these teachers also will start using technology to grow professionally. For example, the Internet provides a vast oppor-

tunity for teachers to learn more about teaching through access to instructional models and materials as well as interaction with other teachers all over the world. Laserdiscs, CD-ROMs, and television, to name a few, are sources of information for the reflective practitioner to use to increase instructional effectiveness.

Using the Internet

The Internet is a worldwide system of interconnected computer networks with countless databases, resources, and methods of communication. This network system may be the most important vehicle for improving education since the invention of the printing press (Ellsworth, 1994).

Students often begin on the Internet by using e-mail to communicate around the world or even to other students in other schools in the same school district. Next, they begin to tap the vast sources of the most current information possible on a seemingly endless list of topics. As students become more enthusiastic, they often become interested in computer programming and other areas of math and science. It becomes obvious to students that the more they know about computers and the Internet, the more information they can access. As Ellsworth (1994) has observed, the Internet is perhaps the greatest source of information ever created.

The Internet provides a seemingly endless number of ways for students to access not only data but people from all parts of the world community. Not only can students use the Internet to learn more about literally any topic, teachers too can use the Internet to learn more about teaching, students, and the content of the curriculum. Students and teachers together can explore the world of information that opens at their fingertips. For example, students can explore environmental problems through conversations with other middle school students using the medium of e-mail. The study of French culture would certainly come alive for the student who was able to immediately try using what was recently learned by communicating with students in France.

It is obvious that to become a more effective middle level teacher, one must have solid technological capability. This competency not only allows teachers to perform teaching tasks more efficiently and effectively, it allows them to facilitate the development of technological competencies in their students. Without technological capabilities, it will be more difficult, if not impossible, for middle level students to become productive citizens in the world community of tomorrow.

Ability to Self-Evaluate

Middle level teachers must become reflective practitioners. A reflective practitioner is a teacher who can, among other things, analyze the ongoing teaching-learning environment and make changes to facilitate students' learning. This concept of the reflective practitioner views the teacher as a professional empowered to conduct formative evaluation and make decisions that affect teaching and learning.

A teacher's self-evaluation should begin with reflective thinking. Teachers need to continually seek ways to improve the learning experiences in their classrooms. Reflective practitioners constantly seek feedback from other teachers, administrators, students, and parents; yet, it is the individual teacher that must analyze this feedback in order to make relevant changes.

Self-evaluation must focus on both personal and professional factors. On a personal level, teachers must analyze their interpersonal skills and their overall personal qualities in order that they may provide a proper model to youngsters at a very formative stage of life while, at the same time, provide the leadership needed to conduct good advisor-advisee relations with the students. For example, when interacting with students the reflective practitioner does not blame problems on the students, parents, or the administration. Reflective practitioners use self-evaluation to determine how they can do something to improve the situation. Reflective practitioners feel in control, a feeling of self-efficacy, because they sense that they are empowered to find answers and solve problems through their own reflection. On a professional level, they must analyze their instructional procedures and the curriculum structures to determine if all students are being given an opportunity to realize success. When students fail to learn, the reflective practitioner does not assume the problem is always with the students or some uncontrollable factor. The reflective practitioner will take the responsibility of finding ways to help students become successful. This all begins with self-evaluation.

Of the many important characteristics common to effective middle school teaching it is hard to imagine a teacher being truly effective if that teacher fails to practice self-evaluation. From John Dewey, to Ralph Tyler, to John Goodlad, to virtually all other students of effective teaching, scholars in the field of education have consistently suggested that teachers must reflect on their own teaching and practice to provide the best learning for their students.

Self-evaluation is never complete, it is a consistent, ongoing process. The reflective practitioner is never satisfied even when others seem content with the status quo. The reflective teacher always will seek ways to improve teaching and learning. This means, of course, that middle school teachers will only reach their full professional potential in schools where they are encouraged and empowered to evaluate themselves and act upon their decisions.

Finally, it should be noted that self-evaluation must be tied to a vision of excellence. All teachers will not share the same vision of excellence; this is as it must be. If teachers are truly scholarly, they will bring a variety of individual ideas and opinions to the school community. Nevertheless, each teacher should have formed a vision that will guide both teaching and self-reflection. Too frequently teachers lack a vision to give consistency to their behavior. Teachers at one moment may claim to be constructivist favoring cooperative techniques and authentic assessment yet at the next moment may want to evaluate the worth of a program based on norm-referenced, standardized test scores. This type of inconsistency in vision is dangerous. When teachers lack a consistent vision of excellence, they have no clear standard to use for self-evaluation. Teachers who lack such vision will behave inconsistently and rarely will they be able to make consistent reasoned adjustments for improvement. It obviously is difficult to grow through self-evaluation when teachers are unaware of the fact that their behavior is inconsistent. Thus, reflection must begin with the formulation of a set of beliefs about teaching and learning. It will be difficult to be an effective teacher in a modern middle school with a vision of excellence for yesterday's junior high school. When the experienced teacher has clearly formulated a vision of excellence, self-evaluation will become a very productive and natural part of the formulation of a consistently effective teaching-learning environment.

Summary

This chapter has focused on the characteristics of the effective middle level teacher: a person who is most instrumental in the functioning of the learning environment. It was noted that teachers must have leadership skills (with students, other professionals, and parents), scholarship and reflective thinking skills, communication skills, interpersonal skills needed for an understanding of cultural awareness, technological skills, and self-evaluation skills. Regardless of how effective a school's curriculum might be, teachers must demonstrate these skills if optimal cognitive and affective growth is to be realized by the students.

REFERENCES

Apple, M. (1990). *Ideology and curriculum,* 2nd ed. New York: Routledge.

Armstrong, T. (1994). *Multiple intelligences in the classroom.* Alexandria, VA: ASCD.

Banks, J. (1994). "Transforming the mainstream curriculum." *Educational Leadership,* 51, 4-8.

Barth, R. (1990). "A personal vision of a good school." *Phi Delta Kappan,* 71(7), 512-516.

Baumrind, D. (1971). "Current patterns of parental authority." *Developmental Psychology Monographs,* 1(1), 1-103.

Bedwell, L., Hunt, G., Touzel, T., & Wiseman, D. (1991). *Effective teaching: Preparation and implementation,* 2nd ed. Springfield, Ill: Charles C Thomas.

Bruer, J. (1994). *Schools for thought: A science of learning in the classroom.* Cambridge, Mass., MIT Press.

Bunting, C. (1994). "Building a school-industrial partnership." *Middle School Journal,* 25, 43-45.

Clarridge, P., & Whitaker, E. (1994). "Implementing a new elementary progress report," *Educational Leadership,* 52(2), 7-9.

Dewey, J. (1897). "My pedagogic creed." *The School Journal,* 54(3), 77-80.

Dewey, J. (1902). *The child and the curriculum.* Chicago: University of Chicago Press.

Dewey, J. (1916). *Democracy and education.* New York: McMillan.

Downs, J. (1993). "Getting parents and students involved: Using survey and interview techniques." *The Social Studies,* 84(3), 104-106.

Eggen, P., & Kauchak, D. (1994). *Educational psychology: Classroom connections,* 2nd ed. New York: Merrill.

Ellsworth, J. (1994). *Education on the Internet.* Indianapolis, IN: Sams Publishing.

Finders, M., & Lewis C. (1994). "Why some parents don't come to school." *Educational Leadership,* 51(8), 50-54.

Gardner, H. (1993). *Multiple intelligences: The theory in practice.* New York: Basic Books.

Gentile, L., & McMillan, M. (1994). "Critical dialogue: The road to literacy for students at risk in middle schools." *Middle School Journal,* 25(4), 50-54.

George, P., Stevenson, C., Thomason, J., & Beane, J. (1992). *The middle school and beyond.* Alexandria, Va: ASCD.

Goodlad, J.I. (1994). *Educational renewal: Better, teacher, better schools.* San Francisco: Jossey-Bass Publishers.

Gordon, T. (1981). "Crippling our children with discipline." *Journal of Education,* 163, 228-243.

Gutheinz-Pierce, D., & Whoolery, K. (1995). "The reality of early adolescence: Using what we know to guide our classroom practices." *Middle School Journal,* 26(4), 61-64.

Haberman, M. (1995). "Selecting 'star' teachers for children and youth in urban poverty." *Phi Delta Kappan,* 76, 777-781.

Hunt, G., & Bedwell, L. (1982). "An axiom for classroom management." *The High School Journal,* 66(1), 10-13.

Jasmine, J. (1995). *Addressing diversity in the classroom.* Westminster, CA: Teacher Created Materials, Inc.

Knight, E. (1969). *Education in the United States,* 3rd ed. New York: Greenwood Press.

Ladson-Billings, G. (1994). "What we can learn from multicultural education research." *Educational Leadership,* 51, 22-26.

Lipman, P. (1993). "Teacher ideology toward African-American students in restructured schools." Doctoral diss., Un. of Wisconsin-Madison.

McCaleb, S. (1994). *Building communities of learners.* New York: St. Martin's Press.

Masucci, J. (1995). "Guarding against gender discrimination in the middle grades." *Middle School Journal,* 26, 39-42.

Moffett, J., & Wagner, B. (1976). *Student-centered language arts and reading, K-8: A handbook for teachers,* 2nd ed. Boston: Houghton Mifflin.

Peck, K., & Dorricott, D. (1994). "Why use technology?" *Educational Leadership,* 51(7), 11-14.

Perrone, V. (1991). *A letter to teachers.* San Francisco: Jossey-Bass.

Renihan, P., & Renihan, F. (1995). "The home-school psychological contract: Implications for parental involvement in middle schooling." *Middle School Journal,* 26, 57-61.

Schlechty, P. (1976). *Teaching and social behavior: Toward an organizational theory of instruction.* Boston: Allyn and Bacon.

Sherman, P., & Banks, D. (1995). "Connecting kids to community with survey research." *Middle School Journal,* 26(4), 26-29.

Swartz, E. (1992). "Multicultural education: From a compensatory to a scholarly foundation." In *Research and multicultural education: From the margins to the mainstream,* edited by C. Grant London: Falmer Press.

Tworek, F. (1994). "Teaching: What's your angle?" *Middle School Journal,* 25(5), 54-57.

Waller, W. (1932). *The sociology of teaching.* New York: Wiley.
White, R., & Lippitt, R. (1960). *Autocracy and democracy: An experimental inquiry.* New York: Harper and Row.
Winfield, L. (1986). "Teacher beliefs toward at-risk students in inner-urban schools." *The Urban Review,* 18, 253-267.
Zeichner, K. (1992). *Educating teachers for cultural diversity.* East Lansing, Mich.: National Center for Research on Teacher Learning.

Chapter 3

THE MIDDLE SCHOOL STUDENT

Basic to the middle school movement is the strong belief that middle school students are at a unique developmental stage of their lives. In this belief, middle school students have developmental characteristics and needs that set them apart from students attending elementary school and high school.

This is not to say, however, that middle school students within their own group are totally homogeneous. In fact, the student body of a typical middle school exhibits great variance. At the middle level, students frequently, though not always, are 10-to-14-year-olds and are characterized by great diversity as they move from preadolescence to early adolescence. Sharing space in any typical middle school are students who fantasize about dating while playing with dolls sitting beside students who are already sexually active. Some middle school students are very much childlike in their attitudes and behaviors and development, while others are deeply involved in the complex lifestyle characteristics of teenagers.

The all important transition from childhood to adolescence takes place during the middle school years and during this period students are developmentally characterized by the transitions they are experiencing. *Transition* can be seen as the thread that runs through the entire middle level program and holds this diverse group of students together. The task of the modern middle school is to provide a supportive environment which allows students to develop socially, emotionally, cognitively, and physically in order to become productive members of society.

Transitions

A Carnegie Council on Adolescent Development (1995) document, *Great Transitions: Preparing Adolescents for a New Century*, describes quite well the developmental characteristics and needs of middle school students. The report focuses on the problems facing adolescent students and how these young people can be nurtured in order that they may mature into healthy, productive members of society.

It is significant that the Carnegie Council on Adolescent Development chose the words "Great Transitions" to describe the stage of early adolescence. The council notes that this period of life can be tumultuous as young people experience both the good and the bad that comes with growth and change. Middle school students are in a transition where they often must redefine their relationship with peers and family while they are searching for a clearer definition of self as they travel a path that will eventually lead to adulthood. Not only do they face difficult, often confusing social change, they also have the sometimes awesome task of adjusting to the physical changes related to the onset of puberty (Carnegie Council on Adolescent Development, 1995).

George and Alexander (1993) have noted that it was not until the decade of the 1980s that researchers began to distinguish that 10-to-14-year-olds had special characteristics that separated them from younger children and older teenagers. Lipsitz (1980) noted at the beginning of the 1980s that less was known about middle school-aged students than any other developmental stage of the life span. One of the early researchers to understand the unique transitional quality of this age group was Eichhorn (1966) who coined the term "transescence" to describe those in the middle school age group. By the end of the 1980s when the Carnegie Council on Adolescent Development (1989) published its benchmark report on the development, nurturing, and education of middle school students, the fact that 10-to-14-year-old students were going through a distinct, defined period of transition was understood and accepted by the community of researchers in human growth and development.

Shave and Shave (1989) and Feldman and Elliott (1990) are among the many developmental specialists who have recognized the uniqueness of early adolescence. These researchers have determined that early adolescence is an important stage where individuals go through a process of being defined as a person as they change physically, emotionally, socially, and intellectually.

Individual middle school students can have vastly different experiences as they progress through the same developmental period. Some students may find this transitional period very stressful and difficult, while others may pass through it with little or no problem. Students differ greatly in their physical and emotional maturity, and certainly, some cope with developmental changes and resulting social pressures easier than do others (Simmons and Blyth, 1987).

The study of this transitional period has resulted in the enumeration of several lists of important developmental group characteristics and needs of middle level students. Thornburg (1980), for example, identified seven developmental tasks common to students in "transescence". Middle level students:

- are becoming aware of physical changes rapidly taking place.
- are able to organize their thoughts in order to come better problem-solvers.
- are learning new social and sexual roles.
- begin to identify themselves with existing stereotypes.
- are beginning to develop important friendships within the peer group.
- gain a feeling of individual independence.
- become more mature in their development of morals and values.

The Carnegie Council on Adolescent Development (1995) has added much to our basic understanding of early adolescent development. The council has challenged certain myths about adolescence as they challenged certain prevailing stereotypes. Table 3.1 provides an overview of these stereotypes and the responses to them.

Again, the Carnegie Council on Adolescent Development (1995) provides important knowledge concerning how best to deal with the needs of middle level students as they function in their transitional stage.

1. Middle school is a critical turning point in life. It is an ideal time for parents and teachers to come together in order to prevent destructive behaviors. Both positive and destructive health behaviors tend to cluster during the middle school years. Therefore, health-promoting behaviors can become a way of life if properly promoted. Good health during the middle school years is of great importance if students are to learn at an optimal level. Good health at this point will have significant lifelong effects.

2. Academic problems and a lack of guidance from nurturing adults are underlying themes that contribute to many behavior problems in middle school students.
3. When parents or teachers attempt to intervene in order to address problem behaviors, the underlying factors causing the problems must be ameliorated.

Table 3.1
CARNEGIE COUNCIL'S CHALLENGE TO PREVAILING STEREOTYPES

Stereotype	Challenge
Adolescents are a homogeneous group	Students even of the same gender and age vary greatly terms of their physical, emotional, social, and intellectual maturity. Students from low-income or working class backgrounds tend to mature earlier than their more affluent classmates.
Hormonal factors influence middle school students to be out of control	Although hormonal changes have significant impact on the changing nature of middle level students in terms of such factors as growth, sexual interest, and emotional stability, this does not mean that these students are inherently difficult, contrary or hard to educate. When social and interpersonal factors are positive, the transitions will go smoothly.
Youth culture is different from that of adults and in opposition to adult values.	Although middle level students will adopt different music, styles, and values than the adult culture, many middle level students rely on parents, teachers, and other adults for guidance. The period of transition can result in a renegotiated interdependence with the family.
Peer influence among adolescents is usually negative.	If a middle school student becomes part of a positive peer group, the peer group can be a source of reinforcement leading to the development of a healthy, problem-solving, and caring individual.
Adolescents are not capable of complex reasoning or of learning challenging content.	Middle level students have the capability for critical thinking and decision making. It is a disservice to these students when challenging instruction is withheld.

The family, in conjunction with schools and other pivotal neighborhood and community institutions, must combine efforts if the essential developmental needs of middle school students are to be successfully addressed.

Obviously, the period of development that coincides with middle school attendance is one of significant transition. The students break away from childhood and enter adolescence as they travel the path to adulthood. Middle school students are on a search to discover who they really are as they move into early adolescence. Some middle school students will find this period of change to be difficult; others will find the transition exciting and enjoyable. However, all middle school students are going through a distinct period of physical, psychosocial, and intellectual change.

Physical Change

A visit to a middle school setting will leave one with the observation that middle level students often vary greatly in their physical development. Some middle school boys and girls will have the outward appearance of young men and women while others still appear to be children. While one might expect there to be a significant difference between 10-year-old and 14-year-old boys and girls, there also will be great diversity among students at the same age level (Brooks-Gunn and Reiter, 1990; Bukatko and Daehler, 1995).

Some boys, for example, may have fully developed genitals before others, of the same age, have begun development. The onset of menarche may vary several years among girls of the same age group. Naturally, middle school students of the same grade levels often will vary widely in their outward physical characteristics. Some boys will develop broad chests, body hair, and whiskers while other classmates may seem childlike in appearance. Many girls will develop breasts and body hair and undergo a widening of the pelvis while some of their age-mates still have the appearance of elementary school girls. This variation in physical development will often impact social development during this period.

Due to such factors as improved nutrition and better health care practices, maturation has been occurring earlier in successive generations (Coleman, 1980; George and Alexander, 1993). Basically, in Western society, the growth spurt and the onset of sexual development and maturity occurs approximately two years earlier in girls than boys. Girls, on an average, reach menarche at 12 years of age while boys hit the peak of the growth spurt around 14 years of age (Frisancho, 1981; Simmons and Blyth, 1987).

Another critical factor associated with physical development is the varying rate at which such development takes place across the middle school population. Typically, males and females who develop early physically are treated differently and perceive themselves differently than males and females who develop late.

Early maturing males may take on some of the more rugged physical traits that our society associates with manliness and adulthood. These males tend to be pleased with their weight gain and other physical changes (Peterson, 1988). Late maturing males, on the other hand, seem to have poor self-concepts compared to their peers. At the same time, they have trouble relating to their classmates and their parents. These late maturing males often compensate through attention-seeking, childish behavior which tends to only add to their problems (Mussen and Jones, 1957). Such experiences as open showers after physical education class can be very difficult for the late maturing male in middle school.

The case for girls is somewhat different. The early maturing girl typically puts on weight which can be seen as negative in our society. The early maturing female also is sometimes not accepted by her peers who frequently put a premium on looking like everyone else. As a result, the early maturing female may find her friends among older students which, in turn, may place pressure on this young female to exhibit rebellious behavior. Early maturing girls are frequently less satisfied with their appearance and have more problem behaviors than girls who develop more along the norm for maturity (Magnusson, Stattin, and Allen, 1986; Bukatko and Daehler, 1995). Girls who mature much later than their classmates, who seem tall and thin with no evidence of sexual maturity, may also have self-concept problems that may lead to withdrawal and embarrassment (George and Alexander, 1993). Because of these factors, middle level females, as a group, have lower self-esteem and higher self-consciousness than their male classmates (Simmons and Blyth, 1987).

Physical maturity clearly is a complex construct. It affects individuals in diverse ways. Moreover, these physical changes do not take place in isolation from the social, emotional, and intellectual changes that are also surely taking place within each individual middle school student. Fortunately, most students handle these changes with reasonable ease. For some, however, change certainly presents more of an ordeal. Regardless, all middle school students are aware that changes are taking place and are interested in their body and how it functions. This curiosity is normal. If middle school students think their bodies are abnormal, this is likely to cause stress and anxiety at a time when, perhaps more than any other time in life, a person wants to "fit in" and be seen as normal and accepted. Students come to middle school as boys and girls and leave as young adolescents who are concerned about personal hygiene and their attractiveness to other early teenagers.

The aspect of physical development which often causes most concern and contention in the family is sexual development. The increase in sexuality which accompanies puberty is a focal point in many discussions involving both parents and teachers of middle school students. There is evidence that early adolescents are becoming more sexually active in Western societies (Schlegel and Barry, 1991; Carnegie Council on Adolescent Development, 1995).

Of all the problems associated with sexual behavior among middle level students, none is a greater concern than unwanted pregnancy. Such cases are often referred to as "children having babies." In 1990, four percent of all babies born in the United States were born to mothers younger than eighteen years of age (Carnegie Council on Adolescent Development, 1995).

Many of these young females are having forced sexual intercourse. Of those girls who have intercourse at the age of 13 years or younger, over sixty percent have been raped (Carnegie Council on Adolescent Development, 1995). Given the increased amounts of overall sexual behavior at an early age, the incidence of forced sexual intercourse, and the increased frequency of sexual intercourse with inconsistent use of contraception, a large number of young girls become mothers before they are emotionally and intellectually equipped to properly care for their offsprings.

The transmission of sexually related diseases is another concern associated with sexual activity among middle school students. In today's society, sexually transmitted disease is a real threat to the life of the victim as well as any child who may be born to an infected mother.

Concerns related to sexual promiscuity among middle school students are not concerns simply of the family. All society is affected as the rate of early pregnancy and sexually transmitted diseases increases. As a result of these concerns, the health and well-being of middle school students must be a major concern of the school. Young adolescents today are exposed to the adultlike problems of AIDS and pregnancy. However, such problems can only be successfully faced through improved guidance and sex education programs and strong community, parent, and school interaction. Such programs and approaches are often attacked by various segments of adult society feeling that the school should avoid this domain (Allen, Splittgerber, and Manning, 1993; Anspaugh, Ezell, and Goodman, 1987).

Most parents, however, want sex education provided in the school; for example, there is evidence that 80 percent of adults want their children to receive education about sexuality at school (Fine, 1988). The question that is so often raised concerns what should be taught in these programs. Some people ask that nothing short of abstaining from sex should be taught, while others feel a less strict approach should be taken (Bukatko and Daehler, 1995). Up to this point, sex education has neither led to less and safer sex, nor has it led to a higher incidence of sexual behavior as some people have feared (Glazer, 1993; Stout and Rivara, 1989).

Why has sex education failed to meet the needs of society and the middle level students? Probably, too often, a less than exciting and relevant curriculum has been offered. Moreover, the curriculum is too frequently taught after the students have already become sexually active (Santelli and Beilenson, 1992).

Psychosocial Development

Psychosocial development during the middle school years is, to a great extent, focused upon the students' interpersonal relationships within peer groups. This is a period of time when students become more and more dependent upon the values and opinions of their contemporaries. Since the peer group tends to be a focal point for socialization, the group often provides an arena for the beginning of dating between the sexes.

However, it is important to note that the psychosocial development of early adolescents is often, to a great extent, related to social and emotional ties to their parents. Sometimes it is easy to recognize the conflict existing between middle school students and their parents and teachers. Many middle school students, however, do not rebel against adult authority, and many experience relatively little stress related to their relationships with parents and teachers.

Attachment to Parents

Research has shown that a relationship exists between social adjustment during adolescence and the students' relationships with their parents. For example, Rice (1990) found that adolescents who could show affection and trust for their parents were more likely to have a high self-esteem and the ability to display social competence. Kobak, Cole, Ferenz-Gillies, and Fleming (1993) found that adolescents who had positive relationships with their parents found it much less stressful to discuss such high-pressure topics as dating and behavior rules with them. Brodzinsky, Schecter, Braff and Singer (1984) found a high frequency of academic and psychological problems among adolescents who were adopted and speculate that this difficulty in these years is due to the separation of the child from the biological mother at an earlier age.

The adolescent who has experienced the very serious problem of child abuse is likely to have many significant problems in social and emotional development. As one would expect, research has shown that when a child is abused the ramifications can be long-lasting leading to many years of dysfunctional behavior (Main, Kaplan, and Cassidy, 1985). Probably, the most damaging type of abuse to occur during late childhood and early adolescence is sexual abuse (Berger and Thompson, 1995). As bad as sexual abuse would be at any time in a person's life, it is perhaps most damaging during the middle school years because the student is at this time in search of personal identity and there are so many other changes that occur due to the onset of puberty. Students in middle school, unfortunately, fall within the high-risk age range for sexual victimization (Finkelhor, 1994).

Finkelhor (1994) has noted that most sexual abuse is committed by men and most of these men are close relatives or family friends. Sexual abuse often will begin when the victim is very young and escalate to more serious violations during the middle school years. The psychosocial damage done to the victim of such assaults is immeasurable. Sexual abuse occurs almost equally across all socioeconomic and educational levels.

The middle school student who suffers sexual abuse is likely to be angry, fearful, and depressed; usually, these students will have problems in school. Abused middle schoolers may exhibit such behaviors as running away from home, substance abuse, inappropriate sexual behavior or even suicide (Briere and Elliott, 1994). Obviously, it is the responsibility of middle school administrators and faculty to provide the necessary support to abused students for healing to begin. In this, it is usually necessary for the school to bring in professionals such as social services or child/adolescent psychologists from the community to form a team of supportive adults for such victims. An abused boy or girl, especially one who has been abused by one or both parents, is likely to endure critical problems in both personal and academic endeavors. Until stability and trust has begun to be regained, there is little chance for growth in academic or social performance.

During this period the middle schooler also has begun to de-idealize parents. As a result, more often than in earlier years, middle school students will have a different point of view from their parents, as well as from their teachers, and conflict is more likely to result. Often parents and teachers treat middle school students in a way that the middle schoolers perceive as childlike when, in fact, they see themselves as being more adultlike. Yet, given all of these new perceptions that may, at times, create friction between middle school students and their parents or teachers, parents and teachers must remember these students still rely on the significant adults in their lives for guidance and support (Berk, 1993). If middle school students are to establish a smooth transition from childhood to late adolescence, a strong attachment to parents will be most beneficial.

Peer Group Identification

As middle school students search for their individual identities, not only do they turn to adults for answers, they also turn to their peers. During the middle school years, students in most cases begin spending more time with peers and less with the family. Teenagers in the United States spend, on an average, 20 hours a week with peer group members outside of the time spent in classrooms (Savin-Williams and Berndt, 1990).

The peer group serves many important, valuable purposes for middle school students; ties to the peer group sustain the psychosocial development of middle school students (Berk, 1993). The peer group traditionally acts as a support group helping the student deal with the problems associated with becoming an adolescent. The peer group can act to decrease a student's depression while, at the same time, uplift the student's self-concept. It also has been found that students who have close peer relationships with age-mates who value academic success tend to perform well in school themselves (Epstein, 1983). When middle school students enjoy being with their friends at school, they often will develop an overall positive outlook on school in general (Savin-Williams and Berndt, 1990). Finally, the peer group gives middle school students an important arena in which to search for their own identity and deep understanding of other people. The peer group allows middle school students to examine their own strengths and weaknesses and their own needs and desires while becoming sensitive to these traits in others (Berk, 1993).

Peer groups evolve in their makeup and nature. At the middle school level peer groups usually begin as same-sex groups. However, groups do sometimes mingle with groups of the opposite sex. For example, a group of boys might join a group of girls at the mall, and all go for hamburgers and then to play electronic games. This behavior will lead to mixed-sex groups by the end of middle school and the beginning of high school (Seifert and Hoffnung, 1991). Parents and the school tend to encourage the development of cliques because adults are certainly aware of the important role peer groups play in the socialization process as middle level students more and more pull away from the family. Too, parents and teachers are very much aware that peer groups can influence students in either a positive or negative direction. For this reason, students are encouraged to make friends with students who have social and academic standards similar to those of their parents and teachers. Students, of course, do tend to conform to the habits and attitudes of their peer group although probably not to the degree that the popular stereotype would have us believe (Seifert and Hoffnung, 1991).

Self-Concept

A major trait of the middle level student is a searching to define oneself. During these years the student is frequently focused on "self" trying to determine strengths, weaknesses, likes, and dislikes. Because most young adolescents experience a growth spurt and many physical changes due to the onset of puberty, they become very focused on their personal appearance at this time of radical change. In fact, they sometimes become so focused on themselves that they feel everyone is looking at them or "checking them out" as if they were on stage.

A positive self-concept is critical to a person who spends a considerable amount of time involved in self-analysis as middle level students do. Middle school students often make contradictory, confusing self-descriptions when asked to describe themselves; for example, a middle school student may use the terms "smart" and "dumb" when offering a self-description (Damon and Hart, 1988). Obviously, when students are showing confusion about who they are and when the self-concept is in a highly formative stage, teachers and parents should send as many positive messages to them as possible to uplift their self-esteem.

Self-concept is related to many factors outside of the students' control. For example, early maturing males tend to develop better self-concepts than late developing males. The early maturing male will receive more positive feedback from his own observation of his body and his physical skills and is likely to receive positive feedback from other people such as parents, teachers, and peers. Even though maturation rates are, for the most part, not controlled, progressive middle schools are structured to allow students to receive feedback in a non-threatening environment. As an example, a dance may be held at the school; however, it will be acceptable for the students to come in same-sex cliques if the students so desire. Essentially, forced dating situations such as formal dances are avoided since it is often too difficult for middle school students to deal with the anxiety and rejection that may come as a result of such affairs. In fact, it is at times difficult for mature adults to deal with this type of stress. Finally, middle schools typically offer intramural athletics which should place the emphasis on participation of all students as opposed to interscholastic team sports where students may be cut from teams because they are not good enough. Such blows to the ego of young males and females who perhaps had dreamed of playing basketball or cheerleading can be harmful and interfere with developing a positive self-concept.

For most young people, becoming an adolescent is a time for the evolution of pride and feelings of self-worth; many young people probably do not go through the emotional turmoil that once was associated with becoming an adolescent (Powers, Hauser, and Kilner, 1989). However, there still exists great diversity in emotional development and self-esteem. Students such as those who are late maturing, those having problems in school, or those who come from lower socioeconomic environments, for example, may have serious problems developing a healthy self-concept. It is important for all middle level students to receive authoritative parenting, positive feedback from teachers, and success in their academic endeavors if they are to have the self-esteem necessary to be successful in later adolescences (Rosenberg, Schooler, and Schoenbach, 1989).

The research of Erik Erikson (1963) is some of the earliest and most important work focusing on the psychosocial development of adolescents. Erikson theorized that people develop psychosocially through eight stages as seen in Table 3.2. These stages, Erikson believed, developed sequentially in such a fashion that problems at one stage would have a negative impact on development in subsequent stages. That is, the inability to resolve psychosocial problems in childhood would hinder normal development during adolescence.

Middle school students will normally fall within two of Erikson's stages. In Erikson's fourth stage called *Industry vs. Inferiority,* which typically concludes around 11 or 12 years of age, the student is oriented toward mastery of basic tasks which build a feeling of high self-esteem as the student enters middle adolescence. Students will become more peer group oriented and use the performance of age-mates as a standard to measure their own competency against. Erikson felt that students who leave this stage feeling inferior or even mediocre when compared to their peers will have long-lasting negative outcomes. Erikson's fifth stage, *Identity vs. Role Confusion,* typically begins around 11 or 12 years of age and lasts usually until the student finishes high school. Normally, students enter this stage near the end of the middle school experience. These students become even more conscious of the peer group influence as they search for the essence of "self." Clearly, Erikson felt that students have a strong desire for a feeling of "independence" from adult authority and, at the same time, acceptance from the peer group. Early in this stage, middle school students look for role models and attempt to make certain characteristics of these models their own.

Possibly one of the most important aspects of psychosocial development among middle school students is its diversity; middle school students clearly will vary widely in their developmental levels. Not only is there a definite maturity difference among younger and older middle school students in general, many individual differences in psychosocial development exist among age-mates. Although most students evolve into well-balanced high school students, some middle

Table 3.2
ERIKSON'S STAGES OF PSYCHOSOCIAL DEVELOPMENT

Stage	Typical Age	Characteristics
1. Basic trust versus basic mistrust.	Birth - 18 months	The infant either learns to trust or mistrust caregivers.
2. Autonomy versus shame and doubt	18 months to 3 years	Autonomy develops when the child is praised for new psycho-motor accomplishments, not shamed for mistakes.
3. Initiative versus guilt	3 to 6 years	The child explores the world socially and physically during conscience development; guilt is the opposite of initiative.
4. Industry versus inferiority	6 to 12 years	Many new skills are learned and practiced. The child who is not successful feels incompetent and inferior.
5. Identity versus role confusion	Adolescence	The adolescent must develop an identity in all aspects of life.
6. Intimacy versus isolation	Young Adulthood	The individual must form meaningful relationships or become an isolate.
7. Generativity versus stagnation	Middle adulthood	Adults seek ways to support future generations.
8. Ego integrity versus despair	Late adulthood	Integrity comes with a feeling of satisfaction with one's own life.

school students have serious problems resulting from low self-esteem and general identity confusion. All who work in the middle school must be sensitive to each student's needs to the degree that this is possible. Maybe more than at any other time in the student's life, middle school is a time when young people should never feel as though they are simply "a number" lost in the crowd. *All middle school students need to know success and have an opportunity to feel personal worthiness.*

Intellectual Development

At one point in time, middle school students were thought of as being "on hold" as far as cognitive development was concerned. Some researchers (for example, Toepfer, 1980) argued that these students had reached an intellectual plateau and should not be over challenged. Today this position is questioned by researchers (Carnegie Council on Adolescent Development, 1989). Middle level educators today are aware that the curriculum must be academically challenging to all students while, at the same time, designed and delivered in such a way as to optimize success. This concept will be further developed under discussions of curriculum, instruction, and assessment (see Chapters 5, 6, and 7). Erb (1995), in an editorial for the *Middle School Journal,* stated the importance of a challenging academic curriculum well.

> Creating climates of caring, promoting positive self-esteem, and fostering cognitive growth are all factors with which we middle level educators should be concerned. . . . We can talk about self-esteem, we can talk about caring, we can talk about laying off the pressure all we want. However, these terms have become code words for some who think that we have "watered down the curriculum" and diverted middle schools to being places where "warm fuzzies" and "feeling good" have supplanted the goal of academic growth. (p. 2)

The message is clear; if middle schools are to challenge the minds of students with academic content and if the curriculum is to be developmentally appropriate, middle school educators must never allow the academic component of the program to suffer as the affective elements are bolstered. Research such as Wigfield and Eccles (1994) and Midgley and Urdan (1992) indicates that middle level students are motivated to learn and can reason and evaluate information. The intellectual development of middle level students clearly allows them to go beyond low-level cognitive processes such of repetitive rote learning (Turner and Meyer, 1995).

Piaget's research (1952) is frequently examined to explain the development of reasoning ability in humans. He, of course, proposed a stage theory of mental development (see Table 3.3) that is widely accepted.

Naturally, according to Piaget's theory of cognitive development, the middle school student is seen as a person in transition. Piaget found that the typical child could reason logically with the use of con-

Table 3.3
PIAGET'S STAGES OF COGNITIVE DEVELOPMENT

Stage	Typical Age	Characteristics
1. Sensorimotor	0 - 2 years	The child moves from reflex action to a more goal-directed behavior.
2. Preoperational	2 - 7 years	The egocentric child begins to think with symbols as language develops.
3. Concrete operational	7 - 11 years	The individual is able to solve problems and think logically with the use of concrete aids.
4. Formal operations	11 years and beyond	The individual is able to solve problems and think logically without the use of concrete aids.

crete aids between the ages of 7 to 11 years. Approximately at the age of twelve, the child would be able to begin reasoning through abstract thought. Of course, it was not proposed that these changes in reasoning would be abrupt and complete; the complete changes would develop over time. Predominantly, the typical student between the ages of 11 years and 13 years of age will use concrete symbols as they reason. However, during this age span students will begin to use internal thought processes (i.e., abstract thinking) more and more (Thornburg, 1982).

Some educators (George and Alexander, 1993) feel that the vast majority of middle level students function primarily at the concrete level of reasoning. In truth, this may be a moot point. Those students who have begun to use abstract thought would only, as a rule, be doing so some of the time at a transitional level. It seems safe to suggest that in a typical middle school most of the reasoning processes will be formed at a concrete level. This has nothing necessarily to do with the intellectual rigor of the curriculum. Whether something is learned at a concrete or abstract level is more a matter of how learning takes place than a matter of what is learned.

One of the more interesting theories of intelligence that helps us to better understand students at all levels is the theory of multiple intelligences, often referred to as MI (Gardner, 1983, Gardner, 1993; Armstrong, 1994). Basically, Gardner has theorized that individuals have more than one type of intelligence and that each person posses varying degrees of each type. There are, he feels, seven types of intelligence, as seen in Table 3.4. Gardner believes most people can develop higher levels of intelligence of each type and that there are many ways to exhibit intelligences within each type (Armstrong, 1994). These seven intelligences interact in a complex fashion (they actually do not exist in isolation of one another) to explain each individual's ability to perform certain tasks (Gardner, 1983).

Table 3.4
GARDNER'S SEVEN TYPES OF INTELLIGENCE

Intelligence	Optimum Example	Characteristics
1. Linguistic	Author-Ernest Hemingway Orator-Jessie Jackson	Great ability to understand the meaning and functions of oral and written language.
2. Logical-mathematical	Mathematician-Issac Newton Scientist-Albert Einstein	Great ability to handle in depth reasoning and to understand numerical patterns.
3. Spatial	Artist-Michelangelo Architect-Frank Lloyd Wright	Very accurate visual perception of spatial reality and the ability to transform those perceptions.
4. Bodily-kinesthetic	Athlete-Michael Jordan Dancer-Martha Graham	Great ability to create high levels of physical movements and skills.
5. Musical	Musician-Ray Charles	Great ability to create and appreciate rhythmic, musical expressions.
6. Interpersonal	Political leader-Bill Clinton Religious leader-Billy Graham	Strong capacity to understand and properly respond to the moods and needs of other people.
7. Intrapersonal	Analyst-Sigmund Freud Reformers-Jesus, Buddha	Keen sense of self-actualization with great insight into self.

In terms of the development of these intelligences, individuals, beginning in childhood and continuing throughout life, have both *crystallizing experiences and paralyzing experiences* (Walters and Gardner, 1986). Crystallizing experiences happen to an individual and allow them to discover an intellectual gift; for example, a teacher gives a mathematical puzzle to a student, and the student displays exceptional logical-mathematical skills and goes on to develop excellent mathematical skills. Or, the parent takes a child to view a dance recital which awakens bodily-kinesthetic intelligence in the child who becomes a professional dancer. On the other hand, students can have paralyzing experiences which squelch their development in a certain type of intelligence. For example, a student writes a poem and reads it to the class; after which, the teacher criticizes the work so harshly the student is embarrassed and comes to dislike writing or reading poetry in the future. Obviously, as middle level students experiment with many ideas within the context of the school curriculum, the intent should be to insure uplifting experiences which are crystallizing in nature as opposed to those experiences which cause guilt, shame, anger, fear, and anxiety and paralyze intellectual development.

Students in Trouble

Unfortunately, many middle school students throughout all segments of society from all across our country are finding it difficult to negotiate the pitfalls on the road from childhood to adolescence. The Carnegie Council on Adolescent Development (1995) illustrates these risks well by supplying data on the increasing problems middle school students face in the sexual, social, economic and educational domains. The problems associated with broken homes, disease, racial tensions and poverty are difficult for all members of society. However, these serious problems can become magnified when students are searching to find their own identity and people to use as models.

Research suggest that low socioeconomic status seems to place students at risk across the nation. When low socioeconomic students come to school, the system often attempts to change their language and much of their culture. Middle-class students, on the other hand, come to school and are, for the most part, reinforced for those qualities their families and community have already instilled as important. Change simply is not as easy or as comforting as is reinforcement;

therefore, many of the academic and behavioral problems associated with dropping out, failure, and socially unacceptable behaviors can be found among low socioeconomic students. There seems to be, however, some good news and the odds against these students can be overcome (Carnegie Council on Adolescent Development, 1995). Students who overcome severe economic and personal adversity need strong attachments with parents or significant adult role models, and they need a support system from their community (e.g., school, church, or youth groups) which provides sustained support and guidance (Carnegie Council on Adolescent Development, 1995). Before these students damage their lives to a point where repair is unlikely, adults must intervene to add the necessary support and guidance system. Most low socioeconomic students have problems, and all middle-class students are certainly not problem free. However, low socioeconomic students tend to be more greatly at risk to have more educational, health, and social problems than other student groups (Wilson, 1993; Brown and Eisenberg, 1995).

Some people still believe that the problems of adolescence are mainly the problems facing our high school, not middle school students. This is quite a false assumption. For example, it has been reported by the Carnegie Council on Adolescent Development (1995) that one-third of all eighth graders have used illegal drugs, almost 15 percent of all eighth graders have participated in binge drinking in the past two weeks, and the rate of births for mothers under 15 years of age is on the increase.

Although many middle school students are well adjusted and experience little stress with the transition years, many do have problems that make the transition years a very difficult time for adjustment. These problems, coupled with the temptations for sexual exploration and abusive life-styles presented by certain segments of the media, make healthy development very difficult for some students.

Developmental Appropriateness

Many important developmental characteristics of middle school students separate middle level aged students from both high school and elementary school students. Given this unique developmental stage of transition that characterizes middle school students, it is important that the modern middle school has a curriculum that is developmentally appropriate for the students. Dorman, Lipsitz, and Verner (1985) noted that middle school students need to experience a variety of learning experiences through diverse scheduling and curriculum formats, experiences that allow for self-exploration, opportunities for meaningful participation in school and community, an environment which provides for positive social interaction with both peers and adults, opportunities for physical activity, a chance to demonstrate competence and achievement, and an environment which provides both structure and clear limits. The educational program needs to be structured to meet the needs of middle school students (see Chapters 4 and 5).

Guidance

Middle school students need a support system of caring adults to guide them as they test their new feeling of independence. Middle school students need guidance in their social and educational endeavors, and this guidance should be augmented by a feeling of community within the school (Oliner, 1986). The feel for community is established, in part, through interdisciplinary instructional teams which offer a family-type structure of students and teachers to offer support. Also, an advisor/advisee relationship should be established with each student and a teacher to add to the strength of the system's support mechanism (see Chapter 4).

School Community Relationships

Naturally, support must come from beyond the walls of the school. A strong relationship among teachers, parents, and significant adults in the community is important. No support system for students can be optimal without a strong connection with the family. Teachers and families working together provide the best possible support for the student in transition. Community resources such as health services, social services, churches and youth groups are also important elements in this support system (see Chapter 4).

Affective Education

As students begin developing a concept of who they are and as they become more oriented to peer group relationships, it is significant that they reflect on their interests, attitudes and habits as well as those of others. Middle level students are becoming more independent of their parents as they start to form their own attitudes and opinions. Students are influenced by peers, family, media, and other diverse sources as they try to sort out good from bad, interest from disinterest, and like from dislike. The messages are often conflicting. For example, taste in music, fashion, and certain television programs may vary greatly from peer groups on the one hand and parents and church groups on the other.

Schools should help students clarify and understand their values. The middle school can help these students develop the skills to face their concerns through such avenues as exploratory courses, advisor/advisee relationships, and team meetings.

Independent Learning

The middle level student needs the independence necessary to explore and experiment with self, peers, and new concepts. These students have a feeling of new-found independence and absolutely need the freedom to express themselves as an individual and as a group member. The middle school teacher should not try to be as controlling as an elementary school teacher yet acknowledging that middle school students often need support and guidance more than high school students may require.

Exploratory courses should be a part of the curriculum in order to give students the independence to make certain choices. These elective-type experiences will also help students develop and explore new interests during this time of important transitions (see Chapter 4).

Academic Excellence

The middle school must offer a curriculum and instruction that is developmentally appropriate along with appropriately high standards for academic performance (see Chapters 5 and 6). In the twenty-first century citizens will need well-developed technological and communication skills to function successfully. All schools must be accountable for offering quality instruction of the most up-to-date content. Students who are going to be prepared for the high-tech future must have sound academic preparation today. Society should accept no less. Middle school students clearly have inquiring minds eager to gain new information and explore new avenues of interest and are ready for "crystallizing experiences" that will open the door to life-long learning and exploration.

Middle school students are ready to be challenged but must be given every opportunity for success. Paralyzing experiences that create anguish or shame in the classroom may squelch the love of learning for years to come. Because of this, the middle school classroom must be supportive and success-oriented while, at the same time, presenting students with academic challenges. Perhaps a key factor in creating such a learning environment for middle level students is the provision of concrete learning materials. Although the transition to the early stages of abstract learning is occurring at least for some students, practically all middle level students are likely to benefit from concrete examples and materials as they are involved in activities that challenge their reasoning abilities. A mix of many concrete activities followed by opportunities to experiment with abstract thought seems to be developmentally appropriate.

Healthier Living

To be appropriate to the needs of middle level students, schools must address healthy living styles. A major area of emphasis by the Carnegie Council on Adolescent Development (1995) is adolescent health. Many American youth are not covered by any type of health insurance (approximately one in every seven have no insurance) and receive limited medical attention. As the Carnegie Council recommends, developmentally appropriate health care services must be provided in a variety of health care settings to include school-based and school-linked care centers. However, even in this day when the threat of AIDS is so real, 80 percent of all school-based health clinics are not allowed to distribute contraceptives to adolescents.

Middle school students, especially those from low socioeconomic situations, must receive sound health care advice and guidance from the school. Millstein, Petersen and Nightingale (1993) have noted the key ingredients that come to a good integrated health program appropriate for middle schools as illustrated in Table 3.5.

Table 3.5
**KEY COMPONENTS OF
AN INTEGRATED MIDDLE LEVEL HEALTH PROGRAM**

Component	Advantage
1. Student information	This aids students to make positive decisions, avoid negative influences of peers and media, resolve conflicts without violence, and cope with stress.
2. Student health services	Services provide preventive care for mental, physical, and dental well-being.
3. Motivation for students to protect their own health	This provides students an opportunity to apply knowledge gained.
4. Support from families, teachers and health care providers	Support is necessary if students are to overcome the many obstacles to sound health practices.
5. Healthy environments	A positive environment provides health role models in the context of an atmosphere free of violence, drugs, and negative forces.

Middle school educators must create an atmosphere and design experiences to the benefit of students in the transition from childhood to later adolescence; middle school students have developmental characteristics that are uniquely different from elementary school and high school students. It is essential that the middle school learning environment be structured to address the specific needs of this singular group of students if developmental appropriateness is to be achieved.

Summary

In this chapter, the salient characteristics of middle level students have been explored. One of the most important concepts discussed is "the student in transition." Middle level students are in transition from childhood to later adolescence; this is basic to the foundation of modern middle level education. Another important factor discussed is the diversity among middle level students. Given there is considerable developmental difference between 10-year-olds and 14-year-olds, it must be remembered that vast developmental differences can exist among middle school students of the same age group as well. Also, it should be noted that the physical, psychosocial, and intellectual development of each student is a complex matter which can only be explained through the interaction of many important factors that take place over a number of years often beginning in early childhood.

The challenge to middle level educators is the creation of a learning environment which is responsive to the developmental characteristics of students in transition. As developmental theorists and researchers collect more data on the unique characteristics of middle school students, it will be possible to create middle schools that are even more developmentally appropriate in the future than those of today.

REFERENCES

Allen, H., Splittgerber, F., & Manning, M.L. (1993). *Teaching and learning in the middle level school.* New York: Merrill/Macmillan.

Anspaugh, D., Ezell, G., & Goodman, K. (1987). *Teaching today's health.* New York: Merrill/Macmillan.

Armstrong, T. (1994). *Multiple intelligences in the classroom.* Alexandria, VA: Association for Supervision and Curriculum Development.

Berger, K.S., & Thompson, R.A. (1995). *The developing person through childhood and adolescence.* New York: Worth Publishers.

Berk, L.E. (1993). *Infants, children, and adolescents,* Boston: Allyn and Bacon.

Briere, J.M., & Elliott, D.M. (1994). "Immediate and long term impacts of child sexual abuse." *The Future of Children,* 4, 54-69.

Brodzinsky, D.M., Schecter, D.E., Braff, A.M., & Singer, L.M. (1984). "Psychological and academic adjustment in adopted children." *Journal of Consulting and Clinical Psychology,* 52, 582-590.

Brooks-Gunn, J., & Reiter, E. (1990). "The role of pubertal processes." In S.S. Feldman and G.R. Elliott (Eds.), *At the threshold.* Cambridge, MA: Harvard University Press.

Brown, S.S., & Eisenberg, L. (Eds.) (1995). *The best intentions: Unintended pregnancy and the well-being of children and families.* Washington, D.C.: National Academy Press.

Bukatko, D., & Daehler, M. (1995). *Child development: A thematic approach.* Princeton, New Jersey: Houghton Mifflin Co.

Carnegie Council on Adolescent Development. (1989). *Turning points: Preparing American youth for the 21st century.* New York: Carnegie Corporation of New York.

Carnegie Council on Adolescent Development. (1995). *Great transitions: Preparing adolescents for a New Century.* New York: Carnegie Corporation of New York.

Coleman, J.C. (1980). *The nature of adolescence.* New York: Methuen.

Damon, W., & Hart, D. (1988). *Self-understanding in childhood and adolescence.* Cambridge MA: Cambridge University Press.

Dorman, G., Lipsitz, J., & Verner, P. (1985). "Improving schools for young adolescents." *Educational Leadership,* 42(6), 4-49.

Eichhorn, D. (1966). *The middle school.* New York: The Center for Applied Research in Education, Inc.

Epstein, J.L. (1983). "The influence of friends on achievement and affective outcomes." In J.L. Epstein and N.L. Karweit (Eds.), *Friends in school* (pp. 177-200). New York: Academic Press.

Erb, T. (1995) "It's academics, stupid! If you care enough." *Middle School Journal,* 27, 1, 2.

Erikson, E.H. (1963). *Childhood and society.* New York: W.W. Norton and Company.

Feldman, S., & Elliott, G. (Eds). (1990). *At the threshold: The developing adolescent.* Cambridge, MA: Harvard University Press.

Fine, M. (1988). "Sexuality, schooling, and adolescent females: The missing discourse of desire." *Harvard Educational Review,* 58, 29-53.

Finkelhor, D. (1994). "Current information on the scope and nature of child sexual abuse." *The Future of Children,* 4, 31-53.

Frisancho, A. (1981). *Human adaptation: A functional interpretation.* Ann Arbor: The University of Michigan Press.

Gardner, H. (1983). *Frames of mind.* New York: Basic Books.

Gardner, H. (1993). *Multiple intelligences: The theory in practice.* New York: Basic Books.

George, P., & Alexander, W. (1993). *The exemplary middle school.* New York: Harcourt Brace College Publishers.

Glazer, S. (1993). "Preventing teen pregnancy: Is better sex education the answer?" *Co Researcher,* 3, 409-418.

Kobak, R., Cole, H., Ferenz-Gillies, R., & Fleming, W. (1993). "Attachment and emotion regulation during mother-teen problem-solving: A control theory analysis." *Child Development,* 64, 231-245.

Lipsitz, J. (1980). "The age group." In M. Johnson (Ed.), *Toward adolescence: The middle school years, Seventy-ninth Yearbook of the National Society for the Study of Education, Part I.* Chicago: University of Chicago Press.

Magnusson, D., Stattin, H., & Allen, V. (1986). "Differential maturation among girls and its relations to social adjustment: A longitudinal perspective." In P.B. Baltes, D.L. Featherman, and R.M. Lerner (Eds.), *Life-span development and behavior* (Vol. 7). Hillsdale, N.J.: Erlbaum.

Main, M., Kaplan, N., & Cassidy, J. (1985). "Security in infancy, childhood, and adulthood: A move to the level of representation." In I. Bretherton and E. Waters (Eds.), *Growing points of attachment theory and research. Monographs of the Society for Research in Child Development,* 50(1-2, Serial No. 209).

Midgley, C., & Urdan, T. (1992). "The transition of middle level schools: Making it a good experience for all students." *Middle School Journal*, 24, 2, 14-15.

Millstein, S.G., Petersen, A.C., & Nightingale, E.D. (1993). *Promoting the health of adolescents: New directions for the twenty-first century.* New York: Oxford University Press.

Mussen, P.H., & Jones, M.C. (1957). "Self-conceptions, motivations, and interpersonal attitudes of late and early maturing boys." *Child Development*, 28, 243-256.

Oliner, P.M. (1986). "Legitimating and implementing prosocial education." *Humbolt Journal of Social Relations*, 13, 391-410.

Peterson, A.C. (1988). "Adolescent development." *Annual Review of Psychology*, 39, 583-607.

Piaget, J. (1952). *The origins of intelligence in children.* Margaret Cook (Trans.) New York: International Universities Press.

Powers, S.I., Hauser, S.T., & Kilner, L.A. (1989). "Adolescent mental health." *American Psychologist*, 44, 200-208.

Rice, K.G. (1990) "Attachment in adolescence: A narrative and meta-analytic review." *Journal of Youth and Adolescence*, 19, 511-538.

Rosenberg, M., Schooler, C., & Schoenbach, C. (1989). "Self-esteem and Adolescent problems: Modeling reciprocal effects." *American Sociological Review*, 54, 1004-1018.

Santelli, J., & Beilenson, P. (1992). "Risk factors for adolescent sexual behavior, fertility, and sexually transmitted diseases." *Journal of School Health*, 62, 271-279.

Savin-Williams, R.C., & Berndt, T.J. (1990). "Friendship and peer relations." In S.S. Feldman and G.R. Elliott (Eds.), *At the threshold: The developing adolescent* (pp. 277-307). Cambridge, Mass: Harvard University Press.

Schlegel, A., & Barry, H. III. (1991). *Adolescence: An anthropological inquiry.* New York: Free Press.

Seifert, K.L., & Hoffnung, R.J. (1991). *Child and adolescent development.* Boston: Houghton Mifflin Company.

Shave, D., & Shave, B. (1989). *Early adolescence and the search for self: A developmental perspective.* New York: Praeger.

Simmons, R.G. & Blyth, D. (1987). *Moving into adolescence.* New York: Aldine de Gruyter.

Stout, J.W., & Rivara, F.P. (1989). "School and sex education: Does it work?" *Pediatrics*, 83, 375-379.

Thornburg, H. (1980). "Early adolescents: Their developmental characteristics." *The High School Journal*, 63(4), 216.

Thornburg, H. (1982). "The total early adolescent in contemporary society." *The High School Journal*, 65, 272-278.

Toepfer, C.F., Jr. (1980). "Brain growth periodization data: Some suggestions for reorganizing middle grades education." *The High School Journal*, 63, 224-226.

Turner, J.C., & Meyer, D.K. (1995). "Motivating students to learn: Lessons from a fifth grade math class." *Middle School Journal*, 27, 1, 18-25.

Walters, J., & Gardner, H. (1986). "The crystallizing experience: Discovery of an intellectual gift." In *Conceptions of Giftedness,* R. Sternberg and J. Davidson (Eds.). New York: Cambridge University Press.

Wigfield, A., & Eccles, J.S. (1994) "Middle grades schooling and early adolescent development: An introduction" *Journal of Early Adolescence,* 14, 102-106.

Wilson, W.J. (1993). "Poverty, health, and adolescent health promotion." *Promoting adolescent health: Third symposium on research opportunities in adolescence.* Washington, D.C.: Carnegie Council on Adolescent Development.

Chapter 4

CREATING A POSITIVE
MIDDLE SCHOOL CLIMATE

The developmental nature of the early adolescent is best characterized as fluctuating and irregular. Because early adolescents exhibit such diverse psycho-social, cognitive and physical behaviors, a middle level teacher's awareness of these developmental differences will
help the teacher make appropriate decisions about creating effective
learning environments. Establishing school and classroom environmental systems that positively impact young adolescent learning and
development is the first step in effective middle level instruction.

Positive School Climate and Student Developmental Needs

The tenth "essential element" of effective middle schools identified
in "This We Believe" (National Middle School Association, 1992) concerns the social, academic, and interpersonal schooling conditions that
promote a "positive school climate." Positive school climate can influence student motivation to learn, student psychological health and
decision making, and academic achievement (Crohn, 1983; Good,
Biddle and Brophy, 1975; Purkey, 1970).

How does one know if a middle school demonstrates a positive
school climate? An excellent way to find out is to ask middle school
students about their perceptions of the school, their teachers, and their
classes. Students usually state honest opinions about their school.
They may respond, "I like school because the rules are fair," or
"School is ok. There are lots of activities to do." They may say, "I hate
school! The teachers are mean and don't listen to anyone." In any
event, student responses provide a general idea as to what the school
climate conditions are and how students feel about them.

Note : Dr. Suzanne Cormier of Winthrop University was the major contributing author to this
chapter.

Another way to determine school climate is by visiting several different middle schools. After meeting the administration and staff, visiting different classrooms, and attending school activities, it will be possible to gain a clear understanding of positive and negative school climate conditions. School climate conditions are displayed in several ways. Student attitudes toward school, the attitudes of the school principal and staff toward students, school rules and procedures, and the behavior of classroom teachers are all ways that school climate is conveyed and maintained.

So, what is positive school climate? School climate is more than a series of rules and procedures implemented by teachers and administrators. In essence, it is a philosophical approach based on a belief system that emphasizes successful learning expectations, mutual respect, and supportive guidance. Based on this belief system, teachers, administrators and school staff strive to develop and maintain specific practices and programs that address student developmental needs that in turn will support effective learning and growth.

Erikson emphasized that the young adolescent's primary developmental task is establishing a personal identity (Elkind, 1994). The journey toward forming a personal identity is complex and requires active exploration. The adolescent's search for successful identity formation is influenced by important cognitive, social, and physical issues (Scales, 1992). Schools can help middle level students through this journey by meeting their primary developmental needs. Scales (1992) identified these needs as

1. positive social interaction with adults and peers,
2. structure and clear limits,
3. competence and achievement,
4 creative expression,
5. physical activity,
6. meaningful participation with families, schools and communities, and
7. self-definition.

Middle school experts believe that schools with positive climates meet the developmental needs of students by providing certain environmental conditions (Lounsbury, 1991; Stevenson, 1992). The environmental conditions stressed most often are those that emulate a sense of family and belonging in young people. This type of family atmosphere emphasizes safety, caring, respect and acceptance (Lounsbury, 1991; Wilmore, 1992).

In summary, the factors or conditions that make up positive school climate must respond to the developmental needs of students. Consequently, it appears that the "supportive relationship" schools have with students is the most important underlying factor in creating exemplary school learning climates. Of course the key ingredient to supplying a supportive relationship is the faculty and staff who provide it.

Schools demonstrate the concept of positive school climate in different ways. Effective middle level schools provide positive learning climates through three distinct types of environmental systems: (1) school-wide systems, (2) classroom systems, and (3) school-community systems. Each of these systems is guided by the underlying philosophical belief system of the school and its leadership regarding the type of activities, interactions and programs that will best foster student learning and growth.

The first environmental system is the school-wide system, one which effects the total student body. This system involves giving students a sense of security, sustaining guidance, and a connection to the school family by offering activities and by defining a set of behavioral expectations. The system also focuses on helping students develop their interests, responsibility, and independence. Advisor-advisee programs, school clubs, student career explorations, student government, and student-administrator interaction are a few examples of school-wide practices that can provide a positive school-wide climate.

The second type of environmental system within the school is the classroom system. This system is shaped and monitored by classroom teachers and concerns the relationship that exists between students and teachers. Consequently, the structure of the class, the nature of the learning activities, the instructional methods, and the interpersonal communication and interactions between students and teachers are the primary factors that influence classroom learning climate. Once again, the teacher or teacher team is the key ingredient.

Finally, the third type of environmental system that conveys school climate is the school-community system. The school community is composed of the families, businesses, service organizations, churches, and agencies that are a part of the school area and environment. The school faculty and staff are responsible for bringing together this system to enhance student and community learning.

If these three school environmental systems are operating with the intent to respond to the learning and developmental needs of young adolescents, then schools will demonstrate an exceptionally positive climate. In the next three sections, these systems are described in detail with an emphasis on the teacher's role in supporting each system. Table 4.1 provides a list of these environments and the components of each system.

Table 4.1
TYPES OF SCHOOL CLIMATE ENVIRONMENTAL SYSTEMS
AND THEIR COMPONENTS

Type of Environmental System	Components of the System
School-wide	• School policies, rules, and procedures
	• Student affairs activities
	• Student guidance and support
	• Teacher advisory
Classroom	• Classroom structures
	• Classroom rules and procedures
	• Teacher behaviors and attitudes
School-community	• Parental involvement
	• Community organizations and services

School-Wide Systems

The middle school must be a responsive learning environment in order that young adolescents feel a part of a supportive and concerned community (Carnegie, 1989; Mac Iver and Epstein, 1993). This type of responsive learning environment insures that students are not alienated, neglected, or abandoned in the schooling process and, consequently, offers opportunities for student leadership development, and student activity participation and self-exploration.

A positive school-wide environmental system will address the learning and belonging needs of students by implementing relevant school policies, programs, and activities. Special break times for student social contact, student mediation training, after school clubs, and advisor-advisee programs are all examples of ways to provide a positive school-wide climate. Four of the most important middle school practices that guide student behavior and provide for student psychosocial and cognitive growth are (1) school rules and procedures, (2) student affairs activities, (3) student guidance and support, and (4) advisory programs.

School Policies, Rules, and Procedures

Middle schools which demonstrate effective school climates create for students an atmosphere of safety and belonging (Wilmore, 1992). The most effective middle schools insure the security and belonging needs of students by providing certain conditions and programs that maintain a positive learning atmosphere. These conditions concern school policies, rules, and procedures designed to protect student rights and responsibilities. Middle schools must communicate to students that they are valued and respected human beings. All policies and procedures must emphasize that students value and respect each other as well as their school as a whole. The middle school must strive to adopt a "family-like" atmosphere where everyone takes responsibility and plays an important part in the schooling process. The middle school philosophy emphasizes that these conditions are most likely to produce effective student learning and development.

To function effectively, good middle schools have written guidelines and expectations for student behavior. How these expectations are conveyed and enforced are important issues to consider when examining the climate of a middle school. The standards and policies for student behavior must be clearly described, defined, and enforced during all aspects of the school day. Once again, the purpose of these standards is to protect student safety and rights while encouraging student responsibility and mutual respect. These standards must be maintained not only in classrooms but also in the hallways, during lunch, and at activities before and after school.

Teachers and administrators in the middle school are responsible for supporting, maintaining, and enforcing school policies and procedures that address student rights and responsibilities. In order to carry out these responsibilities, the concerned teacher should first study the school's handbook for student behavioral standards and rules. Teachers must know and enforce school rules as well as model responsible, respectful behavior. Second, teachers should discuss the importance of school policies and rules with their students and be sure that students have access to the school handbooks in their classrooms. Students must be knowledgeable and understand behavioral expectations. Are these written clearly for students to understand? Third, teachers should observe and analyze how effective and fair these school policies and rules are for their students. Teachers should discuss them with students and their colleagues to be sure that they are effective in protecting student rights, and they are not limiting students in negative ways. *A school that is overly rigid, authoritarian, and punishing is a school with a negative school climate.* Teachers may want to encourage their schools to revise their procedures and policies in order to provide for student input in developing these important standards. Student involvement in defining school rules and procedures insures that students have a sense of control over their environment and that their opinions are important. And finally, teachers must reflect on their own behavior when faced with maintaining and enforcing school rules. Do they ignore inappropriate student behavior in the hallways or do they take appropriate action? How comfortable are teachers in conveying an assertive tone with students? The teacher's commitment to enforcing school standards is important. Whether in the hallways during class changes, attending school activities, or serving on bus duty, the middle level teacher must monitor student behavior effectively.

Unfortunately, safety in schools has become a national concern of parents, students, and teachers. One recent study reported that adolescents between the ages of 10 and 19 are killed by guns at a rate of one every three hours (Sautter, 1995). Such acts of violence are now taking place in schools and are being committed by middle school children. Other acts of aggression are also occurring at the middle school level. Inappropriate touching and caressing, and verbally suggestive comments are examples of sexual harassment behaviors that occur in middle schools (Shoop, 1994). To respond to these issues, the National Middle School Association has approved a resolution promoting the development of intervention strategies aimed at reducing aggressive behavior and increasing the safety of young adolescents in schools.

To insure student safety, some schools have taken a reactive approach to violence by installing metal detectors and closed circuit cameras in school hallways and on school buses to monitor student behavior. Many middle schools have also instituted severe expulsion policies for weapon possession.

These types of interventions, while protective, also may send negative messages seriously affecting the school climate. In comparison, other schools have adopted a more proactive approach to addressing school violence. These schools try to combat the underlying causes of student violence and aggression by providing mediation training for middle school teachers and students (Sautter, 1995). Mediation training involves learning conflict resolution and conflict management behaviors that focus on decreasing feelings of anger and increasing problem-solving communication. Students learn to analyze the consequences of their actions and try to come up with workable solutions other than aggressive behavior. Currently, several school districts offer special mediation training to teachers and administrators who, in turn, are responsible for training students and parents (N. Settlemyer, personal communication, September 12, 1995).

In addition to mediation training, one of the best strategies for protecting student safety rights seems to be the development of a school-wide safety and crisis intervention plan. This plan is created by teachers, students, and parents, and is placed in the general school handbook. The plan describes safety threats and presents strategies and procedures to follow in the event problems occur. Most importantly, in the event of a crisis or school-wide tragedy, specific teacher and student teams can help the entire school family better cope with unexpected happenings. Teachers and students can form a "crisis network" team after they have been through appropriate training on how to respond to others during a crisis at the school.

Student Affairs Activities

In addition to providing students with exceptional classroom learning experiences, Wilmore (1992) stresses that middle schools should offer a variety of student affairs activities that will involve students in other important aspects of school beyond academics. The middle school years are a time when students either connect with or disconnect from the schooling experience which makes this time a critical turning point (Carnegie, 1989). Most importantly, students who either physically or mentally withdraw from school often believe that they are not liked by their teachers and that they do not belong (Gold and Mann, 1984). Conversely, students who are active in school in co-curricular activities such as sports teams or drama clubs may be more likely to increase school attendance and positive behavior in school (Hale, 1993).

Involvement with school activities can result in three important student outcomes. First, students have an opportunity to explore and develop their interests in a structured way. This exploration can guide students in establishing their identity and expand their involvement with leisure time activities. Second, activity involvement allows students to form relationships with members of their peer group who have similar interests. The peer group becomes an extremely important influence on students during early adolescence. Third, the adults that students come in contact with during these activities are influential role models. The majority of these adults are teachers at the school who have an interest in students.

Being involved with student activities demonstrates to students that teachers care about them and that they have other interests besides classroom academic learning (Wilmore, 1992). The personalized contact and interpersonal relationship students form with at least one significant person at a school is critical to their sense of belonging (Carnegie, 1989; Lounsbury, 1991). Having this type of relationship conveys to young adolescents that someone cares about them and that they have a place in the school family.

What are some varied student affairs activities that middle school teachers can lead and sponsor? The list is endless. Of course, the traditional list includes student council, athletic teams, and clubs. To reach more students, educators recommend activities and clubs in such areas as photography, quilt making, student mentor training, the arts, learning strategies, music and dance appreciation, and kite-flying (Stevens, 1992; Wilmore, 1992). These activities may take place before and after school or at special club periods.

In addition to student affairs activities, some middle schools offer specified exploratory programs for students during each school semester. Students are able to choose an area of interest to develop through short courses that may last a 9-week period. Exploratory programs are more fully described in Chapter 5.

Teacher involvement in student affairs activities is helpful in creating a positive middle school climate that meets the developmental needs of young adolescents. Student needs for competence, creative expression, physical activity, and positive social interactions can be met through each of these activities. In addition, being involved with students in areas other than classroom learning can be beneficial for the teacher. Becoming aware of the interests and issues that young adolescents face can help teachers become more sensitive to students as they create more relevant learning opportunities for them.

Student Guidance and Support

Middle schools with rules and procedures in place and planned student affairs activities have practices that positively respond to student developmental needs for safety, belonging and identity formation. To further address these needs, effective middle schools offer special programs and practices that focus on students' affective learning. These affective programs are frequently called student advisory and student advocacy programs (Campbell, 1992).

Affective learning deals with such variables as student self-esteem, values, anxiety, motivation, self-understanding, and creativity (Brown, 1975). Furthermore, affective education as a practice can encompass all aspects of student development including social, emotional, physical, vocational, recreational, and intellectual needs (Allender, 1982). The common theme evident in the literature on affective learning is that it demonstrates a student-centered focus which addresses student feelings, emotions, and attitudes especially in relation to student learning in an academic setting (Anderson, 1981; Newberry and Loue, 1982). Learning in classrooms involves a strong interaction between the social, psychological and cognitive domains.

The student guidance and support program must respond to student developmental needs. Traditionally, student affective issues have been handled by the school guidance departments and, thus, have not been seen as issues for teachers to address. In addition to individual counseling, guidance departments have been responsible for maintaining student records, instituting academic referrals, coordinating testing, sponsoring career days, and conducting parent-teacher conferences. Because of the multitude of responsibilities that guidance counselors have and their limited time allotted for individual and group affective-based guidance and counseling, middle schools have instituted extended student support programs that directly involve classroom teachers. The awareness that students must have a significant relationship with at least one adult in the school has influenced middle school guidance counselors to expand their outreach services to other faculty. Hence, the total school is now assuming more responsibility for student affective learning by providing student-centered programs such as "teacher advisory."

Teacher Advisory

Because such programs are based on early adolescent developmental needs, middle school teacher advisory programs are one of the most frequently recommended components for effective middle schools (Clark and Clark, 1993; Hertzog, 1992; Merenbloom, 1991; Stevens, 1992). Unfortunately, these programs are also the most difficult to implement and maintain because of the new role responsibilities that teachers must assume. Still, effective middle schools offer some form of advisory that is worthy of consideration.

Advisory programs are also referred to as advisor-advisee, class guidance, TA (teacher advisory), and homebase (Ames & Miller, 1994). In advisory programs, a teacher adopts a guidance role with a defined group of students. The teacher-advisor tries to help students adjust to the diverse physical, moral, and social-emotional developmental conflicts they may be experiencing at school and perhaps out of school. Claire Cole (1992), who has written extensively on teacher advisory, defines the concept as "a time structure when items of importance, some unplanned, can be discussed by small groups (of students) with higher levels of trust and concern than is found in the classroom" (p. 7).

These meetings, or advisory sessions, are led by an adult (e.g., a teacher, administrator, or counselor) who meets with the same group of twelve to fifteen students on a daily basis (Cole, 1992, Ziegler and Mulhall, 1994). The sessions run from ten to thirty minutes, or longer if necessary, and they are scheduled at various times during the school day. Some schools have advisory after first period class while other schools may offer advisory after lunch period. The schedule varies from school to school.

The topics discussed during advisory are unlimited and include such issues as death, war, divorce, peer relationships, violence, school policy, shoplifting, sexual harassment, and coping skills (Ayres, 1994;

Cole, 1992; Shoop, 1994). In many cases, the topics steer away from academics and address more affective issues that students face on a daily basis. However, advisory programs that also include academic support and assistance with subject area activities and teacher team assignments may be integrated into the program. In any event, advisory programs must include student input into the topics and themes, and teachers must be comfortable with facilitating learning in these areas.

Teacher advisory serves many purposes and can result in important consequences. First, teacher advisory can foster better relations between students and teachers (Ayres, 1994). The program allows students and teachers to learn about each other in a setting other than a strictly "academic" classroom. Through class discussions, students are given the opportunity to express their views on subjects that concern them. Most importantly, this type of sharing gives teachers a better understanding of the issues and concerns that young adolescents face. Zeigler and Mulhall (1994) assert that the mutual understanding that develops in the teacher advisory relationship can influence student motivation to learn. They also emphasize that the relationships can encourage teachers to become more motivated to guide, teach, and listen to their students.

Second, teacher advisory can foster better relations among students who come from diverse backgrounds which, in turn, can result in building stronger group cohesiveness (Campbell, 1992). The peer group has a strong influence on young adolescents with their ensuing concern for fitting in and belonging. By conducting activities that encourage student interaction and communication, advisory can expand the knowledge students have of each other and may help students develop more supportive relations with others who do not typically fall in their circle of friends. Depending on the skill of the advisor, the students may become more knowledgeable of, and accepting toward, student cultural and ethnic differences. For example, students should be given the opportunity to discuss the unique ways their families celebrate certain holidays and participate in certain customs and rituals. Also, differences in language expression and their origins are worthy issues that influence social perspectives. These activities may be especially helpful when new students enter the school from different locations.

Third, there is some evidence that teacher advisory can increase student motivation and improve the behavior of at-risk students (Mac Iver and Epstein, 1993; Ziegler and Mulhall, 1994). Literature on advisory suggests that these programs may lower student absences, improve student attitudes toward learning, and lower student dropout rates. Further, these programs, when administered appropriately, can ease the transition students experience in schools as they progress from a smaller, more intimate, learning environment of the elementary school to the larger, more impersonal, environment of the high school where pressures increase and demands can be overwhelming (Hertzog, 1992). Through advisory, students can think and reflect about their behavior in school and learn new ways of coping with school pressures (Ayres, 1994).

Advisories appear to provide many benefits to students by helping them with their developmental needs. Unfortunately, studies are showing that only 75 percent of the middle schools report that they have advisory programs (Mac Iver and Epstein, 1993). This data is especially disturbing since the researchers also report that schools with effective advisory programs were also schools with strong guidance programs and lower dropout rates.

What makes an advisory program a successful one? After reading the above section, it can be seen that the teacher is the critical factor in determining the success of the program. In addition to having at least two years of program planning, advisory programs must have exceptional teachers as advisors. Effective teacher-advisors demonstrate important personal and professional attitudes and behavior. Many of these characteristics were discussed in Chapter 2.

Cole (1992) contends that some of the problems with teacher advisory stem from the fact that many teachers do not know how to express feelings of caring and concern. She believes that many teachers lack adequate training and that many teachers suffer from shyness and a lack of confidence when attempting personal communication. Whereas teachers may be able to get their subject matter across to their students, they may not be as successful guiding student discussions on sensitive issues such as friendship and peer relations. Ayres (1994) asserts that teachers also may lack an understanding of the philosophy and purpose behind advisory and thus may be fearful of their role. In reality, many teachers are not comfortable with this type of activity.

Without question, conducting advisory sessions requires a great deal of skill, knowledge and commitment. The characteristics that many teachers have reported as being important for advisory effectiveness are listed in Figure 4.1.

THE EFFECTIVE TEACHER ADVISOR:

1. sincerely cares about all students,

2. demonstrates enthusiasm toward all students,

3. listens to and values student opinions,

4. models respect and effective communication skills,

5. guides student self-reflection and group cooperation,

6. plans developmentally appropriate advisory activities,

7. identifies students needing more intensive guidance and support,

8. assesses the progress of the advisory program,

9. understands the teacher advisor's role and responsibilities, and

10. participates in training to improve advisory skills.

Figure 4.1. Characteristics of effective teacher advisors.

In summary, teacher advisory may be one way for middle schools to meet the developmental needs of students. However, only through effective school planning and the participation of well-trained and committed teachers will the advisory be beneficial to students in the middle school. School-wide policies, activities and programs all play a significant role in addressing student developmental needs.

Classroom Environmental Systems

A major school environmental system that reflects the climate of the school is the relationship that exists between the students and teacher in the classroom. This relationship is established and maintained by the interactions that occur primarily during instructional activities in the classroom. Teachers are constantly communicating and responding to students. Of critical importance are the interpretations students make about their teachers' verbal and nonverbal behaviors. Sometimes, messages are unclear and result in student confusion and frustration, which in turn can often lead to classroom management problems. Teachers who create a positive learning climate often avoid management problems by planning for student needs.

The primary goal of the middle school is to create a positive learning climate that meets the academic and social needs of all students (Stevens, 1992). In order to meet student needs in the classroom, teachers must have specific elements in their learning environments for students. Educators have identified the elements of a good learning climate (Vars, 1988) These elements include:

• a meaningful curriculum,
• active and age-appropriate teaching methods,
• clear expectations and guidelines,
• student and teacher rapport, and
• student success.

Teacher knowledge of early adolescent development is imperative for these elements to be maintained. Reflect a moment about early adolescent development. As noted in Chapter 2 the early adolescent is changing intellectually, socially, emotionally, and physically. The developmental nature of these young people should guide teaching, communication, and learning structures in the classroom. Young adolescents are becoming more self-conscious and egocentric. They are beginning to engage in abstract problem solving, and they can understand satirical situations. They have a thirst for stimulating experiences and exploration, and often, they look to their peer group for these experiences. In addition, because of physical changes, they are adjusting their postures, the way they dress, and their self-image. Sitting still for an entire class can be a problem. To maintain an effective learning climate that is orderly and conducive to learning, the teacher must take these developmental issues into consideration. Obviously, a fifty-minute lecture on the use of pronouns would be a poor instructional strategy to use with middle school students (see Chapter 6).

Classroom Structures

Teacher behaviors and strategies help maintain a positive learning climate. The first step in the teaching process, however, focuses on the physical structure and environment of the classroom and how this can influence student learning and behavior. The physical environment of the classroom can create student behavior problems (Vars, 1988). The way desks and chairs are arranged, the view outside the window, and the ability to see the chalkboard, overhead transparencies, and other instructional materials are all factors to consider.

Ideally, the desks and chairs in a classroom must be arranged so that the teacher can move freely around to each student without barriers. This arrangement allows the teacher to make contact easily with each student in all parts of the room. Also, the arrangement must allow the teacher to have a clear view of each student in order that student behavior may be monitored. Equally important, students must be able to see their teacher and make eye contact during instruction. Beyond seeing the teacher, the classroom should be designed so that students can view the board and other visual learning materials without obstruction. When views are blocked, students find other activities to occupy their time, and this could be a source of behavioral problems.

The placement of resources, materials, books, computers, and student work folders must allow for easy access. The classroom must be pleasing and comfortable, yet it must convey a learning atmosphere where student interest is stimulated. Supplemental material enhances instruction and learning. Maps, magazines, software, and student resources should be organized and in place for student involvement. The teacher must have all instructional items and resources neatly organized and available quickly when needed. These materials need to be accessed and put into use without losing instructional time and with a minimum amount of disruption.

Seating arrangements in middle school classrooms must be designed to support a variety of learning activities. These activities include individual work, small group work and team projects. Many teachers prefer arranging desks in groups of four; others prefer a classroom with two semicircles. There is no ideal desk arrangement that has demonstrated increases in student learning and attention. Teachers should experiment to find the one that works best for them. Certainly, one that allows easy transition to student group work would be preferred.

Finally, middle school teachers, because they are teamed, have the benefit of working closely with their peers. This relationship can help teachers share environmental structures and strategies that work best for them and their students. Teaming allows teachers to learn from each other and also can support new ideas and approaches that teachers may try. A major philosophical approach of the middle school is one of collaboration between faculty. This concept is further discussed in Chapters 2 and 7.

Classroom Rules and Procedures

All classrooms have rules and procedures that help guide and facilitate student learning and behavior (see Figure 4.2). As noted, one of the seven developmental needs of young adolescents is for structure and clear limits. Rules identify expected behavioral standards for the classroom while procedures institute the practices and routines to follow to accomplish certain tasks. "All students will be in their seats when the bell rings" is an example of a rule. A procedure, for example, might concern how students turn assignments in to the teacher (e.g., putting them in the assignment box or passing them forward). In any event, rules and procedures can help provide the necessary structure for a positive learning climate. To be effective, rules should be limited in number (Campbell, 1992).

---

1. Be punctual, polite, and pleasant.

2. Be prepared for class with materials/homework ready to go.

3. Stay on task.

4. Keep hands, feet, and objects, and remarks to yourself.

5. Raise your hand before speaking.

Figure 4.2. Sample classroom rules.

In determining the rules and procedures of a middle level classroom, individual interdisciplinary teacher teams and students should both be involved (Purkey and Novak, 1984; Schurr et al, 1995). There are several advantages to having the team draw up initial classroom policies. First, there is one defined set of policies and procedures rather than separate ones for each teacher on the team. Having one set makes it less confusing for the adolescent who, during this developmental stage, frequently needs repetition and consistency (Campbell, 1992). Second, the team has determined what constitutes misbehavior. Thus, more consistency can be provided throughout the school day in maintaining appropriate behavior. Third, when major infractions occur, the team can meet together with the student to determine the appropriate course of action. Teaming also allows a group of teachers to know a specific group of students very well; students will view the teacher team as a unit that functions cohesively.

Students must also be involved in determining classroom rules and expectations. Stevenson (1992) asserts that young adolescents are striving for individual identity by trying out independent thinking and decision making. They question authority and assert their beliefs more so than in previous years. Subsequently, he contends that in areas where decisions can be shared, such as classroom policies, student input is necessary. Moreover, Stevenson claims that young adolescents are usually very cautious and conservative in making decisions that impact others. A major benefit of student involvement is that the rules and procedures will be more meaningful and relevant to the entire class. By eliciting student input, teachers convey a respect for student views and communicate that students are important in the decision-making process (Purkey and Novak, 1984).

Teacher Behaviors and Attitudes

When examining teacher behaviors that influence classroom climate, first look closely at the curriculum and instruction taking place in the classroom. Middle school educators agree that the curriculum in middle level classrooms must be stimulating, and the instruction must be fast-paced to avoid student boredom and low motivation (Wilmore, 1992). Student engagement in learning activities can be related to the pacing and transitions that take place in classroom.

Most importantly, teachers must be able to provide students with meaningful content that connects them to the real world (Kovalik, 1994). Middle school classroom learning should encourage a variety of student expression including, for example, media technology, writing, music, and computer activities (Scales, 1992). In an eighth grade English class, students can develop their own poems and create a corresponding computer graphic poetry presentation that is set to music. In this instance the students are able to make poetry come to life in a way that is more meaningful to them compared to the more traditional methods of teaching poetry through reading and writing. This instructional approach encourages active student learning through exploration and use of different skills.

Middle level educators also emphasize that students must experience success in the classroom (Scales, 1992; Stevenson, 1992). Classroom activities should be varied and individualized so that students can be recognized and rewarded for their effort and perseverance in learning, as well as for achievement. The goal orientation of the class should be focused on student learning and improvement with effort and cooperation being recognized. In addition to a student of the month who has demonstrated high grades, teachers should also include a student of the week for different qualifications (Schurr et al, 1995). Negative labeling of students should be avoided at all costs (Strahan, 1989), and limiting recognition to one type of achievement measure is an exclusionary practice that may neglect the majority of students.

It is important that the classroom atmosphere convey mutual respect and recognize students who put forth a great deal of effort in their schoolwork. To support student exploration in learning and motivation, students must feel safe to make mistakes in the classroom and not fear looking stupid (Wilmore, 1992). Being laughed at by the peer group or embarrassed by the teacher in front of others are horrible experiences for middle school students to bear. Once again, a caring and safe classroom environment where student dignity and self-worth is maintained is necessary (Vars, 1988). To insure this type of atmosphere the teacher must emphasize respect and model it as well.

Student motivation and perseverance in the classroom depends greatly on student self-efficacy. Self-efficacy is the belief that people have about their ability to succeed at a given task or situation. This construct is very important to student engagement in learning tasks. To build student self-efficacy, teachers must communicate to students that they believe in them, and they know that all students have the strength and ability to succeed in school. Therefore, middle level teachers must show students, both verbally and nonverbally, that they have appropriately high expectations. This communication must indicate to students that they are able, valuable, and responsible young people (Strahan, 1989). Teacher communication and feedback to students must be given carefully, not effusively. Praise must be appropriate and specific while not drawing unnecessary attention to the young adolescent. A subtle note or a quiet whisper may convey praise best. At all costs, do not embarrass the student; students must be treated with respect.

Effective middle school teachers model fairness, composure, and respect. This modeling is often conveyed through the language used in the classroom. Good and Brophy (1994) recommend that teachers phrase rules and directives in positive, not negative terms. Figure 4.3 provides examples of positive and negative statements. Positive statements are more accepting and cue students into an understanding of the behavior. Negative statements can put students on the defensive and often cause resentment.

POSITIVE	*NEGATIVE*
• Put your materials away neatly.	• Don't leave a messy desk.
• Talk to your partner quietly.	• Don't be so loud.
• Move quickly and quietly into your discussion groups.	• Don't be so slow and noisy.
	• Don't be lazy and just guess.
• Be prepared to tell us why you chose this response. Think it through carefully.	

Figure 4.3. Examples of positive and negative directives.

In summary, certain teacher behaviors can promote and maintain a positive learning climate in the classroom. A positive school classroom climate has an atmosphere of respect, clear guidelines for behavior, and a learning orientation that emphasizes exploration, participation and success.

School-Community Environmental System

Two of the eight recommendations of the Carnegie Report, *Turning points, preparing American youth for the 21st century* (1989), concern increasing involvement of families and community groups with middle schools. Middle schools and students do not exist in isolation from families and communities. Education occurs both in and out of the middle school and, therefore, involves parents, businesses, governmental agencies, civic groups, and other organizations (South Carolina Middle Level Project, 1994). Collaborative partnerships between families and community organizations are necessary to create an effective learning climate in the school and the community.

The third school environmental system that further defines the climate of the school is the interaction that occurs between the school and the family and the school and the community. The community is composed of businesses, places of worship, governmental agencies, recreational and youth serving organizations, and health and family support agencies. To develop the life skills they need to survive and contribute to our society, young adolescents need (1) parental support for learning, (2) access to health services for physical as well as psychological issues, and (3) exposure to the business world (Scales, 1992). The education of young people involves parents, family members, and the total community.

Parental Involvement

Two predominant types of parent involvement have been identified (Henderson, 1981). These types are general school program involvement and child-focused involvement. Examples of parent participation in school program functioning are volunteer work at the school, serving on school advisory councils, and sponsorship of school activities such as field trips, PTA presentations, and booster clubs. This level of parental participation has several benefits. First, parents become more aware of the many dimensions and facets of schooling that go beyond academics. Second, this awareness helps increase the parents' understanding of the school system functioning which in turn can help promote schools to others who may not understand. Third, parents have much personal and professional expertise they can share with teachers and administrators in such areas as finance, business, leadership, and educational resources. Parental participation is of significant importance because it can have a powerful effect on the school faculty, staff, and students (Myers and Monson, 1992).

An excellent example of parental participation in school program review and development occurred when a local school district adopted a strategic planning agenda whereby each school was directed to formulate specific committees to study and define school goals for the next three years and to determine programs and activities that would support these goals. These committees, which met for several months during the school year, were composed of teachers, administrators, students, parents, community representatives and non-teaching staff members, such as custodians and cafeteria workers. Serious dialog occurred between the many diverse groups of people on these committees, and many different views were presented in such areas as student learning, school rules, and special programs. Even though opinions differed in many respects, the committee groups were able to reach an agreement on what the school goals and activities should be for their middle school. Once finalized, the plan was presented to the principal for implementation. Because of the high level of involvement and input from the different planning team members, the principal then had additional support from the community to reach school goals.

The second type of parental involvement is child-focused and concerns the learning and development of the young adolescent in the family. Here, parental involvement is directly related to the child's functioning in the school. The traditional form of parent involvement deals with teachers informing parents through letters, phone calls or conferences about their child's learning progress and behavior in school. In addition to keeping parents informed, middle school advocates recommend that parents be educated about early adolescent development (Renihan and Renihan, 1995). Parents must have information about young adolescent characteristics and issues, ways to communicate with them, and what schools are doing to meet student needs (Clark and Clark, 1993).

Research on parent involvement in education has demonstrated that significant parent participation will promote successful learning in young adolescents (Johnston, 1993). Middle schools encourage parental involvement through frequent communication and by providing relevant activities and programs. Newsletters, special seminars on student learning, parent discussion groups, and a sharing of resource materials on adolescent development and learning are examples of parental outreach activities.

The teacher plays an important role in developing parental involvement and support for student learning. Teachers must design and implement a system for communicating with parents that is effective and that meets teachers', students', and parents' needs. Teachers must build rapport with parents to lessen the distance that typically exists between parenting and schooling responsibilities and expectations (Renihan and Renihan, 1995). Through communication and collaboration teachers and parents can jointly participate in activities that support student learning both during and after school hours. For example, teachers must, at least once each month, call or communicate with parents in writing about student learning and behavior. This communication should include both student strengths and areas needing change, and it should be presented in a simple and direct manner. Communication should always include something positive.

Teachers in their communications must provide suggestions for home learning activities that parents can provide. For example, if students need to measure items in the home for a mathematics assignment, parents should help them find appropriate items. Further, if students must interview neighbors about careers, parents could recommend to students who they can call. Home assignments to involve parents must emphasize the value of work and connect school to normal experiences in the student's environment (Johnston, 1993). Often, parents may doubt their abilities and knowledge level when it comes to helping their children learn. Teachers must, therefore, give parents reassurance and non-threatening relevant activities; for example, parents should be encouraged to help students with homework schedules and provide them with quiet time for studying.

Johnston (1993) presents specific teacher characteristics to enhance parent involvement. He states that teachers must (1) have knowledge of changes in family structure and design new ways to connect with parents, (2) alleviate their prejudices toward families who are led by single parents or families from a lower socio-economic level, (3) learn about family needs through dialogue and listening, and (4) be specific in communicating with parents. Instead of saying, "Paul is adjusting poorly," tell parents that "Paul has missed handing in two assignments this week." Clear, concerned communication must be emphasized.

Mr. and Mrs. John Doe
Main Street
Anywhere, USA

Dear Mr. and Mrs. Doe,

Your daughter Joan has been making adequate progress in all of her content courses over the last month. She has a very pleasing attitude and has always been polite and courteous to the teachers in the team. Moreover, Joan is very well liked by her classmates.

In the last month, her teacher noticed that Joan has not met the same standards she was meeting earlier in the school year. Although her work is at an acceptable level, her teachers feel she is capable of much more and has done better work in the past. We hope that you can help us determine what problems Joan may be having and work with us to eliminate them.

The team has noted the following changes in Joan's behavior:

1. She is not completing all of her homework.

2. She seems to "daydream" too frequently during class.

3. She has, especially in the past two weeks, been late to several classes.

As you know, we are always happy to meet with you to discuss your child's progress. Please feel free to call and set an appointment at your convenience.

Sincerely,

Figure 4.4. An example of effective home communication.

Finally, to support teacher communication with parents, the school administration must provide flexible scheduling and appropriate time for meetings and conferences. Teachers may need to meet with parents at other times during the day and in other locations besides the school. Also, teachers may need additional training in how to communicate effectively with parents. Teacher teams could work together toward improving their conferencing skills.

Community Organizations and Services

The relationship between the school and community organizations must be highly interactive and positive. Community involvement, as does parent involvement, provides many benefits to the entire learning community. First, student understanding and exploration of careers can be enhanced through business participation in schools. Teachers can utilize business resource people in their classes to demonstrate different types of careers related to specific subjects. Moreover, the abilities and skills needed for certain careers can be tied into subject matter with the participation of business people (Martorella, 1990). Besides work skills needed, students will gain a better understanding of the work ethic required to get and maintain a job. Ideally, students and teachers need to visit people on the job in addition to having class discussions.

Second, students can become engaged in community service learning projects that are conducted in collaboration with schools and community/business organizations. For example, a team of sixth grade classes may become involved with a project that provides services to the local nursing home. Depending upon the needs of the nursing center, students may be given opportunities to work with older adults, perform programs, or help improve the outdoor grounds of the center. Community service projects can help enhance meaningful learning about the community and encourage students, at a young age, to be supportive and involved citizens. Also, there is some indication that service learning can promote achievement, self-confidence and problem-solving skills by having students work cooperatively on community projects (Lewis, 1992). In turn, the businesses and organizations involved with these students can learn more about young adolescent developmental needs and be more supportive of their families and schools.

Third, health and social service agencies that provide services to families and young adolescents can be more accessible during the school day. Disadvantaged families are in constant need of services; unfortunately, these services often require time away from school for students and time away from work for the parents. Service agencies could collaborate and arrange times during the month that they would be available at the school site. Middle schools, of course, need to identify the needs of their students and families to coordinate the services required. Special agreements must be made with area agencies to participate in providing these services at the schools, and schools must provide adequate office space for these supportive agencies. By offering these services at the schools, student absences may be decreased and parents may perceive the school system as being concerned and more responsive to their needs.

The climate of the school depends greatly on the interaction that occurs between the school and the community. Effective learning environments can be created in schools with the support of the parents and community. With this community support, effective learning environments can also be created in homes, businesses and community organizations.

Summary

This chapter has described three types of school environmental systems that convey the learning climate of the school. These systems include school-wide programs and policies, classroom learning, and school-community activities. In an effective middle school, all of these systems are designed to support the developmental needs of young adolescents.

The chapter also describes the creation of a school-wide learning environment that emphasizes each student's personal worth and opportunity for success. Such an environment will certainly lessen classroom management problems. Regardless of how well constructed the school environment is, however, there will be times when middle school students will exhibit problems. In solving these problems, teachers must focus on the causes of misbehavior, not react negatively to symptomatic behavior. Middle level faculty can draw from one of the many books and training programs that will help develop school-wide approaches to addressing such problems.

Research evidence suggests that the environment needs to be developed in its entirety, not in isolated pieces (Felner, Jackson, Kasak, Mulhall, Brand and Flowers, 1997). That is, the most effective middle schools where students make the most significant academic gains address the entire environment (size, student/teacher ratio, amount of team planning time, etc). Schools that, for example, have adequate planning time (i.e. four times per week) but have teams of students that are too large with student/teacher ratios around thirty are not likely to be as effective. Also, it helps little to go from one planning period per week to two periods or from 200-student teams to teams of 180 students. (Serious adherence to the principles of middle level education as discussed in Chapter 1 must be enforced if true effectiveness is to be realized.)

REFERENCES

Allender, J. S. (1982). Affective education. In H.E. Mitzel (ED.), *Encyclopedia of Education Research* 5th ed. New York: The Free Press, pp. 94-103.

Ames, N. L., & Miller, E. (1994). *Changing middle schools.* San Francisco: Jossey-Bass.

Anderson, L. W. (1981). Assessing affective characteristics in the schools. Boston: Allyn and Bacon, Inc.

Arnold, J. (1994). Towards a middle level curriculum rich in meaning. *Middle School Curriculum,* Nov., 8-12.

Ayres, L. R. (1994). Middle school advisory programs: Findings from the field. *Middle School Journal,* 25, 8-14.

Brown, G. I. (1975). The training of teachers for affective roles. In Ryan, K. (Ed.), *Teacher Education* (pp. 173-203). Seventy-Fourth Yearbook of the National Society for the Study of Education, Part 2. University of Chicago Press, Chicago, Illinois.

Campbell, S. H. (1992). How do we meet the needs of early adolescents? *The Education Digest,* 58, 8-12.

Carnegie Council on Adolescent Development. (1989). *Turning points: Preparing American youth for the 21st century.* New York: Carnegie Corporation.

Clark, S. N., & Clark, D.C. (1993). Middle level school reform: The rhetoric and the reality. *The Elementary School Journal,* 93, 447-480.

Cole, C. (1992). *Nurturing a teacher advisory program.* Columbus, OH: National Middle School Association.

Crohn, L. (1983). *Toward excellence: Student and teacher behaviors as predictors of school success.* ERIC Document Reproduction No. ED 242 704.

Elkind, D. (1994). *A sympathetic understanding of the child.* Boston: Allyn and Bacon.

Felner, R.D., Jackson, A.W., Kasak, D., Mulhall, P., Brand, S., & Flowers, N. (1997). "The impact of school reform for the middle years: Longitudinal study of a network engaged in Turning Points-Based comprehensive school transformation." *Phi Delta Kappan ,* 78(7), 528-532; 541-550.

Gold, M., & Mann, D. W. (1984). *Expelled to a friendlier place.* Ann Arbor: The University of Michigan Press.

Good, T., Biddle, B., & Brophy, J. (1975). *Teachers make a difference.* New York: Holt, Rinehart & Winston.

Good, T. L., & Brophy, J. E. (1994). *Looking in classrooms.* New York: Harper Collins College Publishers.

Hale, R.P. (1993). Clubs reach urban middle level students. *Schools in the Middle,* 2, 23-25.

Henderson, A. (1981). *The evidence grows.* Columbia, MD: National Committee for Citizens in Education.

Hertzog, C. J. (1992). Middle level advisory programs: From the ground up. *Schools in the Middle,* 2, 23-27.

Johnston, J. H. (1993). *The new American family and the school.* Columbus, OH: National Middle School Association.

Kovalik, S. (1994). *Integrated thematic instruction: The model.* Kent, WA: Susan Kovalik and Associates.

Lewis, A. (1992). *Urban youth in community service: Becoming part of the solution.* ERIC/CUE Digest. New York, NY: ERIC Clearinghouse on Urban Education. (ED351425)

Lounsbury, J. H. (1991). A fresh start for the middle school curriculum. *Middle School Journal,* 23, 1991.

Martorella, P. H. (1990).The community as laboratory for learning. *Middle School Journal,* 22, 20-23.

Mac Iver, D. J., & Epstein, J. L. (1993). Middle grades research: Not yet mature, but no longer a child. *Elementary School Journal,* 93, 519-533.

Merenbloom, E. Y. (1991). *The team process.* Columbus, OH: National Middle School Association.

Myers, J., & Monson, L. (1992). *Involving families.* Columbus, OH: National Middle School Association.

National Middle School Association. (1992). *This we believe.* Columbus, OH: National Middle School Association.

Newberry, N. A., & Loue, W. E. (1982). Affective education addresses the basics. *Educational Leadership,* 39, 489-500.

Personal communication N. Settlemyer (personal communication, September, 12, 1995).

Purkey, W.W. (1970). *Self-concept and school achievement.* Englewood Cliffs, NJ: Prentice-Hall.

Purkey, W. W., & Novak, J. M. (1984). *Inviting school success.* Belmont, CA: Wadsworth Publishing Co.

Renihan, P. J., & Renihan, F. J. (1995). The home-school psychological contract: Implications for parental involvement in middle schooling. *Middle School Journal,* 26, 57-61.

Sautter, R.C. (1995). Standing up to violence. *Phi Delta Kappan,* 76, 1-12.

Scales, P. C. (1992). From risks to resources: Disadvantaged learners and middle grades teaching. *Middle School Journal,* 23, 3-9.

Schurr, S. L., Thomason, J., & Thompson, M. (1995). *Teaching at the middle level.* Lexington, MA., D. C. Heath and Co.

Shoop, R. J. (1994). Using advisor-advisee to eradicate sexual harassment. *Middle Ground,* Summer, 1-12.

S.C. Middle Level Project. (1994). *Characteristics of effective middle level teachers and recommended middle level teacher preparation standards.* Unpublished report, Coastal Carolina University, S.C.

Strahan, D. (1989). Disconnected and disruptive students. *Middle School Journal,* 20, 1-5.

Stevens, R. L. (1992). Caught in the middle: The tracking dilemma. *Schools in the Middle,* 2, 35-37.

Stevenson, C. (1992). *Teaching ten to fourteen year olds.* New York: Longman.

Vars, G. (1988). Maintaining order in the classroom. *Middle School Journal,* 20, 4-6.

Wilmore, E. L. (1992). The "affective" middle level school: Keys to a nurturing school climate. *Schools in the Middle,* Summer, 31-34.

Ziegler, S., & Mulhall, L. (1994). Establishing and evaluating a successful advisory program in a middle school. *Middle School Journal,* 25, 42-46.

Chapter 5

DEVELOPING APPROPRIATE CURRICULUM

Imagine you are on a job interview. It is the teaching job you have always wanted–teaching middle level students. Thus far, the principal interviewing you has asked a series of general questions. Then, she says, "I would like you to imagine you are at a party among mostly strangers. Someone asks you, 'What do you do?' How would you answer?" You wonder what this person wants you to say. What would be the "right" thing to say? A little panicked, you blurt out, "I'm a science teacher." The middle school principal interviewing you suddenly seems a little less interested in your qualifications than before.

Perhaps a better response would be, "I help middle school students learn science. I am a teacher." Middle school principals are typically seeking teachers who have the ability to develop a sound curriculum in the chosen content area while, at the same time, implement instruction in a student-centered fashion. To stress that you are a science teacher emphasizes the important fact that you have knowledge in an area of academic inquiry. However, the response fails to stress the necessary emphasis on your total role as a teacher in offering developmentally appropriate instruction to enhance the social, emotional, and intellectual growth of your students. The middle school curriculum, therefore, must achieve a balance between academic-centeredness, on the one hand, and student-centeredness on the other hand.

The integrated curriculum, one that traces themes within subjects and that shows the interrelatedness of subjects, has been adopted by many middle schools as a preferred approach to offering experiences that aid in the development of student-centered learning while maintaining content relevance. Trying to offer an academically challenging curriculum while still meeting the holistic needs of middle level students is a true challenge to educators. Efforts to meet the social, personal, and academic needs of early adolescents has been addressed through the use of interdisciplinary teams, integrated curriculum, and exploratory activities in many exemplary middle schools (Kellough and Kellough, 1996).

Philosophical Rationale

Curriculum can be developed, at one extreme, using a subject-centered curriculum. At the other extreme, curriculum can be developed using a student-centered framework. A continuum can be formed with these extremes at each end and degrees of student-centeredness or subject-centeredness falling somewhere between these polar opposites. That is, one can have levels of student-or subject-centeredness.

Subject-centered curriculum tends to be formatted on either a discipline base, a broad fields base, or a structure of the knowledge base (Myers and Myers, 1990). Regardless of the base used, a subject-centered curriculum emphasizes the learning of specific content over all else. The teacher's primary concern is offering instruction in the content area while students are oriented toward the acquisition of knowledge in a specific field of inquiry.

The *discipline* base was the first subject-centered organization used. Scholars decided what content belonged in the discipline and that content was used to form the scope and sequence of the curriculum. An example might be the discipline's "history" or "literature" with subsets such as "U.S. history" or "American literature." The concept of a *broad fields approach* to subject-centered curriculum simply combines subsets into bigger units. For example, "language arts" is a broad field combining reading, writing, speaking, and listening skills and knowledge. *The structure of the knowledge* organization was introduced by Bruner (1960) and is essentially the notion that within each discipline there are important, major ideas or concepts that should form the framework for the curriculum. For example, the concepts of "identity number" and "communitive properties of addition and multiplication" might help form the structure of the knowledge in mathematics.

Student-centered curriculum, as compared to subject-centered curriculum, is based on the personal needs and interests of students as well as the social needs evolving from their everyday activities. An important contribution to the student-centered framework for curriculum development came from a group of educators called "Humanists" who were very influential in the 1970s and early 1980s (Maslow, 1970; Combs, 1982). These educators strongly stressed the importance of concepts such as self-concept, individual needs, and the worth of all individuals. The community service components of many current middle school curricula are indicative of the social function of a student-centered curriculum (Allen, Splittgerber, and Manning, 1993). An essential of the student-centered organization is the opportunity for students to have input in the decisions made concerning the structure and format of ongoing learning experiences.

As noted earlier, curriculum integration is essential to a movement toward more student-centeredness in the curriculum. Many schools today are attempting to integrate curriculum around themes that not only run through basic ideas within subjects but also show the interrelationships among subjects (Ornstein and Hunkins, 1988). There can be degrees of student-centeredness; over the years, there have been several curriculum designs that have evolved with varying degrees of content integration. Some of these are identified here.

Correlated Subjects

Correlated subjects was an early attempt at curriculum integration. In the correlated subjects design similar topics might be taught in two or more content areas without doing away with the boundaries of any of the subject areas. For example, in history class students might study colonial American history while studying literature from the same period in English class.

Broad Fields

"Broad fields," as discussed earlier, is seen as a type of integrated curriculum design (Shepherd and Ragan, 1992). This is the fusion of subsets of the curriculum into a larger unit (e.g., history, geography, economics, sociology, psychology, government, and anthropology come together to form social studies).

Multidisciplinary or Interdisciplinary

At this level of organization a common theme runs through the instruction of the different content areas. Typically, as Shepherd and Ragan (1992) note, the theme is one of the "tions." For example, "pollution" might be studied as a central theme and instruction in several of the "ics" (e.g., mathematics, economics, politics, etc.) are focused on a central theme. The existence of a theme is a major difference between correlated and multidisciplinary curriculums.

Integrated Thematic

In this design, teachers work together using student input to a central theme or themes, and instruction is built around such themes. In this model, the boundaries that separate the content areas fade away as the total curriculum becomes integrated. At the highest level, all teachers and students involved focus on the theme or themes together. There are variations in how these thematic approaches are developed; however, most agree that such a design has great value but takes time to fully implement. Kovalik (1994) has suggested that it takes three to five years to fully implement her model for Integrated Thematic Instruction. While a time investment will be needed, it is of singular importance that middle schools strive toward an integrated thematic organization if they wish to provide developmentally appropriate instruction for their students.

Theoretical Rationale

Due to the importance of providing an integrated, student-centered curriculum in today's middle level schools, persistent effort has been put forth to develop an appropriate model for such a curriculum. An appropriate curriculum for middle level students must be personally and socially relevant, interesting, and, at the same time, academically challenging to the learner. It is truly not a matter of the student taking precedence over the curriculum; the needs of the students and the need to provide an appropriate academic program must be meshed into a single driving force of the school.

A number of theorists have added to our knowledge of the integration of the middle school curriculum. An early discussion of middle level integrated curriculum was developed by Eichhorn (1966) who described a two-part curriculum. Eichhorn described an "analytical" and a "physical-cultural" component of the curriculum. The "analytical" component was composed of traditional academic content (i.e., language, mathematics, science, and social studies) while the "physical-cultural" component was composed of physical education, practical arts, fine arts, and cultural studies.

The "analytical" component would be integrated as much as possible to focus on the thought processes inherent in each of the academic areas. The physical-cultural component would be addressed in an integrated fashion to focus on the social and physical development of students. Eichhorn stressed that students needed to be involved in curricular planning. Discovery learning and independent behavior were stressed as students develop physical skills, individual interest, socialization, self-acceptance, cultural appreciation and a range of varied experiences (Eichhorn, 1966).

Lounsbury and Vars (1978) discussed the need to integrate middle school curriculum with emphasis on the personal and social developmental needs with problem-solving strategies being emphasized throughout the curriculum. Lounsbury and Vars proposed the use of 'blocks of time" (sometimes referred to simply as "blocks" by many teachers) to organize for integrated instruction. Actually, the blocks of time were organized around mathematics, science, social studies, and language arts along with art and music. Moreover, Lounsbury and Vars proposed the development of what they called a *continuous progress* component which focused on a sequential development of skills and knowledge in mathematics, science, reading and foreign language. Also, they proposed a *variable component* which integrated exploratories, independent studies, enrichment activities, electives, and other student projects.

Wiles and Bondi (1986) have suggested an integrated curriculum based on the developmental characteristics of middle school students. Wiles and Bondi divide the curriculum into three integrated components: Personal Development, Education for Social Competence, and Skills for Continuous Learning. The focal areas are used to integrate the core content areas with personal and social issues that are significant to the developmental stage that characterizes middle level students.

An exciting proposal for curriculum integration has come from James Beane, another middle school curriculum expert. The Beane (1990) curriculum is organized around thematic units. In turn, each theme will be addressed from both early adolescent developmental concerns and from society's concerns. For example, if technology were a theme, it would be examined from the middle school student's perspective (e.g., video games, television as entertainment, or the personal computer as a learning tool) and from a societal perspective (e.g., global telecommunications, the impact of the Internet on society, or technology's impact on environmental protection). These themes, according to Beane, must be selected in order that the curriculum may focus on three essential learnings: (1) *democracy,* (2) *human dignity, justice, and peace,* and (3) *cultural diversity.* According to Beane (1990, 1991, 1993), the curriculum must be focused on common problems and needs which impact the middle level students. These common problems and needs must be shown to have relevance in society as a whole. Table 5.1 delineates the major issues Beane sees as important to the life of middle school students and the major social issues middle school students should address in the curriculum.

Beane clearly differentiates between multidisciplinary or interdisciplinary and integrated curriculum (Sadowski, 1995). Beane feels that in order to have an integrated curriculum boundaries between content areas must disappear. Jacobs (1989) also refers to the dissolution of subject area boundaries as the highest level of integration of curriculum which she labels as the *integrated day.* To Beane, teachers teaching about the same theme, to the same students, in separate content areas are involved in interdisciplinary instruction—not integrated instruction.

Table 5.1
POSSIBLE THEMES USING BEANE'S MODEL

Personal Issues	*Social Issues*
1. Coping with personal changes (physical, intellectual, and socio-emotional)	1. Interdependence in a global society
2. Identity and self-concept development	2. Diversity of cultures
3. Morals, ethics, and values	3. Environmental issues
4. Peer group relations	4. Governmental processes and organizations
5. Developing a balance between independence and adult dependency	5. Economic issues in a global society
6. Commercialism as it impacts fashion, music, and leisure activity	6. Technological issues
7. Relating self-worth to commitments to other people	7. Self-destructive behaviors in a global society

A strength of Beane's framework is its balance among academics, personal concerns, and societal issues. It seems most significant that students are able to learn the connection between their concerns and those of greater society while, at the same time, learning the necessary skills and knowledge to function productively in today's world while preparing for the complexities of the future.

Beane has noted the integrated curriculum approach has pitfalls as does any educational endeavor. His greatest fear comes from the realization that some teachers will try integrated instruction and curriculum design without understanding how it should be applied or even what it fully means. "I have worked with teachers who plan with students but never press them" (Sadowski, 1995, p. 6). Beane feels that teachers who do not truly understand the necessary processes will not stress the necessary content and skills and cause integrated curriculum to receive unwarranted criticism.

Teaming

Team teaching is an organizational structure which is currently being examined as an important means for meeting the developmental needs of middle school students while providing a method for delivering an interdisciplinary curriculum. Teaming has been used in one form or another since the 1930s (Shepherd and Ragan, 1992). As a result of the recommendations of *Turning Points: Preparing American Youth for the 21st Century* (Carnegie Council on Adolescent Development, 1989), *This We Believe* (National Middle School Association, 1992) and middle level education leaders such as Beane (1990), George (1982), Erb and Doda (1989) and Vars (1987), interdisciplinary teams have become a common characteristic of many middle schools.

The interdisciplinary team can be an effective means of giving more personal attention to the middle level student. Through the use of teams, the school is broken down into subgroups of teachers and students serving to create, in essence, "schools within a school." Now, the student no longer is one of 900 students; the student becomes one of 100-125 students. A group of teachers (usually two to five in number) will team together to work with a group of students forming a family or team atmosphere. The team should have a name and a logo which adds to the bonding of the group. The teachers will come together to plan instruction and discuss the special needs of individual students in the team. This allows students and teachers to know one another better and to increase the chances for improved communication (Powell, 1993). Surveys indicate that approximately half of the nation's middle schools are using interdisciplinary teams, and every indication leads us to believe the number of schools using this organizational pattern is on the increase (Willis, 1995; Shillington, 1994).

The interdisciplinary team provides teachers an opportunity to plan the curriculum in such a way as to provide instruction around themes without having to maintain traditional subject matter boundaries. As Schurr, Thomason, and Thompson (1995) have noted, developing a functional teaching team that can provide an integrated curriculum approach takes both time and effort. The interpersonal dynamics of the teaching team must evolve in order that the teachers can openly and honestly collaborate together in order to develop units of instruction and plan and implement daily instruction. Through this type of collaboration and interaction teachers share with each other the rewards and frustrations of daily instruction (Powell and Mills, 1994).

Schurr, Thomason, and Thompson (1995) have outlined a suggested process for teaching teams to use as they move from single subject instruction to a more interdisciplinary curriculum. *Step one,* the team should discuss their students in a team planning session. This discussion will allow teachers to share with one another specific techniques and strategies that are successful with certain students. As teachers share these ideas in their planning, they are taking the first steps toward curriculum integration. *Step two,* the teachers should begin trying to coordinate homework assignments and assessments. Through their discussions, teachers should find certain common threads that tie the different content areas together; such skills, topics, and themes can form the connections needed to integrate the curriculum. *Step three,* teachers should enumerate the goals common to their personal content area. The team can then designate certain goals common to all discipline areas that can be emphasized through interdisciplinary study. *Step four,* the team should develop a scope and sequence chart that will allow common themes to be taught at the same time in each content area. *Step five,* the team should develop at least one integrated thematic unit each semester. Obviously, some units are much more complex than others; Schurr, Thomason, and Thompson (1995) suggest that the team can begin with a simple unit and progress to more complex plans. The team should see immediate value and receive positive feedback from students. Obviously, such a five-step process helps the team to evolve from single subject teaching through correlated and multidisciplinary approaches to, ultimately, an integrated thematic approach. Cook and Martinello (1994) described how interdisciplinary teams can be rather direct in curriculum development initially and become more open-ended with experience. That is, teachers prepare thematic units (see step five above) then proceed to a true integrated thematic curriculum which does away with content area boundaries over time.

Thematic Unit

A truly integrated thematic unit should, first of all, have high, challenging content presented in such a fashion that it will have relevance to the lives of middle level students. The teaching and assessment strategies associated with the content must be relevant to academic understanding while, at the same time, being both interesting and enjoyable to the developmental age group involved. That is, the unit must be student-centered while maintaining standards of academic excellence. As Erb (1995) noted, student-centeredness is most important; however, it is a hollow accomplishment without academic growth. The middle school must not be characterized by a curriculum that fails to realize its primary focus of providing an excellent academic program.

Theme Selection

The use of themes to provide the means of developing an integrated curriculum is a quite practical way to proceed. *Themes* are learned ideas which may be used to combine (integrate) traditional subject matter areas. Themes are easy to formulate and have the potential for making learning exciting. Properly stated, themes allow important aspects of the subject matter content to be included for each subject area of the curriculum. Consider the theme *THE FUTURE*. A little imagination by subject matter specialists serving on an interdisciplinary team could produce an interesting and exciting integrated curriculum with just that theme as a starting point.

Some teams prefer to develop themes that deal with issues and problems present in the local community or even problems relevant on a much larger scale. Themes are especially useful for addressing current events and issues; an issues approach to theme development tends to capture the imagination and enthusiasm of middle level students. This is true because themes involving, for example, local environmental issues often prove to be quite relevant to the middle level student. As any teacher knows—youthful idealism in dealing with issues and solving problems can be an important asset.

Content study is structured in order to lead to the construction of learning; themes help to outline and form the structure so learning is not fragmented, isolated, and irrelevant. Using a thematic approach, students are better able to realize the interconnectedness of the major subject areas. As a result, middle level students will tend to better understand the artificiality of subject boundaries. A primary benefit of themes is that they help in the organization of content and help teachers restructure both what they teach and how they teach it.

Fogarty (1994) presents an acronym which might be used to develop quality themes for either an interdisciplinary or integrated curriculum. The steps described by the acronym (THEMES) are shown in Figure 5.1.

When developing themes, whether using Fogarty's model or some other procedure, the primary source of themes should be student interests and needs. If teachers follow this advice, one should expect far fewer student queries such as "Why do we have to learn this?" Teachers should use virtually all available resources to produce and develop themes related to student interests, needs, and concerns. For example, many young adolescents are concerned about finding their place in a group so a theme "INTERDEPENDENCE" would be very appropriate. Each subject area contributes to the formation of the theme. Extensive use should be made of topics in textbooks, sources of current events, community resources and sites, and adolescent literature just to name a few examples. Use of the seemingly limitless resources of the information age is particularly opportunistic to the development of a quality integrated curriculum.

Think:	According to Fogarty, this very important first step consists primarily of brainstorming activities with as many different people involved as possible. Themes are developed in all areas without any thought about categorization at this point.
Hone:	Once the list of themes is produced, the list is analyzed and divided into categories. The procedure is to put the themes into lists and then refine or hone the lists. Following this, an attempt is made to identify what are termed "champion themes" in each category.
Extrapolate:	Team members then work to extrapolate the criteria that were used to develop the themes, particularly the champion themes. Individual team members thus complete a bit of self-reflection to decide why they chose a particular theme. From that, they extrapolate criteria which are then shared with other members of the team. This aids the decision-making process of selecting themes for further utilization.
Manipulate:	In this stage of theme development, the team members try to think of all possible ramifications (the hows, whys, and wherefores) of given themes. Fogarty further recommends that the team develop a question around the chosen theme(s). Each question is further refined as the manipulation process continues.
Expand:	Expand refers to expanding the theme and associated question by developing ideas for activities. The teachers involved produce all the activities they possibly can using a webbing process (Fogarty, 1991). They "web out" the theme to include the various curricular areas and further develop the theme through the elucidation of activities.
Select:	Select refers to the selection of valued outcomes related to the themes produced. The team has now reached the point where activities may be examined to determine if each fits into expected outcomes related to the theme. Thus, an activity sorting process is involved and activities are selected which support valued outcomes. Once the activities are thoroughly analyzed, the team may quite readily develop assessment procedures to judge the attainment of valued outcomes.

Figure 5.1. Fogarty's THEMES model for selecting themes for integrated curriculum.

Unit Development

An interdisciplinary thematic unit involves a blending of the subject matter disciplines into a segment of work focused upon a central theme (see Figure 5.2). Typically, when working with middle level students, a range of two to four weeks is a common length and is appropriate to maintain student attention and interest; however, some units can last as long as the entire school year. Regardless of length, a unit is essentially an organization of information related to a particular topic. In the development of units, the instructional team attempts to organize the curriculum around a body of knowledge that is manageable within the context of the curriculum. The use of themes facilitates unit organization; lesson plans are prepared to prescribe the daily activity of the unit learning that goes on in the classroom.

Typically, teachers work together as teams to develop interdisciplinary thematic units. Development is often followed by individual teachers, in their own classroom, implementing daily lesson plans related to that unit. Ideally, the interdisciplinary team determines time, place, and method of implementation of daily lessons related to the unit. In this way the unit acts as an organizer for everyone involved; its main function is to unify several subject matter areas around a specific theme.

The unit planning process consists of the identification of unit goals, selection and/or development of themes to realize the goals, development/selection of activities, and, finally, estimating how much time and materials should be allotted for the unit.

When teachers have unit plans developed by their interdisciplinary teams, it makes it much easier for them to develop their daily lesson plans because the material is, for the most part, already outlined by the developers of the thematic units. Teachers implementing the interdisciplinary unit through the use of daily lessons also will tend not to rely so heavily on a single textbook approach; therefore, they will have the opportunity to be more creative within the framework of the unit.

The planning of an individual lesson, usually referred to as a "daily lesson plan," involves the completion of three basic parts: (1) Objectives, (2) Procedures/Activities, and (3) Assessment. First, the teacher has to determine the objectives for the lesson. This is a relatively simple task; all one has to do is to ask the question "What do I

Title: ***Hispanic Culture and Its Impact on the United States***

Hispanic Unit
Seventh Grade Yearlong Interdisciplinary Unit

Goal: To familiarize our students with the Hispanic culture and to develop an understanding of the growing influence of the Hispanic culture on the United States.

Grade level objectives: The students will:

- sponsor a Hispanic child through Children's International by sending financial aid monthly and for Christmas and for the child's birthday, correspond with the child

- adopt a school with a Hispanic population, share in a cultural exchange of letters and videos

- participate in a field trip to. . .

Culminating activity: The student will participate in a end-of-year celebration, Cinco de Mayo. This will be a festival of food, song, dance, games, costumes, drama, and displays.

Departmental objectives:

Math: The student will:

- read and interpret graphs and charts

- given statistics, students will create bar, line, and circle graphs

- determine population density by substituting in a formula

- calculate mileage using map scales

- solve word problems relating to the Hispanic world

- make models of Hispanic villages to scale
- plan a family budget according to Latin American standards

Language Arts: The student will:

- complete a novel study of Scott O'Dell's *Shark Beneath the Reef*

Figure 5.2. Seventh grade yearlong interdisciplinary unit used at Whittemore Park Middle School, Conway, South Carolina.

- read and respond to various short stories by Hispanic authors (Gary Soto, Pat Mora, Ricardo Alegria, Sandra Cisneros, etc.)

- research and present oral reports on Hispanic holiday customs

- write friendly letters to pen pals from sister school in Florida and the adopted child

- write business letters to obtain information

- research and write reports on famous Hispanics

- read Indian mythology and Latin American folktales

Science: The student will:

- simulate the food and land requirements for selected rain forest animals

- demonstrate the effects of lumbering, cattle ranching, and conservation efforts on the delicate balance of the rain forest ecosystem

- recognize that a rain forest has layers: the emergents; the canopy; the understory; and the forest floor

- observe the characteristics of each layer

- reproduce a layer of the forest containing the trees, flowers, animals, etc., that live there

- name several characteristics of a tropical rain forest. Describe the differences and similarities between a tropical rain forest and a forest in our area

- name some of the common products that originate in a tropical rain forest

- investigate rain forest problems and describe several initiatives that are helping to protect the forest

Social Studies: The student will:

- identify and describe the major physical features and climate of Latin America

- understand how Indian and Spanish cultures impact on the modern Latin American countries

Figure 5.2. *(continued)*. Seventh grade yearlong interdisciplinary unit used at Whittemore Park Middle School, Conway, South Carolina.

- identify the most important natural resources and industries of Latin America

- analyze the impact of religion and overpopulation on modern Latin America

- describe the growing influence of Hispanic culture on the United States

Art: The student will:

- study the history of art as it relates to the Hispanic culture (pre-Columbian Americans)

- study criticism and appreciation of works of art created by Hispanic persons and cultures (artists: El Greco; culture: Mayan)

Music and band: The student will:

- make Hispanic music

- study the history of music as it relates to the Hispanic culture

- listen and analyze music created by Hispanic persons and cultures

Home arts: The student will:

- study the food and textiles of the Hispanic culture

- prepare food according to Hispanic cuisine

- create Hispanic costumes for the Cinco de Mayo celebration

Physical Education: The student will:

- play games from the Hispanic culture

- dance traditional folk dances

Spanish: The student will:

- learn Spanish grammar and vocabulary

- speak Spanish

Video production: The student will:

Figure 5.2. *(continued).* Seventh grade yearlong interdisciplinary unit used at Whittemore Park Middle School, Conway, South Carolina.

- produce a video to share with sister school

Learning Model

Bloom's Taxonomy: Following is an example of how we will use Bloom's Taxonomy in our unit to encourage higher-order thinking skills.

Knowledge:

1. Students will be able to name six countries that have a Hispanic culture.

2. Students will be able to list five characteristics of the Latin American culture.

Comprehension: After research, students will be able to explain the significant elements of the Latin American/Hispanic culture—language, religions, food, music, clothing, etc.

Application: Construct a working Latin American community; e.g., village, ancient city, etc.

Analysis: Students will be able to distinguish between traditional American and Hispanic cultures and explain the reasons for the differences.

Synthesis: Students will create a new nation using the premise that the U.S. did not win the Mexican War and a new nation was formed from the current states of Texas, New Mexico and Arizona, and the northern states of Mexico.

Evaluation: Students will evaluate classroom oral presentations based on student-developed criteria.

Letter to Parents/Teachers/Business Partners

1. Inform "customers" about the unit and its objectives.

2. Ask for support in the form of classroom volunteers, guest speakers, and resources.

3. Identify materials that are needed to facilitate the unit.

Resources

Books

George, Jean Craighead. *Shark beneath the reef.* New York: Harper Trophy, 1989.

Figure 5.2. *(continued).* Seventh grade yearlong interdisciplinary unit used at Whittemore Park Middle School, Conway, South Carolina.

Textbook

A World View. Silver Burdett & Ginn.

Persons

Guidera, Bonner, Conway High School Spanish Teacher.

Organizations

Children's International.

Latin American Tourist Bureaus.

Audio Tape

South America: Amazon rain forest. Gordon Hempton.

Magazines

Demarist, Arthur. "Violent saga of a Maya kingdom." *National Geographic,* February 1993: 95-111.

Holiday, David "Building the peace in El Salvador." *Journal of International Affairs.* Winter 1993: 415-438.

Kane, Joe. "Roaring through Earth's deepest canyon." *National Geographic,* January 1993: 119-138.

Rhoades, Robert E. "Corn, the golden grain." *National Geographic,* June 1993: 92-117.

Stuart, George E. "Maya heartland under siege." *National Geographic,* November 1992: 94-106.

Stuart, George E. "Murals of ancient Cacaxtia." *National Geographic,* September 1992: 120-136.

Pretest/Posttest

Pretest: Within the first week of school all seventh grade students will be asked to list everything they know about Latin America and Hispanic culture. The results will be placed in an individual student folder.

Posttest: Following the Cinco de Mayo festival, students will again be asked to list everything they know about Latin America and Hispanic culture. Their pretest will then be returned for comparison. This should demonstrate to the students a dramatic increase in knowledge and understanding.

Figure 5.2. *(continued).* Seventh grade yearlong interdisciplinary unit used at Whittemore Park Middle School, Conway, South Carolina.

Project Page

1. Have the seventh grade class sponsor a child from a Latin American country through Children's International. This will involve regular correspondence with the child, and monthly financial support and special gifts at Christmas, Easter, and the child's birthday.

2. Establish a special relationship with a school in Mexico through corresponding with pen pals and exchanging videos.

3. Participate in a field trip related to early Spanish influence in the United States.

4. The end-of-year Cinco de Mayo festival will be the culminating activity. This will be a festival of food, song, dance, games, costumes, drama and displays.

Evaluation/Assessment

1. Student portfolio.

2. Student-produced encyclopedia.

3. Student-produced dictionary.

4. Various written projects and oral presentations.

Activities

Internet Research Paper

The research paper must be a minimum of two pages, word-processed, double-spaced. Pages must be numbered and font size is to be 12. Font styles must be either Arial or Times New Roman. The paper must include a reference page. Standard Microsoft Word margins are to be used.

Each original paper must have a minimum of three separate Internet sources. No more than one source other than Internet sources can be used.

The subject of the research paper is to be any specific country having a Latin American culture. Topics such as foods, religions, occupations, customs, and politics are some that may be examined.

The paper will be evaluated on *content* which should be informative and original, *organization* which includes all necessary parts and proper writing style,

Figure 5.2. *(continued).* Seventh grade yearlong interdisciplinary unit used at Whittemore Park Middle School, Conway, South Carolina.

punctuation/usage which includes correct spelling, grammar, and comma usage.

Boundary Breakers:

Where would you like to visit in Latin America? Why?

What kind of Mexican food have you eaten?

What sounds might you hear in a rain forest?

If you traveled to a Latin American country, how would you like to travel? Why?

What is one Spanish word you know?

When you think of Latin America, what color do you think of?

Scampering:

1. While planning a vacation along the west coast of Mexico and Central and South America, north along their east coasts, and finally over the Caribbean islands before returning to Mexico, the students will draw an outline of their trip, pointing out countries, physical and water features, and general impressions of what they saw in their minds.

2. Student closes his/her eyes and starting on the Pacific side pilots a ship through the Panama Canal. Following the teacher-led voyage, the student will describe the working of locks, vegetation, direction of travel and other observations along the way.

Values Clarification:

1. Rank ten Latin American countries in the order you would like to visit them.

2. Imagine you are a child in Latin America, prioritize a list of possible purchases if you were given a gift of $14 – book, underwear, shoes, ice cream, socks, sandals, jeans, party, movie, toilet paper, fruit, water, cola, immunization, etc.

3. Prioritize the following issues by importance to Latin America: cultural preservation, economic development, educational opportunities, saving the environment, economic imbalance (a few rich; many poor), availability of food, health care, overpopulation, and political freedom.

Figure 5.2. *(continued)*. Seventh grade yearlong interdisciplinary unit used at Whittemore Park Middle School, Conway, South Carolina.

Forced Choices:

Are you castenettes or a guitar?

Are you a hot tamale or a taco?

Are you a jalapeno or a banana pepper?

Are you an afternoon thunderstorm or a morning mist?

Are you the Panama Canal or the Amazon River?

Are you the forest canopy or the forest floor?

Are you an Aztec or a Conquistador?

Are you a hacienda or a ejido?

Role Playing:

Scenario: An Organization of American States (OAS) to discuss the development of newly found oil reserves in a rich farming area of Peru.

Characters: Environmentalist/naturalist; industrialist; farmer; political leader of Peru; and representatives of the OAS.

Matrix Method of Creating: Create the name of a new country by uniting two Latin American countries (for example, Peruba for Cuba and Peru).

	BRAZIL	COLUMBIA	PERU	BOLIVIA	ARGENTINA
HAITI					
CUBA					
JAMAICA					
GRENADA					
BAHAMAS					

Figure 5.2. *(continued).* Seventh grade yearlong interdisciplinary unit used at Whittemore Park Middle School, Conway, South Carolina.

Mystery Box: What's in the box? Pass a closed box around the room that contains an item associated with Latin America–feel the weight, shake, and listen to the sound. Each student asks one question or may guess. Give the class unlimited guesses.

Mystery Item: Pass around an artifact from Latin America that may be unfamiliar to the students. Have the students come up with as many uses for the item as possible.

Logic Problem: A Latin American farmer has a snake, a rat, and a sack of corn. He must move them from one room to another, but can only move them one at a time. The snake will eat the rat if left unattended, and the rat will eat the corn. How can he move them safely?

Sequencing:

1. Joe Hayes, *The Day It Snowed Tortillas.* Read each of 10 short stories/fables individually and have students put them in chronological order based on context clues.

2. Build time lines sequencing the prehistoric to modern development in a region/country in Latin America. This could also be done for the European exploration of Latin America and/or countries gaining their independence.

Classification: List as many things as possible–

Things in a hacienda.

Things in a rain forest.

Things exported from Latin America.

Things found in an Aztec ruin.

The island nations of the Caribbean.

Things made of pottery.

Languages spoken in Latin America.

Things you would take on a vacation to Latin America.

Figure 5.2. *(continued).* Seventh grade yearlong interdisciplinary unit used at Whittemore Park Middle School, Conway, South Carolina.

Field Experiences:

- Mexican restaurant.

- Archeological dig of the possible early Spanish settlement near Georgetown.

- Florida–Miami; Epcot Center.

Speakers:

- Foreign exchange students; Latin American students at Coastal Carolina University.

- Local farm workers.

Audio-Visual:

- Travel videos.

- *West Side Story.*

- Video production and exchange with students in a mostly Hispanic school in the U.S. and/or Latin American country.

Figure 5.2. *(continued).* Seventh grade yearlong interdisciplinary unit used at Whittemore Park Middle School, Conway, South Carolina.

want the students to be able to do after they have completed this lesson?" In other words, the teacher must try to focus on some type of student performance or desired outcome as evidence of learning. Thus, the focus is on what students will be able to do. It is a good idea to get in the habit of starting all objectives with the phrase, "Each student will be able to...." For example, the following is one of the objectives for a lesson dealing with pollution: *Each student will be able to define the term "biodegradable."*

Objective writing can, of course, be much more complicated; Mager (1962) advocated a three-part performance objective that is rather elaborate. The objective must contain a performance, a criteria, and a condition statement. For example, *each student will define 22 of 25 keywords from Unit Six on a closed-book examination.* However, all the teacher really needs is a sentence that states what the student will be able to do following instruction. The sentence must be structured around a measurable verb such as *describe, define, construct, measure,* and *explain.* Sentences such as, *each student will be able to understand pollution,* are avoided because of the vagueness of the term *understand.* Thus, in planning to implement daily lessons for the thematic unit, the teacher should prepare a group of measurable sentences representing the unit objectives.

Following the selection or development of objectives, the teacher must decide upon the appropriate activities or procedures to be used to facilitate the mastery of the daily objectives and enable students to exhibit their new learnings. The procedures portion of the plan describes what the teacher plans to do in order to help the students to the point of being able to do new things. In other words, this section of the plan enumerates activities to facilitate student learning. Activities, especially in the case of middle level students, must be developmentally appropriate and be presented through a variety of implementation procedures or methods which will actively involve students in the learning process, for example, cooperative learning circles (Johnson, Johnson, and Holubec, 1994), student-directed plays, student-developed projects (group or independent) and community resource volunteers, to name a few. The use of a variety of methods and materials helps teachers attend to the fact that there are a variety of developmental levels among the students in the classroom. The term *authenticity* denotes that instructional tasks should focus on experiences which are common to the real life of middle level students. A teacher could use cooperative learning groups for some activities, inquiry procedures for others, and other activities could involve student project work (see Chapter Six). Of course, the teacher must also make use of various tools especially including computer technologies.

It is further suggested, as an aid to accommodating individual differences, that teachers or teams develop procedures which attend to Gardner's concept of seven intelligences (Gardner, 1993). Activities should be developed which span the entire range of intelligences. Campbell and Burton (1994) suggest that, although some overlap exists among the intelligences, a good framework is provided for developing plans and activities (see Figure 5.3).

Gardner's Seven Intelligences	*Sample Activity*
Linguistic: Emphasize reading, writing and storytelling skills.	Read a short story and tell the story in your own words.
Logical/mathematical: Involve numbers and the use of reasoning, questioning, and sequential thinking.	Given one-half acre of land, calculate the cost of seeds, fertilizer, and equipment needed to plant a garden.
Spatial: Make use of mental and physical pictures, model building, and imagination.	On the vacant parking lot, design and construct a basketball court.
Music: Use rhythm, pitch, lyrics, and melodies.	Students play and sing the folk songs of various countries.
Kinesthetic/body: Use activities which are tactile, involve physical activity, dance and/or drama.	Perform folk dances common to various countries.
Intrapersonal: Use individual activities involving reflective thinking.	Each student will develop an individual plan to improve his/her physical well-being.
Interpersonal: Group activities that emphasize social leadership and cooperative learning.	Work in teams to develop a self-propelled vehicle.

Figure 5.3. Activities based on the seven intelligences adapted from Campbell and Burton (1994).

The final portion of the lesson plan involves assessment: a necessary step to determine if the teacher was successful in facilitating student mastery of the objective(s). The assessment used must match very carefully with the objectives of the lesson so that everyone involved knows the degree to which the subject has been mastered. Learning may be assessed through a variety of formal and informal means ranging from paper and pencil tests to student portfolios. The keys to quality assessment are clarity, fairness, and authenticity (see Chapter Seven). Figure 5.4 presents an example of a completed lesson plan.

Exploratory Programs

In order to address the developmental characteristics of middle level students, the curriculum must allow students to explore and experiment with their own interests and ideas. Certainly, a middle level school that wishes to provide a developmentally appropriate curriculum must offer students broad exploratory experiences in a non-restrictive environment (Lounsbury, 1991). An exploratory program should give students elective opportunities that allow them the chance to express their natural desire to explore their special interests. The exploratory program should compliment the basic core requirements to offer students a relevant, viable learning experience.

While strongly emphasized in the middle school, the concept of exploratories is not new; throughout the years, these courses have had various names: unified arts, related arts, specials, and "explo" for example (Schurr, Thomason, and Thompson, 1995). With the back-to-basics movement of the 1970s and the standardized testing movement of the 1980s, many of the so-called exploratory courses implemented at that time were no more than samplers of high school courses (Fedor, 1994). However, starting in the 1990s, exploratory programs took on new importance as a program component to provide middle level students needed opportunity to explore their own interests. Due to such milestones in middle level education literature as *Turning points: Preparing American youth for the 21st century* (Carnegie Council on Adolescent Development, 1989) and *Exploration: The total curriculum* (Compton and Hawn, 1993), the exploratory program is being seen as a key component of the total middle school curriculum.

Subject_____   Grade Level_____

Time_____

Objectives	Procedures	Assessment
1. Students will give examples of antonyms, synonyms, homophones, and rhyming words.	1. Students will review examples of homophones, antonyms, synonyms, and rhyming words.	1. Each group of students will hand in completed job reports for a group grade.
	a. Chalkboard	a. Originality of verse
	b. Group work	b. Number and use of antonyms, synonyms, homophones and rhyming words.
2. Students will create a new verse for the poem using antonyms, synonyms, homophones, and rhyming words.	2. Students will be divided into designated groups according to ability (higher level working with lower lever).	
	3. Each group will be given a job description to perform, using a commercial poem, *Excuses* by Susan Paprocki (see attached job cards).	
	4. As each group finishes students will move to the next job lev-el as time permits.	
Materials:		
1. Chalkboard and chalk	5. Students will move back into a large group format to share their findings and verses, orally.	
2. *Excuses* by Susan Paprocki		
3. Job cards		
4. Paper and pencils, pens		

Figure 5.4. Sample lesson plan.

This, unfortunately, is not to say that all middle schools are characterized by exploratory programs. Middle schools vary widely in the methods chosen to provide exploratory experiences for students. To a large measure, the variance in programs is accounted for by the fact that such experiences must be tailored to local conditions; for example, some schools must deal with problems of space, personnel, and finances.

In fact, exploratory experiences are not yet a dominant feature of middle level curriculum, and exploratory experiences have not frequently been incorporated into the subject matter areas of language arts, social studies, mathematics, and science (Irvin, Valentine, and Clark, 1994). It would seem that middle schools have been somewhat slow in adopting this important curriculum characteristic. However, many schools are taking significant strides in providing exploratory experiences.

Irvin, Valentine, and Clark (1994) have noted three avenues through which exploratory programs are typically implemented: short courses, co-curricular activities, and intramural activities. In each case, student choice is determined by interests and abilities. Table 5.2 presents several examples of each major format for implementing exploratory experiences outside of the basic core courses.

Table 5.2
EXAMPLES OF EXPLORATORY EXPERIENCES

Exploratory Courses	*Co-Curricular Activities*	*Intramural Activities*
Life Skills	Student Government	Basketball
Creative Writing	Career Days	Track
Drama	Musical Groups	Tennis
Keyboarding	Student Clubs	Golf
Creative Design	Drama	Chess
	Publications	Bridge
		Co-ed Softball

There are obviously many examples of good exploratory programs across the country. An important characteristic of such programs is their dynamic nature; that is, they are constantly changing from year to year. This change is necessary because the interests and needs of new groups of middle level students will change from year to year. The following example (see Figure 5.5) of an exploratory program was developed at Irmo Middle School in South Carolina for grades six through eight (Fedor, 1994).

Sixth Grade Options:

Most sixth grade options are nine-week quarters with the exception of physical education. Students in yearlong band or strings elect only two courses from exploratory electives.

FINE ARTS

Fine Arts rotation (music, art, crafts, and drama)

Band

Strings

EXPLORATORY

Home Alone (a living arts class)

Quest

Study Skills

Second Voyage of the *Mimi*

AGP EXPO!

PHYSICAL EDUCATION

Seventh Grade Options:

Most seventh grade options are also quarter courses. Some fine arts courses are full year.

Figure 5.5. An example of an exploratory sequence used at Irmo Middle School, Irmo, South Carolina (Fedor, 1994, p. 12).

FINE ARTS

Band (beginning and continuing)

Strings (beginning and continuing)

Chorus

Performing Arts

Drama

Arts and Crafts

EXPLORATORY

Computer Keyboarding

Project Design

Staying Alive (health)

Sew! What's Cooking (living arts)

World Traveler

Foreign Language Wheel

AGP EXPO!

Day in Court

Current Issues and Answers

PHYSICAL EDUCATION

Eighth Grade Options:

     Eighth grade options vary in length from quarter to semester. All fine arts options are either semester or full-year courses. Because only one language arts class is taught on the core team, eighth grade students select a language arts elective.

FINE ARTS

Band

Figure 5.5. *(continued)*. An example of an exploratory sequence used at Irmo Middle School, Irmo, South Carolina (Fedor, 1994, p. 12).

Strings

Chorus

Art

Arts and Crafts

Drama Performing Arts

EXPLORATORY

Computer Keyboarding

Health

Day in Court

U.N. Forum

R.S.V.P. (living arts)

AGP EXPO!

PHYSICAL EDUCATION

LANGUAGE ARTS ELECTIVES

Application

Language Arts Extension

Effective Communication

Introduction to Journalism

Yearbook

Introduction to French

Introduction to German

Introduction to Latin

Introduction to Spanish

Figure 5.5. *(continued).* An example of an exploratory sequence used at Irmo Middle School, Irmo, South Carolina (Fedor, 1994, p. 12).

Summary

In this chapter, three of the major characteristics of a quality middle school program have been described: (1) interdisciplinary teaming, (2) integrated curriculum, and (3) exploratory activities as they relate to the development of appropriate middle level learning experiences. We also took the position that these three elements are among the most basic ingredients found in any quality middle school. Without these present, at least in some degree, it is difficult to argue that the school in question is a true middle school. Currently, middle level schools are consistently developing interdisciplinary teaming and integrated curriculum. Exploratory activities seem to be developing more slowly; however, middle level educators across the country acknowledge the importance of such programs and are attempting to add quality exploratory programs to the existing core curriculum. When this is accomplished, students will have a richer and more rewarding learning experience as a part of their academic and personal development.

REFERENCES

Allen, H., Splittgerber, F., & Manning, M.L. (1993). *Teaching and learning in the middle level school.* New York: Macmillan Publishing Company.

Beane, J.A. (1990). *Middle school curriculum: From rhetoric to reality.* Columbus, OH: National Middle School Association.

Beane, J.A. (1991). "The middle school: The natural home for integrated curriculum." *Educational Leadership,* 49(2), 9-13.

Beane, J. A. (1993). "Problems and possibilities for an integrative curriculum". *Middle School Journal,* 25(1), 18-23.

Bruner, J. (1960). *The process of education.* Cambridge: Harvard University Press.

Campbell, M., & Burton, V. (1994). Learning in their own style. *Science and Children,* April, 22-24; 39.

Carnegie Council on Adolescent Development. (1989). *Turning points: Preparing American youth for the 21st century.* Washington, D.C.: Carnegie Corporation.

Combs, A. (1982). *A personal approach to teaching.* Boston: Allyn and Bacon.

Compton, M.F., & Hawn, H.C. (1993). *Exploration: The total curriculum.* Columbus, Ohio: National Middle School Association.

Cook, G., & Martinello, M. (1994). "Topics and themes in interdisciplinary curriculum." *Middle School Journal,* 25(3), 40-44.

Eichhorn, D. (1966). *The middle school.* New York: The Center for Applied Research in Education.

Erb, T. (1995). "It's academics, stupid! If you care enough." *Middle School Journal.* 27(1) 2.

Erb, T., & Doda, N. (1989). *Team organization: Promise, practice, and possibilities.* Washington, D.C.: National Education Association.

Fedor, S. (1994). "Interest in everything and nothing very much: Exploratory programs, the hallmark of the middle school." *The South Carolina Middle School Journal,* 2 (1), 11-13.

Fogarty, R. (1991). *The mindful school: How to integrate the curricula.* Palatine, IL:IRI/Skylight.

Fogarty, R. (1994). "Thinking of themes: Hundreds of themes." *Middle School Journal,* 25(4), 30-31.

Gardner, H. (1993). *Multiple intelligences.* New York: Basic Books.

George, P. (1982). "Interdisciplinary team organization: Four operational phases." *Middle School Journal,* 13(3), 10-13.

Irvin, J., Valentine, J., & Clark, D. (1994). "Essential elements of a true middle school: What should be vs. what is." *Middle School Journal,* 26(1), 54-58.

Jacobs, H. (Ed.). (1989). *Interdisciplinary curriculum: Design and implementation.* Alexandria, VA: ASCD.

Johnson, D., Johnson, R., & Holubec, E.J. (1994). *The new circles of learning: Cooperation in the classroom and school.* Alexandria, VA: ASCD.

Kellough, R., & Kellough, N. (1996). *Middle school teaching: A guide to methods and resources.* Englewood Cliffs, New Jersey: Prentice-Hall.

Kovalik, S. (1994). *ITI: The model integrated thematic instruction.* Kent, Washington: Kovalik and Associates.

Lounsbury, J. (1991). *As I see it.* Columbus, Ohio: NMSA.

Lounsbury, J., & Vars, G. (1978). *A curriculum for the middle school years.* New York: Harper and Row.

Mager, R. (1962). *Preparing instructional objectives.* Palo Alto, California: Fearon Publishers.

Maslow, A. (1970). *Motivation and personality.* New York: Harper and Row.

Myers, C., & Myers, L. (1990). *An introduction to teaching and schools.* New York: Holt, Rhinehart and Winston.

National Middle School Association. (1992). *This we believe.* Columbus, Ohio: NMSA.

Ornstein, A., & Hunkins, F. (1988). *Curriculum: Foundations, principles, and issues.* Englewood Cliffs, N.J.: Prentice-Hall.

Powell, R. (1993). "Seventh graders' perspectives of their interdisciplinary team." *Middle School Journal,* 49-57.

Powell, R., & Mills, R. (1994). "Five types of mentoring build knowledge on interdisciplinary teams." *Middle School Journal,* 26(2), 24-30.

Shillington, N. (1994). "Four components for promoting team development." *Middle School Journal,* 48-52.

Sadowski, M. (1995). "Knowing no boundaries: A conversation with James Beane." *The Harvard Education Letter,* 11(5), 5-7.

Schurr, S., Thomason, J., & Thompson, M. (1995). *Teaching at the middle level: A professional's handbook.* Lexington, Mass: D.C. Health and Co.

Shepherd, G., & Ragan, W. (1992). *Modern elementary curriculum.* New York: Harcourt Brace Jovanovich.

Vars, G.F. (1987). *Interdisciplinary teaching in the middle grades.* Columbus, OH: NMSA.

Wiles, J., & Bondi, J. (1986). *The essential middle school.* Tampa, FL: Wiles, Bondi, and Associates.

Willis, S. (1995). "Refocusing the curriculum: Making interdisciplinary efforts work." *Education Update,* 37(1), 1-8.

Chapter 6

PROVIDING DEVELOPMENTALLY APPROPRIATE INSTRUCTION

In order to successfully respond to such a diverse student population with a variety of emotional, social, and cognitive attributes, as is found in the middle school, middle level teachers must be prepared to plan, implement, and assess a number of appropriate teaching strategies and techniques (Stowell, Rios, McDaniel, and Christopher, 1996). Of crucial importance is that teachers know when to use these strategies as well as how to use them; the teacher is the critical key in providing developmentally appropriate instruction. This, of course, is not meant to imply that all students must be instructed through the use of all possible teaching strategies. To the contrary, as just stated, effective teachers need a repertoire of teaching strategies at their disposal in order that they may attempt to match the best possible methodology to the learning needs and styles of a given set of students. The effective middle level teacher can provide multiple "avenues of learning" to students.

As within all levels of schooling, middle level teachers must be concerned about the instructional needs of the specific content areas under study. At the middle school level, teachers must be aware of the best and most current knowledge concerning instruction and learning environments common to their content areas. Effective instruction requires a knowledge of student developmental characteristics and a fundamental familiarity with content and how best to help students learn it.

In this chapter, the generic instructional attributes of middle level teachers who have constructivist classrooms will be discussed. Next, specific teaching strategies that are typically used in middle level learning environments will be examined. Some of these strategies will emphasize direct teacher instruction others will emphasize the role of teacher as a facilitator.

Methodology Based on Constructivist Principles

The ideal model for teaching middle level students features instruction based on constructivist principles. Simply put, the constructivist classroom is one where students are encouraged and guided to construct deep understanding of significant concepts. The emphasis is placed upon the students developing their own knowledge as opposed to always being given answers and being told what and how to think. Such a learning environment capitalizes on students' cognitive dissonance (inner cognitive conflict) and their ability to reflect upon their experiences.

Brooks and Brooks (1993) have provided guidelines for constructivist teaching (see Figure 6.1). The twelve behaviors they have described are also seen as the characteristics of the effective middle level teacher.

Encouraging and accepting student autonomy and initiation is central to the middle level learning environment (Schurr, Thomason, and Thompson, 1995; Kellough and Kellough, 1996). Students must be encouraged to take the initiative for their own learning in order that they might become independent problem solvers. Such students learn to ask questions and then answer those questions on their own without waiting to be told what to think. The use of primary sources and raw data (e.g., bank statements, box scores from a sports page, or census reports) allow students to generate their own inferences and develop their own strategies. Studying only secondary sources (e.g., public school textbooks) allows students to memorize the solutions and conclusions drawn by other people rather than to develop critical thinking skills on their own.

When student responses are allowed to shape instruction, the teacher can adapt the curriculum to focus on themes that have immediate interest and importance to students. Using a student-driven curriculum does not mean that certain things will not be taught because students lack initial interest in the topic; rather, it means that what students study, because it interests them, will be related to their real-life experiences. When an event occurs that captures the interest and imagination of the students, continuing with preplanned lessons will often result in missing a very teachable moment (Brooks and Brooks, 1993).

Constructivist teachers should:

1. encourage and accept student autonomy and initiative;

2. use raw data and primary sources as well as manipulative, interactive, and physical materials;

3. use terms such as "classify," "analyze," "predict," and "create," when eliciting student performance;

4. allow student responses to drive lessons and alter instructional methodology and content selection;

5. allow students to form and clarify concepts before sharing their own understandings and perceptions of the concepts under study;

6. encourage student dialogue with both the teacher and other students;

7. encourage student inquiry by asking open-ended questions and reinforcing student-to-student collaboration;

8. ask students to elaborate on their initial responses;

9. engage students in activities that will engender contradictions to their initial hypotheses and encourage discussion;

10. allow adequate wait time after asking questions;

11. provide time for students to construct relationships and create metaphors; and

12. nurture students' natural curiosity by using the learning cycle model for instruction.

Figure 6.1. Twelve essential characteristics of constructivist teachers as adapted from Brooks and Brooks.

A close look at the Brooks and Brooks description of the characteristics of constructivist teachers shows that the verbal interaction that transpires in the classroom is highly important. A constructivist teacher will not have a quiet classroom; the classroom will have the sounds of a busy workplace where students share ideas with the teacher and fellow learners. The teacher will be asking appropriate, eliciting questions and encouraging students to dialogue with one another as well as the teacher. The classroom will be an environment where students experience frequent cognitive dissonance as teachers consistently attempt to develop activities which challenge students to rethink their original hypotheses while encouraging group discussion.

Constructivist teachers who use the learning cycle model of instruction allow student inquiry and rely on the student's natural curiosity for learning new concepts. The learning cycle model of instruction describes in the learning process: *exploration, invention,* and *discovery.* The learning cycle model was used as the organizational focal point for the Science Curriculum Improvement Study (SCIS), an elementary science program with instructional units organized around the learning cycle approach (Weber and Renner, 1972; Atkin and Karplus, 1962). Other educators have used the same concept but with slightly different terminology. For example, Barman (1989) used the terms *exploration, concept introduction,* and *concept application* which have become frequently used terms.

A classroom activity using the learning cycle concept would proceed as follows: In the first phase, students would be provided with materials for open-ended exploration. Students would be provided with the time and support to generate questions and hypotheses while exploring these materials. In phase two, instruction would be more direct. The teacher would provide information to help students frame their questions, develop new vocabulary, and set up further exploration. In the third phase, students would work on new problems with the potential for applying concepts learned in the previous phases. Brooks and Brooks (1993) take the position that the learning cycle stands in contrast to traditional teaching techniques. They note that in traditional models concepts are first introduced through more direct methods of instruction after which students are given opportunities to apply the concepts. Any discovery learning that takes place in the traditional format occurs after the introduction and application processes and often involves only the more able students because they finish the application activities before the end of the allotted period of time. Figure 6.2 provides an example of a learning cycle lesson.

As previously stated, the effective middle level classroom is based on constructivist principles. Teachers who want to apply these principles can utilize a variety of teaching techniques to provide the

Phase 1–Exploration

Materials for exploration

- German coins 1917 - 1945

- German stamps 1917 - 1945

- popular German songs 1917 - 1945

- popular German art 1917 - 1945

Procedure

- Ask students to examine the coins, stamps, art works, and song lyrics.

- Have the students generalize about the society from which these materials came.

- Ask students to share their findings or observations with classmates.

Phase 2–Invention

Teacher-led discussion which can use a combination of films, books, slides

- Introduce key facts about life in Germany in 1917 - 1945.

- Introduce any key vocabulary.

- Introduce key historical figures.

- Internet materials and discussion.

- Ask students to identify any components of their exploration in Phase 1 which support the discussions in Phase 2.

Phase 3–Discovery

Materials for analysis

- Film related to Nazi atrocities

- Excerpts from the written accounts of a teenage Jewish girl in Germany in 1940

Figure 6.2. An example of a learning cycle lesson.

- Popular American material describing Germany during the World War II era

Procedure

- Ask students to describe what characteristics of German society after World War I may have led to the rise of Nazism.

- Ask students to theorize about what might have happened to have prevented these problems in Germany.

- Ask students to analyze if the perception of Germans held by Americans during World War II were all accurate.

- Ask students to conjecture what society had done to shape the thoughts and emotions of teenage Jews during World War II.

- Ask students to describe a parallel event in history.

Figure 6.2. *(continued)*. An example of a learning cycle lesson.

best possible instruction to their students. The first methodologies described are student-centered, open-ended techniques for instruction. The second group of methodologies described are teacher-centered, direct methods of instruction. These techniques are standard strategies in high school instruction. They will be examined here in relationship to their effectiveness in middle level instruction and as to how they can be successfully adapted to student-centered learning.

Direct Methods	*Indirect Methods*
• Lecture	Guided Inquiry
• Demonstration	Simulations/Role Playing
• Drill	Independent Study
• Teacher-led Discussion	Cooperative Learning
	Contracts
	Learning Centers

Figure 6.3. Types of instructional strategies.

Direct Methods

Direct methods of instruction rely on the teacher to organize and present information to students in the form they are expected to learn. An example would occur with the teacher who, at the chalkboard, demonstrates to a group of students the proper way to set up a math problem. The teacher expects the students to observe the work at the chalkboard, learn the method, and apply it whenever confronted with similar math problems in the future. The teacher, in fact, shows the students how to do it.

Is there an important place for such instruction in the modern middle school? Yes. Should it be the only type of instruction taking place in the classroom? Absolutely not! While directly imparting information and demonstrating skills is an important part of the middle level teacher's role, it must be remembered that teachers should use visuals, hands-on activities, and opportunities for movement and student talk throughout the instructional episode. Moreover, when using direct instructional methods, teachers should involve students in reflective discussion sessions using open-ended questions to elicit critical thinking (Stowell, Rios, McDaniel and Christopher, 1996).

Basically, direct teaching, also referred to as systematic, active or explicit teaching, imparts information or demonstrates skills. That is, information is provided to students in its final form; students typically are not asked to create or discover new knowledge or skills. Teachers present information; students apply knowledge; practice a skill; and teachers give feedback. This section focuses on four teaching methods that are usually used to directly convey information to students in its final form: *lecture, demonstration, drill,* and *teacher-led discussion.*

Lecture

The lecture method is perhaps the most direct of all forms of instruction. In this method, teachers provide information to students through an oral presentation. This can take place in an early childhood setting or a high school classroom; the emphasis is on the teacher giving students information that they are expected to learn just as it is presented (Bedwell, Hunt, Touzel, and Wiseman, 1991).

Among middle level educators the lecture method is often seen in a negative light. There are, we think, obvious reasons for this attitude.

First, historically, some very poor teaching has taken place in the lecture format. Too frequently, students have been bored by ill-prepared teachers who showed little enthusiasm for the content or teaching in general. In other cases, teachers have lectured about material that they loved, yet they have done it without regard for the readiness of their students to learn or for their own ability to adequately communicate in a meaningful and enjoyable fashion. Second, there is, as it certainly should be, a major emphasis being placed on students taking an active role in their own learning; lectures, of course, tend to create very passive learning environments. Constructivist teachers certainly want students to be active learners interacting with one another as they manipulate learning materials in a responsive environment. Lecturing, with its negative connotations, obviously may not be embraced by teachers with a student-centered orientation. Kellough and Kellough (1996) in their review of middle school instructional techniques use the term *formal talk* instead of lecture for the form of direct instruction appropriate for middle school students.

In the many instances when teachers need to present information to middle level students, as Kellough and Kellough (1996) note, one of the major considerations in using this strategy is the length of the oral presentation. Middle level students have a tendency to tune out teachers who talk too much no matter how motivating they are trying to be. Lectures at the middle school level should be structured in a format similar to what Schurr, Thomason and Thompson (1995) refer to as a minilecture. At the middle level, this type of direct instruction should be highly organized, brief, goal directed, and, if at all possible, interactive. The lecture should focus on a single concept and should be complemented with questions to check understanding throughout the lesson.

As noted earlier, if done properly, a lecture can be useful in a middle level classroom. Figure 6.4 provides suggestions for presenting an effective lecture.

The "attention grabber" is recommended to motivate and capture student interest at the beginning of the lecture. An "attention grabber" (such as a picture, a story, a song, or a poem) does not have to be a singularly dramatic event; it is simply something at the beginning of a lesson to solicit student attention.

A key consideration in developing an effective presentation is relating new material to concepts which students have previously

1. Begin the lesson with an "attention grabber."

2. Follow a well-planned logical sequence.

3. Tie new information to concepts that students have already learned.

4. Project confidence in your mastery and understanding of the material.

5. Vary stimulus through the appropriate use of audiovisual aids.

6. Be as brief and to the point as possible.

7. After lecturing, provide application experiences through a more student-centered approach.

8. Be receptive to student questions throughout the presentation.

9. Monitor student nonverbal behavior to determine their receptivity.

10. Ask questions to solicit verbal feedback.

11. Use voice inflections and animated body movements.

Figure 6.4. Suggestions for presenting effective lectures as adapted from Bedwell, Hunt, Touzel, and Wiseman (1991).

learned. David Ausubel (1963) is probably best known for developing his concept of *advanced organizers* which, he noted, would aid in making lectures more meaningful. Ausubel believed that to tie previous learnings with new material the teacher should provide an introduction to the lecture that helps students make this important connection; he called this type of advanced organizer a *comparative organizer*. Ausubel felt that making a match between new concepts and ideas and past learnings is critical if verbal learning is to be meaningful. Further, Ausubel felt that when it was impossible to relate new material to previously learned content the teacher should provide students with some type of conceptual arrangement of the material to be presented (e.g., an outline) which he called an *expository organizer*.

Self-confidence is an important factor in a teacher's ability to perform successfully; it becomes especially important when using a teacher-centered technique such as the lecture. Confidence, of course, is related directly to the teacher's organization and preparation. Novice teachers often must plan in much more detail than more experienced teachers in order to feel spontaneous and relaxed. When teachers are uneasy with their mastery of the content, the probability of making mistakes in front of the class seems to increase.

Teachers, when lecturing, must be constantly aware of student receptivity. Basically, teachers judge student receptivity by surveying the class to monitor student nonverbal behavior (e.g., looks of confusion, enjoyment, lack of interest, etc.) and by asking questions to determine the level of student understanding. As teachers lecture, they should continue to survey the students for nonverbal reactions while frequently asking questions to insure that the students are understanding the verbal messages being given.

Obviously, a major concern with the lecture method is the possibility of an uninspiring presentation. Middle school students are not likely to tolerate a steady monotone or an irritatingly high-pitched voice. Teachers must communicate an enthusiasm for learning through their method of presentation. Using voice inflections and body animation makes the lesson stimulating. Also, the use of humor within an oral presentation is likely to increase student attention and enjoyment. Stale, boring oral presentations are a "breeding ground" for classroom management problems. Teachers who demonstrate enthusiasm and humor are much more likely to keep their students focused and attentive.

When poorly planned and executed, lectures can certainly promote much that is negative about middle school instruction. In a school setting where active, student participation is held as a premium, the lecture method relegates students to a very passive role. However, if a middle level teacher tries to follow the eleven guidelines provided in Figure 6.4, lecture presentations can be used to make a positive instructional impact.

Demonstration

One of the most classic methods of instruction is the *demonstration*. This direct method of teaching primarily involves the teacher showing students how to do something. Typically, teachers will complement their demonstrations with oral explanation (i.e., lecture). Demonstrations take a variety of formats; for example, the math teacher may work a problem using the overhead projector, the art teacher may show students how to mix paint to create a new color, the science teacher may conduct an experiment as the class observes, or the English teacher may rewrite a paragraph on the chalkboard. Sometimes, teachers will allow a student to demonstrate a skill or process for the rest of the class. Perhaps, the home arts teacher may ask a student to demonstrate the proper method of applying icing to a cake, or the physical education teacher may ask a student to demonstrate the proper method of dribbling a basketball for the other students to observe.

It is important to plan a demonstration before the presentation; adequate preparation requires that teachers practice the demonstration in order to be certain that the procedure works and that they can clearly explain the process as the demonstration is taking place. Teachers should include in the plan a set of guiding questions to accompany the narrative explanation. When the demonstration is complex (especially when dealing with abstract concepts) teachers may provide the students with guide sheets or other written materials to help structure their observations.

If done properly, the demonstration is an effective direct method of instruction. Figure 6.5 outlines the major responsibilities for teachers who wish to use effective demonstration lessons.

1. Begin the demonstration with a short explanation or overview.

2. Be certain that all students can see and hear the presentation without obstruction.

3. Provide an outline of the main points to be observed.

4. Elicit student participation and feedback through questioning.

5. Summarize the main points for clarification.

6. Give students an opportunity to apply what has been learned.

7. Teach at a slow enough pace so that students can reflect on the process while demonstration is in progress.

8. Make certain that all safety precautions have been taken when conducting a demonstration with a potential hazard.

Figure 6.5. Suggestions for presenting effective demonstrations.

There are a number of positive factors to be considered when using the demonstration method. Middle level students typically enjoy demonstration lessons which are often more engaging than a lecture. The opportunity to see something is usually better for learning than a more abstract format. The demonstration is economical in terms of material cost and availability. Frequently, it is impossible to put the necessary materials in every student's hands to conduct student inquiry and experimentation. Yet, teachers may have enough supplies for one person (perhaps the teacher and possibly one or more student helpers) to conduct the experiment while the class observes the demonstration. Finally, it should be noted that demonstrating can aid students in the development of the important skills of *observing* and *listening*.

Drill

Teachers often use drill as a method of providing practice of a skill recently learned. Drill is the repetition of a learned performance. For example, after the students in a physical education class learn to perform a proper handspring, the teacher requires that each student perform twenty handsprings. Or, in a math class after the students learn the procedure for calculating simple interest, the teacher assigns twelve simple interest problems for homework. With drill, teachers attempt to provide overlearning which can make a learned behavior become automatic.

Drill exercises provide teachers with the opportunity to give their students immediate feedback concerning their performance. It has been shown that immediate feedback can be an essential instructional event (Good and Brophy, 1986; Gagne, 1985). Feedback must be as immediate as possible if it is to have its optimal effect. If teachers wait several days to evaluate and return drill assignments to the students, much of the value of the exercise will be lost. One criticism of the drill method has been that it has often been used as "busy work" to fill time and keep students occupied when the teacher has not planned an activity to engage students in learning. When drills are given and not evaluated for their immediate return to students for feedback, the activity can, in effect, evolve into a type of "busy work" with little learning benefit.

Drill typically takes place in the classroom or as a homework assignment immediately following the learning of a new skill or the review of a previously learned skill. The purpose of the drill is to provide students with an opportunity to practice the skill in order that its function will become automatic. The drill exercise also provides a type of formative evaluation feedback to teachers allowing them to determine if certain students are having problems and if reteaching will be necessary.

The drill process is developed upon the notion that students must understand how to do the skill involved prior to being drilled in its function. Students who are given drill exercises before they have mastered the material are likely to make errors and then practice them repeatedly. When this occurs, teachers must help students unlearn these practiced mistakes in order that the proper procedure can be learned and practiced. As a result, pages of homework or classwork drill should never be given to students until the teacher feels that students have a basic understanding of the processes involved. Again, this emphasizes the importance of teachers immediately correcting and returning such work to the students in order to correct any errors taking place before they become even more ingrained.

If drill exercises are not overused to the point of becoming a boring, everyday routine, this strategy has the important advantages of providing both teachers and learners with immediate feedback concerning students' progress. Retention can be aided through the provision of practice followed by immediate feedback. Figure 6.6 provides guidelines for the effective use of the drill method.

---

1. Do not assign a drill exercise unless you are certain that the students have an understanding of the necessary skills and concepts prior to the assignment.

2. Do not drill as a punishment.

3. When possible, monitor student work in progress to prevent the possibility of practicing errors.

4. Provide feedback as soon as possible.

Figure 6.6. Suggestions for the effective use of drills in the middle level classroom.

Teacher-Led Discussion

Students in the middle school want and need to think about the world in which they live, and the teacher-led discussion can be used to elicit high-level thinking of this nature. When characterized by open-ended, critical questions, the teacher-led discussion holds an important place in a responsive middle level classroom (Stowell, Rios, McDaniel, and Christopher, 1996). Moreover, the teacher-led discussion has an advantage over most other types of direct instruction in that it typically provides more opportunities for student participation. The teacher-led discussion is not merely an informal conversation among students and teachers. The class discussion should be designed to achieve some stated objectives, and teachers must guide student participation to reach these desired outcomes.

The success of effective teacher-led discussions often depends upon the teacher's ability to use proper questioning techniques. Silvernail (1986) has noted several important factors concerning teacher questioning based on his review of educational research:

1. teaching techniques based on questioning tend to be effective.
2. there is a positive correlation between the number of teacher-directed questions and student achievement.
3. when teachers repeat correct student answers, it tends to enhance learning.
4. there seems to be no best pattern to use when asking questions around the classroom.
5. a mixture of *low-level* factual questions along with *higher-order* questions seems to produce better results than using either type of question exclusively.

Obviously, the ability to ask questions is an important aspect of middle level teaching especially as it helps teachers focus and structure discussion sessions.

As Silvernail (1986) noted, a teacher should be able to pose both low-level and high-level questions in order to provide the proper balance for optimal learning to occur. Within the context of a teacher-led discussion, an important question type is the *clarifying question*. Research indicates that a positive correlation exists between the teacher's use of clarifying questions and students' understanding of how they think and learn (i.e., metacognitive skills) (Costa, 1991).

Clarifying questions basically restate the ideas or opinions of a student. For example, "I believe you are saying that you think we need to give the plants more light–is that correct?"

Cognitive questions have been classified by several researchers; however, one of the most functional systems was developed by Gallagher and Aschner (1963). This system is based on Guilford's classic model for illustrating the structure of the intellect (Guilford, 1959). Among the levels of questions denoted by Gallagher and Aschner are two lower-level cognitive questions: *Cognitive-memory* and *convergent thinking*. The researchers also classified two higher-level cognitive questions: *divergent thinking* and *evaluative thinking*. The middle level teacher should be able to lead discussion, in part, through the use of these four question types along with the clarifying question discussed earlier.

Table 6.1
EXAMPLES OF GALLAGHER AND ASCHNER QUESTIONS

Question Classification	Example
1. Cognitive memory	Who was the second president of the United States?
2. Convergent	How many square feet of carpet would be needed to completely cover our classroom floor?
3. Divergent	If you were the principal of this school, what are some of the changes you would like to make?
4. Evaluative	Would you rather live today or in the eighteenth century? Why do you feel this way?

Cognitive memory questions are questions with one correct answer that require the student to recall or recognize factual information that has been put to memory (see Table 6.1). Convergent questions also will have one correct answer; however, the answer cannot be memorized. Students are asked to put facts or concepts together to make comparisons, explain facts, state relationships, or solve problems (see Table 6.1) (Bedwell, Hunt, Touzel, and Wiseman, 1991). Divergent questions, on the other hand, are higher-level questions and require students to predict, hypothesize, or make inferences. There will not be a single correct answer as the emphasis is placed more on a student's creative thought processes. Finally, evaluative thinking requires the highest level of cognition. Students are asked to both make a judgment and defend their position (see Table 6.1).

The teacher's ability to use these various types of questions is an important factor in leading effective presentations. The guidelines presented in Figure 6.7 produce questioning techniques that provide for optimal learning.

- Write out the questions in the sequence they are to be asked prior to the discussion session.

- Be certain to ask some of each question type (i.e., cognitive memory, convergent, divergent, evaluative, and clarification).

- Provide adequate time for students to respond to questions. Students need time to reflect before answering, especially when responding to higher-level questions.

- Questions must be tailored to the ability level of the student. Many middle level classrooms have a wide range of ability levels. A question which might properly challenge one student could be frustrating for another.

- Remember to space clarification questions throughout the discussion session.

- Expand upon student responses to questions. This is an excellent technique designed to make students feel their contributions are important and wanted.

- Encourage reticent students to take part in the discussion by asking them questions without making them feel threatened.

- Encourage students to ask questions and respond to one another.

- When students give an incorrect response to a question, give them supportive feedback. Students are less likely to respond in the future if they are made to feel embarrassment because of an incorrect response.

Figure 6.7. Guidelines for questioning techniques used in teacher-led discussions.

The teacher who remembers to follow the guidelines in Figure 6.7 and practices good questioning techniques should find that better discussion sessions will be the result. If teachers focus on developing their questioning skills, keep digressions to a minimum, and use short summaries throughout, they should find that middle level students greatly profit from teacher-led discussions.

Indirect Methods

Given an understanding of middle level students and their desire to be active and participate in learning, it is clear that educators must give young adolescents an opportunity to develop ideas and concepts as they discover new and interesting things about their world. Student exploration should be at the heart of middle level instruction (Rubinstein, 1994). Often in the modern middle level school, inter-disciplinary teams of teachers teach through the use of thematic units providing a more student-centered, less direct, teaching methods (Vars, 1993).

Indirect methods of teaching emphasize student self-learning through exploration while emphasizing the teacher's role as facilitator and guide. Seven indirect teaching methods provide student-centered instruction in middle level classrooms: *guided inquiry, simulations, independent study projects, cooperative learning, learning activity packages, contracts,* and *learning centers or stations.*

Guided Inquiry

Guided inquiry is a method of instruction based on the students' need to learn through actively seeking knowledge rather than by receiving knowledge through direct teaching methods. At the middle level, an inquiry lesson would be one that is conducted by having students identify a problem to solve, design a method to collect data and solve the problem, and identify a solution to their problem. The teacher's role is one of facilitating the inquiry process. That is, teachers can help students identify and define their problem (in some cases teachers actually assign problems for inquiry), guide students in data collection and classification, and elicit from students clear and consistent conclusions and inferences (Kellough and Kellough, 1996).

A typical guided inquiry lesson is made up of six procedural steps:

- statement of the problem,
- development of hypotheses,
- data collection,
- data analysis,
- interpretation of results, and
- reporting of conclusions and generalizations.

As the students move through these steps, teachers ask eliciting questions, provide data for research and analysis, and give general directions to guide students as needed (see Figure 6.8).

1. Ask questions to guide students to a clear definition of the problem. Help students in the formulation of a problem relevant to the stated curriculum objectives which is, at the same time, relevant and meaningful to students.

2. Ask questions that aid students in the development of a manageable number of clearly stated hypotheses.

3. Guide students toward relevant resource material when needed. Provide adequate time in order that students can complete data collection.

4. Ask eliciting questions to guide students through a meaningful organization and classification of the data.

5. Guide students in their interpretation of data in order that conclusions relate to the originally stated hypotheses.

6. Aid students as they select the best way to present their reports of the conclusions and generalizations.

Figure 6.8. Teacher responsibility in conducting guided inquiry lessons as adapted from Bedwell, Hunt, Touzel, and Wiseman (1991).

Middle level students are natural inquirers. They are interested in their world and wish to explore and learn about interesting aspects of their environment. Classical teaching methods, which too frequently emphasize rote memorization to the neglect of exploration and critical thinking, can have the effect of squelching the natural curiosity of these otherwise curious learners. Teachers who desire to encourage discovery learning through the use of guided inquiry techniques must focus on creating a classroom environment conducive to exploration and open-ended learning.

Teachers must first focus on learning activities that will stimulate exploration; open-ended problem solving should be at the center of such learning, not rote memorization. These learning activities must be supported by a collection of suitable learning materials to sustain students' exploration of the topics under investigation. In order to stimulate interest in such exploratory, self-directed activity, teachers must develop an introductory activity that will stimulate students to think and explore with little direct teacher instruction. Such introductory stimuli include the presentation of an open-ended problem, question, or hard-to-explain contradiction. When students begin such study, teachers must be prepared to field a wide range of questions and ideas as students approach problems from a variety of angles.

As students are involved in their own inquiry the classroom environment should be one where they are free to communicate with one another in order to discuss and exchange ideas. When teachers talk to students in this environment, more often it should be to ask questions than to provide information. Teachers should listen carefully to the things students say and make statements and ask questions to clarify and reinforce these student comments. When students ask teachers for specific information related to the problem under study, the teacher should attempt to redirect their questions in order to encourage them to explore and evaluate their own ideas while arriving at their own solutions to problems.

The inquiry process leads students to understand that answers and solutions are often tentative. Students will learn to reserve judgment until as much data as possible has been collected and to rely on themselves to find and create solutions to their own problems. Their critical thinking and problem-solving abilities will be enhanced through the process.

Simulations or Role Playing

In simulations, students play out specific roles in an attempt to authenticate a real-life action or experience. Through the use of this strategy, a vicarious experience is created where students take on roles within a scenario that allows them to experience an important lifelike situation in a controlled, safe classroom environment. In order to answer questions about parenthood, students could, for example, role play parents and children in a contrived situation designed to allow them to gain insights into the problems of parenting that could not be gained from a book or a discussion.

Obviously, a potential danger exists in this strategy: reality can be oversimplified. However, if teachers guard against this oversimplification by guiding students to clarify their concepts, role playing or simulations can be a most valuable technique for middle level instruction. Middle level students are inherently social in nature which makes role playing appealing to them. Middle level students also tend to be curious about other people's points of view which, of course, is an interest that can be developed through simulations (Stowall, Rios, McDaniel, and Christopher, 1996).

According to Freiberg and Driscoll (1992), the typical simulation lesson will have four distinct parts. In the first phase of the lesson, teachers orient the students to the problem to be studied and the simulation process to be used. In the second phase, students should do the necessary background work to play their roles. Simulations used at the middle school level may be complex enough to require several days of research to develop the adequate background information necessary for the roles to be played appropriately. In the third phase of the lesson, students actually play out their roles within the prescribed scenario. Finally, after role playing has been completed, teachers will lead a discussion and critique of the session to enhance learning and critical thinking processes.

An important task for the teacher is to make certain that all participants are focused on learnings related to the instructional objectives. Teachers must do what is necessary to insure that all students benefit from the experience. In some cases due to the nature of the scenario, the entire class may not be directly involved in role playing. When this is the case, teachers should attempt to actively involve those students who form the audience in the fourth phase of the lesson by asking them questions to clarify their thoughts and insights.

The simulation lesson is sometimes time consuming and may require considerable preparation by the teacher in the formation of the scenario and the casting of the roles. Due in part to the nature of middle level students this is a technique that can be used with excellent results within the middle level classroom.

Independent Study

The most pedagogically responsive instructional strategy that can be used in the middle level school is the independent study project where students are allowed to choose a topic to research (Stowell, Rios, McDaniel,and Christopher, 1996). Even though this activity allows middle level students the opportunity to explore issues that are truly important to them, teachers must be certain to provide students with guidance and structure if learning is to be optimal. The structure of a successful independent study lesson requires frequent teacher-student conferences as well as opportunities for students to confer with one another as the research is being completed.

Certainly the notion of students being given opportunity to work independently on open-ended project assignments is a method of instruction which has been recognized as effective for many years; the Progressive educator William Heard Kilpatrick (1918) stressed the importance of the project method in the early twentieth century. The independent study project has proven to be quite effective when teachers follow the guidelines presented in Figure 6.9.

There are special advantages to using the independent study method of teaching in the middle level classroom. First, this method of instruction allows students to present and display their personal work; middle level students typically enjoy and benefit from this opportunity to share with others. Also, independent study projects provide an excellent opportunity for students to increase their study habits and their research skills. In this age of rapid technological advancements, such activities will allow students an opportunity to learn to use the Internet to gather data and communicate with living resources on the World Wide Web. Finally, the independent study project provides an ideal opportunity for the study of integrated thematic topics. The topic of study can combine the content areas of music, art, social studies, language arts, math, science, or any other field of study as specific topics are studied by the student. For example, Albert Einstein could be studied as a historical figure who made significant contributions to science. His interest in the arts or mathematics could be included in a report which could be delivered through both written and spoken language. Other students, of course, could develop their listening and questioning skills as they take part in the discussion session at the end of the report. Overall, this is an extremely valuable experience which would integrate many curriculum areas.

1. Provide students with a list of possible project topics. Students can choose topics not on the list; however, the list provides a framework for topic selection.

2. Approve topics prior to the beginning of research. It is the teacher's responsibility to insure that the topics under study are in conjunction with appropriate educational goals and instructional objectives for the students involved.

3. Guide students' exploration. Sometimes teachers may find it necessary to help students access data on certain topics.

4. Give students the necessary training to use library materials (e.g., journal and microfilm indexes), computers (e.g., Internet access), and other data sources.

5. Conduct conferences with students while the research is in progress.

6. Develop a rubic for evaluating the project and discuss it with the students when the activity is introduced.

7. Collect all written reports and listen to any oral reports or presentations on the predetermined date.

8. Conduct a teacher-led discussion session with the class where students contribute, through group interaction, information learned while completing the project.

9. Evaluate all components of the project and communicate the results to students in a timely manner.

Figure 6.9. Guidelines for conducting the independent study project in a middle level classroom.

Unfortunately, teachers must carefully plan independent study projects to avoid a number of problems. Anytime students work independently on projects teachers must be concerned about the originality of the students' projects. The activities must be structured so that teachers can follow the students' work and insure that the work is not completed by someone else and that students use their time effectively. Stories about parents competing against one another to produce the winning project at the "science fair" have been told for decades.

The question of just how much help from friends and family members is acceptable has been a question facing teachers since projects first became a popular method of instruction. The best way to avoid problems associated with students not doing their own work is to have teachers allot more classroom time to monitoring and guiding student projects. This solution may seem too time consuming to some teachers; however, with more classroom instructional time available to students doing projects, students can reap optimal benefit from the activity.

Cooperative Learning

Cooperative learning is a method of instruction in which students work together in a constructive manner for the benefit of each individual as well as for the entire group. This method became very popular in the early 1980s (Bartz and Miller, 1991).

Slavin (1994) and his colleagues at Johns Hopkins University have developed a set of instructional techniques designed for cooperative learning called *Student Team Learning.* Slavin has stated that there are three central concepts that are most important to the Student Team Learning model for cooperative learning: *team rewards, individual accountability,* and *equal opportunities for success.*

In using this strategy students are divided into cooperative learning teams. Achievement goals are set for each team, and the teams may earn rewards if they reach or exceed the designated criterion. The teams are not in competition with each other; the success or failure of one team is in no way connected to the performance of any other team. That is, all or none of the teams may receive a reward.

In the cooperative learning method, each student is accountable; that is, the team's success is dependent on the individual performance of all team members. Each member of the team must perform without the help of teammates on each assessment. Therefore, the emphasis is placed upon team members helping each other (they study in groups and use peer tutoring) prepare for assessments. However, all students must be evaluated on their own work; grades are not given to the team as a whole. This aspect has a great advantage over classical group work where students worked together on a task or project and every student in the group received the same grade. Teachers have long felt that giving all group members the same grade for a single group project is a practice which is unfair to some students and often encourages a few students to do all the work while other group members do very little. Cooperative learning, on the other hand, provides students with the opportunity to take responsibility for their own work.

Cooperative learning can be an excellent avenue in which to provide instruction for students of varying ability levels (Stowell, Rios, McDaniel, and Christopher, 1996). Equal opportunities for success, Slavin's (1994) third central concept, means that cooperative learning should be structured in order to insure that high, average, and low achievers are equally challenged to work at their highest levels of ability. Since students are competing against their own previous personal performances, all students, regardless of their achievement levels, have an equal impact on their team's possibility for success.

A cooperative learning group optimally will be composed of four students usually of different ability levels, gender, and ethnic background. This type of diversity encourages students to increase communication and develop stronger friendships which, in turn, results in better self-concepts and improved academic achievement (Kellough and Kellough, 1996).

There are many different formats for instruction through cooperative learning. Figure 6.10 provides generic guidelines for teachers who wish to incorporate cooperative learning techniques in their middle level classrooms.

Slavin's (1990, 1994) *Student Teams Achievement Divisions* (STAD) is a very popular model for cooperative learning in middle level classrooms. In this model the teacher presents a lesson and the students study the material in their team groups helping one another learn as effectively as possible. After the time in cooperative groups is over, the teacher quizzes the students on the material individually without help from peers. Each student receives his or her own grade, and the teacher compares the student's score to his or her previous performance. Each team earns rewards based on the degree that team members equaled or exceeded criteria based on their past performance.

All cooperative learning does not have to be done to receive a grade (Johnson and Johnson, 1989). The circle of knowledge model is a brainstorming type activity where the team is given a question or prompt in order for group members to respond. Taking five to seven minutes, group members are allowed to respond in any fashion they wish. One student, the recorder, takes notes writing down each student's comments. Each team member signs the recorder's notes, and the notes are turned in to the teacher who may react to the work but will not grade it. Later, the student comments from each group can be shared on an overhead projection or at the chalkboard as the focus of a class discussion.

---

1. Discuss rules for group learning with the students. For example, students should be responsible for their own work, help one another when needed, and refrain from using "put-downs."

2. Place students in heterogeneous groups or teams of approximately four students.

3. Assign roles to each team member such as *facilitator* (keeps the group on task), *reporter* (informs the teacher or class about group activities), *timer* (keeps track of time), *artist* (illustrator of displays), and *recorder* (keeps notes on group processes).

4. Provide the groups with a learning task to perform.

5. Move around the classroom from group-to-group observing and providing help where needed.

6. Ask students questions to help them evaluate their performance when the activity is complete.

7. Evaluate the student's learning. Assign grades to individuals and rewards to teams as appropriate.

Figure 6.10. Guidelines for conducting cooperative learning in middle level classrooms.

There has been a considerable amount of favorable research done to sustain the value of cooperative learning as a teaching strategy. Johnson and Johnson (1992) found that cooperative learning settings had more frequent use of discovery and higher-level reasoning than traditional classes where learning was more competitive and individualistic. Johnson and Johnson also found that cooperative learning teaches students to further appreciate other people's viewpoints while enhancing students' ability to communicate their own ideas. Moreover, studies have shown that cooperative learning will enhance student achievement (Johnson, Johnson and Maruyama, 1983; Johnson, Maruyama, Johnson, Nelson, and Skom, 1981).

Cooperative learning certainly has instructional advantages for the middle level classroom. Messick and Reynolds (1992) have suggested that, optimally, it should be used approximately sixty percent of the time.

Learning Activity Package

A Learning Activity Package (LAP) is a self-contained, self-instructional set of materials designed to allow students to work independently to achieve stated instructional objectives. Students are given a set of materials (the LAP) that is structured in such a way as to allow them to independently learn certain concepts or skills by working through the materials on their own.

Learning Activity Packages are basically a form of programmed instruction though they are usually teacher-made materials specifically designed to address the teacher's instructional objectives. Typically, a LAP will have five parts: instructional objectives, pretest, learning activities, self-tests, and evaluation.

In preparing a LAP, objectives should be written by the teacher in terms of what the students will learn as a result of completing the package. Remember that the objectives are included here as a method of communicating purpose to the students; therefore, language should be chosen that will be easily understood by middle level students.

Pretests are included in the package for two reasons. First, they serve to introduce the material to students, establish a focus for expected outcomes, and can have instructional value as a result. Pretests also give feedback to the teacher and the students concerning the strengths and weaknesses of given students on certain topics. Based on the information gained from a pretest, the teacher may ascertain that some students are not prepared for a certain LAP, while other students may have previously mastered the material. Answers to the pretests are included in the LAP (usually at the end) in order that students can correct their own responses.

The learning activities constitute the bulk of the LAP. The number of these activities will vary greatly from LAP to LAP due to the nature of the material under study. Many packages may have from seven to twelve activities; however, there will be LAPs with more than a dozen activities. The teacher must include enough activities to insure that students receive sufficient practice to master the stated objectives. The self-pacing and self-instructional nature of the LAP should be sustained by the selection of activities. Some of the activities are likely to take the format of paper-and-pencil workbook type exercises; however, to the degree that is possible the activities should have manipulative, activity-based components. Directions must be complete and easily understood. If students cannot complete the exercises without going to the teacher for help or clarification, the advantages of the LAP as an instructional technique are lessened. As was the case with the pretests, the answers to the learning activities are to be included in the package in order that students can assess their own responses.

Self-tests, like the pretests, are used for both instruction and feedback. The self-test is placed after the learning activities in order that students can determine if they have mastered the content or need further study. Too, the self-test provides the student with a review of the learning activities. The answers to the self-test, as with the pretest, are included in the package to provide students the opportunity to evaluate their own progress.

The final evaluation, unlike the pretest, learning activities, and self-test, is not included in the package presented to the students, nor are the answers included in the LAP. This evaluation is typically summative in nature; the instrument is kept by the teacher and assessed by the teacher. Usually students who are not successful on the final evaluation are directed to readdress certain portions of the LAP or are given additional learning activities.

Teachers obviously can use LAPs in a variety of ways. Units can be conducted in an individualized manner using LAPs to replace textbooks or other curriculum materials. Teachers can supplement the existing curriculum materials with complementary Learning Activity Packages designed to augment or strengthen the students' learning. Teachers may assign certain packages to specific students due to their learning needs at a specific time during the school year. Various approaches may be taken in terms of how teachers might record grades made on the final evaluations. Some will record the grades much the same way they will record grades on other activities. Some others will prefer to award special credit to students who successfully complete a LAP that may be used as an additional or extra credit.

Learning Activity Packages have been popularly used in many middle level schools. Creation of these packages becomes easier when teachers work together and share their products. The advent of instructional teams provides an excellent opportunity for teachers to work together in the development of instructional materials.

Contracts

A learning contract is a prearranged agreement between a teacher and an individual student. In this agreement the student will agree to complete certain learning activities while meeting all requirements with an agreed upon time frame. In turn, the teacher typically agrees to award a certain grade or other reward upon completion of the described activity.

Bedwell, Hunt, Touzel and Wiseman (1991) have indicated that typically a contract will consist of seven distinct parts:

1. *Title* – With middle level students a "catchy" motivational title should be seen as a plus.
2. *Introduction* – A short statement is provided to students with an overview of the material to be studied.
3. *Objectives* – Objectives, written in language understandable to middle level students, are provided explaining what the students are to learn.
4. *Alternative Activities* – A variety of activities should be presented; some may be required by the teacher while students may be able to choose from others. All activities should be designed for active student involvement.
5. *Learning Materials* – A listing of possible learning materials should be provided.
6. *Reporting Procedures* – Specifics as to the acceptable manner students are to submit their final products should be delineated.
7. *Closing Agreement* – A clear statement of the amount and quality of work to be presented for a designated grade is included. A place for the signature of the student and the teacher should be provided.

Contracts are designed, much like Learning Activity Packages, to provide students with an opportunity for independent learning and decision making. A goal of this teaching strategy is to have a minimal level of direct instruction. This should create a learning environment where teachers are free to work with individuals who need one-to-one or very small group instruction because the majority of the students will be working in a self-directed manner. Figure 6.11 provides guidelines for teachers who want to create an environment conducive to independent learning through the use of contracts.

---

1. Develop instructional objectives to guide learners through the material to be covered by the contract.

2. Develop the required and optional learning tasks for the contract.

3. Develop rubrics for grading along with any needed assessment instruments.

4. Gather resources to be used by students in their independent learning.

5. Present the contracts to the students while delineating procedural rules and responsibilities.

6. Schedule meetings with students to monitor their progress toward the objectives.

7. Provide time in the beginning for students to review the contract before meeting with the teacher.

8. Sign the contract with each student involved.

9. Provide ample in-class time for students to work on their contracts in order that their work can be monitored.

10. Allow ample time for reports and other sharing experiences which should include a teacher-led discussion.

Figure 6.11. Guidelines for middle level teachers for the use of instructional contracts.

In a middle school setting, students typically work on a contract for two to three weeks. Obviously the ability of the students, their familiarity with the use of contracts, and the difficulty of the content are all factors in determining adequate instructional time. Remember, teachers who decide to use contracts do not have to use them in every class or for all students. Flexibility and individuality are strengths of this process; teachers should feel free to be creative in the use of contracts as a teaching strategy.

Learning Centers

Learning centers, much like contracts, provide students with an opportunity to become involved in self-directed, individualized learning activities. Like the LAP, learning centers provide a self-contained set of self-instructional materials which provide students an opportunity for indirect instruction.

A learning center is a specified area in the classroom designed for the students to take part in indirect, self-instructional learning. Materials will be provided in the learning center that will be self-correcting and will allow for different styles and rates of learning. Such learning centers have been used commonly in elementary schools (especially in the early childhood grades) at least since the 1970s; however, many educators have made a strong case for the use of learning centers as an effective instructional method at the middle school level as well (Gilstrap, Bierman, and McKnight, 1992).

There are a number of different formats that can be used to develop learning centers; the format used will be dependent upon the learning purpose the center is designed to address. Table 6.2 provides a listing of types of learning centers and their purposes. It should be remembered that different teachers and authors may use various labels for the same type of center.

Table 6.2
TYPES AND PURPOSES OF LEARNING CENTERS

Type	*Purpose*
Skill center, skill development center, content-skill development center, or direct learning center	To provide indirect, individualized instruction designed so that students can learn a specific skill or related information. Typically, this is done through a series of stations so that learning develops from concrete to more abstract forms.
Interest center, exploratory center, or open-learning center	To expose students to an array of topics that may stimulate further reading or study. This is less structured than a skill center.
Reinforcement center or remediation center	To provide students application opportunities to reinforce new skills or knowledge or to recycle and review skills students have had difficulty learning.
Enrichment center or extension center	To complement and supplement skills and information previously introduced through other methods. This is very similar to the interest center.

Learning centers are designed to provide students with independent learning opportunities while their teachers work more directly with students who need such instruction. To be effective, learning centers must be self-contained, self-correcting learning environments. Directions must be clear and easy to follow. Due to differences in learning ability and styles so often found in middle level schools, many teachers use audiotapes or videotapes to supplement written directions. Learning materials must be designed to give students self-correctional feedback (see the earlier discussion of LAPs) so that teachers do not have to provide as much direct feedback. The final assessment instrument, of course, is to be evaluated by the teacher and will not be self-correcting. Figure 6.12 provides guidelines to teachers who wish to use learning centers in their classrooms.

1. Decide on a topic for the proposed learning center that relates to the scope and sequence of the curriculum.

2. Prepare specific learning objectives for the learning center.

3. Decide what type or types of learning center is needed for the topic under consideration (i.e., skill center, interest center, reinforcement/remediation center, or enrichment center).

4. Consider the room arrangement needed to provide for the center or centers.

5. Develop the directions to be given the students for each learning activity (e.g., task cards, audiotapes, etc.).

6. Create the learning alternatives and decide how these activities are to be formatted.

7. Adjust the activities to address the varying abilities, rates, and styles of learning common to middle level students.

8. Develop a management system for the learning center. Questions concerning the number of students allowed in the center at one time, how long students can stay in the center on a given visit, and which times of the day the centers will be used must be answered.

9. Determine a system for evaluating student performance while in the learning center.

10. Orient all students and adults (e.g., student teachers, aides, volunteers) to the center.

Figure 6.12. Guidelines for using learning centers in a middle level classroom

Learning centers are an excellent method for providing individualized instruction in such a way as to develop independence and responsibility in students. Teachers are provided with a format that will give them opportunities to work independently with students who most need it while other students are involved in indirect instruction. Moreover, the learning center provides an excellent avenue for integration of curriculum. Learning centers allow for content crossing several disciplinary boundaries to be integrated within the theme of a single center (Kellough and Kellough, 1996). Of course, central to their use is the philosophy that learning centers must focus on stated instructional objectives that are compatible with the ongoing curriculum and that student performance in the learning centers must be evaluated in terms of these instructional objectives.

Technology and Instruction

Computer technology has had a vital impact on almost every aspect of our lives. It is popularly felt that the integration of traditional teaching strategies with computer technology will provide improved learning in middle level classrooms. The success of this dependent integration is, perhaps more than anything else, on an attitude of educators to be willing to combine technology and teaching into a productive experience that moves students to a new level of understanding.

It is important that the computer be seen as a learning and teaching tool and that computers can be used to enhance learning through the use of virtually any of the direct or indirect strategies discussed in this chapter. For example, the Internet can be used as a source of information to support student inquiry or be used as a resource to help the teacher who is gathering information for a short lecture session. A computer with certain software packages often can become a focal point in the development of a learning center. The examples are virtually infinite. The computer along with the use of CD-ROMs and videodiscs provide students with a vast array of valuable information. Telecommunications, through the use of e-mail and bulletin boards on the Internet, provides middle level students an opportunity to communicate with other students and sources of data all over the world.

The computer, however, is not the only important technological instructional device. The video camera also is an excellent tool in a middle level environment. Due to their nature, middle level students enjoy producing and taking part in video productions. Video productions not only enhance learning, the production of a video can be used as a form of alternative assessment. That is, a produced tape can be evaluated where, in the past, a test or an essay may have served the same purpose.

Teachers must develop confidence in their use of technology and must be in control of the technology instead of being frightened or controlled by it. Also, teachers must accept that educational technology is always changing. This fact alone requires a major commitment for study and professional development on the part of middle level teachers. Teachers should visit other classrooms where teachers are taking advantage of new advancements whenever they can and must be patient and willing to seek help (Schurr, Thomason, and Thompson, 1995).

Teachers should:

1. show an understanding of the basic concepts related to the use of software and hardware in classrooms.

2. understand the capabilities and limitations of computers and related programs.

3. have the ability to discuss the impact of technology on society.

4. demonstrate the ability to use a computer for instructional purposes.

5. master word processing, computer graphics, and telecommunications.

6. be able to use and operate a computer network.

7. have a working knowledge of software evaluation and integration of technology in the curriculum.

8. be able to use electronic spreadsheets and data bases.

9. be able to use an authoring program (e.g., HyperCard, HyperStudio, and Compel).

10. be able to use software related to classroom management (e.g., electronic gradebook, e-mail, and statistical and data analysis).

Figure 6.13. South Carolina's technology competencies for all educators.

The *South Carolina Educational Technology Plan* (1995) has provided that state's framework for the use of technology in public schools. Figure 6.13 outlines those technological competencies South Carolina expects of its educators.

There are many network service providers for middle level teachers who wish to have their classrooms on line (Kellough and Kellough, 1996). A few of such providers are

- TERC which is devoted to math and science education: (617) 547-0430.
- Classroom Connect which is an educator's guide to the Internet: (800) 638-1639.
- I*EARN which is the International Education Resource Network which allows for international telecommunications: (914) 962-5864.
- K12Net which is a bulletin board for professionals, students, or others interested in quality education.

Teaching in Teams

Much of the instruction offered in today's middle level schools is delivered by instructional teams (see Chapter 5 for a detailed description of teaming). Many teachers have found that working in teams to plan and carry out groupwork along with a colleague, though demanding, is both rewarding and educational (Cohen, 1994).

Within the context of an instructional team, teachers may no longer work alone to plan the best instruction procedures. Teachers in teams plan together taking input from all team members to make the best possible decisions. There is research to support the position that such team planning leads to more effective instruction especially when dealing with complex instructional issues (Cohen and Intili, 1982).

Typically an interdisciplinary team at the middle level will have an English teacher, a social studies teacher, a science teacher, a mathematics teacher, and, perhaps, a reading specialist (Vars, 1993). In some teams, an interdisciplinary unit may be planned and delivered by two or three teachers in the group. For example, math and social studies teachers may work together in the teaching of an economics and finance unit. Although teams often spend a great deal of time reflecting on management problems rather than instructional concerns, the collegial nature of team teaching creates an atmosphere conducive to better instruction.

The teaming aspect of middle level schools has certainly impacted instruction. Middle level teachers must be willing to collaborate with other teachers. As teachers reflect on their instruction, it is no longer possible in most modern middle level schools to think of isolated teachers working unilaterally with a single group of students.

Summary

The most important aspect of a middle level school is the teaching and learning that goes on within its walls. For that reason, teachers must make a rather extensive examination of many of the instructional options from which middle level teachers can choose. This chapter surveyed several methods of instruction, both direct and indirect in nature, with the knowledge that effective middle level teachers will blend many of these strategies together in order to offer students the optimal opportunity to learn.

The chapter also examined the impact that technology has on instruction. Educational technology should not be seen as a separate methodology or an end in itself. Technology must be seen as a tool provided to both teachers and students as they strive to prepare and explore a learning environment.

Finally, the chapter examined the impact of instructional teaming on instruction. Many middle level schools organize around interdisciplinary teams. When done properly, planning in instructional teams can provide real advantages for students and teachers alike. More and more, middle level educators are coming to see instruction as something to be developed and carried out by a group rather than an individual where students play a major, active role in orchestrating their own learning.

REFERENCES

Atkin, J.M., & Karplus, R. (1962). "Discovery or invention?" *Science Teacher,* 29, 5:45.

Ausubel, D.P. (1963). *The psychology of meaningful learning.* New York: Grune and Stratton.

Barman, C.R. (1989). "The Learning cycle: Making it work." *Science Scope,* February, 1989, 28-31.

Bartz, D.E., & Miller, L.K. (1991). *12 teaching methods to enhance student learning.* Washington, D.C.: National Education Association.

Bedwell, L., Hunt, G., Touzel, T., & Wiseman, D. (1991). *Effective teaching: Preparation and implementation.* Springfield, IL: Charles C Thomas, Publisher.

Brooks, J.G., & Brooks, M.G., (1993). *The case for constructivist classrooms.* Alexandria, VA: Association for Supervision and Curriculum Development.

Cohen, E.G. (1994). *Designing groupwork: Strategies for the heterogeneous classroom.* New York: The Teachers College, Columbia University.

Cohen, E.G., & Intili, J.K. (1982). *Interdependence and management in bilingual classrooms:* Final report II, (NIE Contract # NIE-G-80-0217) Stanford, CL: Stanford University, Center for Educational Research.

Costa, A.L. (1991). *The school as a home for the mind.* Palatine, IL: Skylight Publishing.

Freiberg, H.J. & Driscoll, A. (1992). *Universal teaching strategies.* Needham, Massachusetts: Allyn & Bacon.

Gagne, R. (1985). *The conditions of learning.* New York: Holt, Rhinehart and Winston.

Gallagher, J., & Aschner, M. (1963). "A preliminary report of the analysis of classroom interaction." *Merrill-Palmer Quarterly,* (9), 183-194.

Gilstrap, R.L., Bierman, C., & McKnight, T.R. (1992). "Improving instruction in middle schools." *Fastback 331.* Bloomington, Indiana: Phi Delta Kappa Educational Foundation.

Good, T,. & Brophy, J. (1986). *Educational psychology: A realistic approach.* New York: Holt, Rhinehart, and Winston.

Guilford, J. (1959). "Three faces of intellect." *American Psychologist,* 1959, (14), 469-479.

Johnson, D.W., & Johnson, R.T. (1989). *Leading the cooperative school.* Edina, MN: Interaction Book Company.

Johnson, D.W., & Johnson, R.T. (1992). "Encouraging thinking through constructive controversy." In N. Davidson and T. Worsham (Eds.) *Enhancing thinking through cooperative learning* (pp. 120-137). New York: Teachers College Press.

Johnson, D.W., Johnson, R.T., & Maruyama, G. (1983). "Interdependence and interpersonal attraction among heterogeneous and homogeneous individuals: A theoretical formulation and a meta-analysis of the research." *Review of Educational Research,* 53, 5-54.

Johnson, D.W., Maruyama, G., Johnson, R.T., Nelson, D., & Skon, L. (1981) "Effects of cooperative, competitive, and individualistic goal structure on achievement: A meta-analysis." *Psychological Bulletin,* 89, 47-62.

Kellough, R.D., & Kellough, N.G. (1996). *Middle school teaching: A guide to methods and resources.* Englewood Cliffs, New Jersey: Prentice-Hall, Inc.

Kilpatrick, W.H. (1918). *The project method.* New York: Teachers College, Columbia University.

Messick, R.G. & Reynolds, K.E. (1992). *Middle level curriculum in action.* New York: Longman.

Rubinstein, R.E. (1994). *Hints for teaching success in middle school.* Englewood, Colorado: Teacher Ideas Press.

Schurr, S.L., Thomason, J., & Thompson, M. (1995). *Teaching at the middle level: A professionals' handbook.* Lexington, Massachusetts: D.C. Heath and Company.

Silvernail, D.L. (1986). *Teaching styles as related to student achievement.* Washington, D.C.: National Education Association.

Slavin, R.E. (1990). *Cooperative learning: Theory, research, and practice.* Boston: Allyn and Bacon.

Slavin, R.E. (1994). *A practical guide to cooperative learning.* Needham Heights, Massachusetts: Allyn and Bacon.

South Carolina Educational Technology Plan. (1995). Columbia, SC: South Carolina State Department of Education.

Stowell, L.P., Rios, A.R., McDaniel, J.E., & Christopher, P.A. (1996). *Working with middle school students.* Westminster, CA: Teacher Created Materials, Inc.

Vars, G.F. (1993). *Interdisciplinary teaching: When and how.* Columbus, Ohio: National Middle School Association.

Weber, M., & Renner, J. (1972). "How effective is the SCIS science program?" *School science and mathematics,* 72(8): 729-734.

Chapter 7

ASSESSING AND REPORTING PROGRESS

An important characteristic of the modern middle level educator is the ability to communicate with students in an honest and supportive manner. Central to this discussion is the type of communication needed to assess student performance. The effective middle level teacher assesses student performance with two major purposes in mind. First, assessment allows the teacher, through data collection, to determine if the curricula and instructional experiences have been effective in educating the students involved. Second, assessment provides students with feedback concerning their personal growth. Consequently, the teacher is challenged to communicate results in an effective manner that supports future learning to achieve these two purposes.

The role of the teacher is clear. First, assessment instruments or procedures must be developed that are, in themselves, part of the learning experience. Second, teachers must devise methods of feedback which relate to students a clear picture of their progress while, at the same time, providing the type of insight and motivation necessary to encourage the students to continue their search for greater learning.

Many middle level teachers are beginning to modify their assessment strategies to better address these purposes. Traditionally, teachers have often graded students normatively (i.e., they have compared students' performance to the performance of their peers). Today, teachers more and more seek techniques that will allow them to evaluate their students' performances based on a set of criteria relevant to both group and individual performance. For example, teachers will have certain performances all students in the class should exhibit in order to maximize academic achievement. At the same time, there may be subgroups of students or individuals within a class who have specialized criteria to reach due to special giftedness, interests, or remedial needs.

As discussed in Chapter 3 middle level students vary due to multiple intelligences, diverse interest and motivation, learning styles, and cultural backgrounds. As a result, teachers may find it necessary to provide a variety of objectives and learning experiences based on the individual learning goals of the students in a class to augment the standard course objectives. Naturally, if different students have unique needs requiring a variety of learning experiences, the middle level teacher must have available a cadre of assessment strategies to evaluate what can be a diverse population of learners in any given class.

Constructivist thought, which has influenced much of the current change in middle level education, has presented teachers with a new way of thinking about the evaluation of student growth. No longer do teachers think about learning in terms of isolated behaviors to be evaluated normatively. Today, mastery of learning is more often seen in terms of clusters of behaviors to be demonstrated in a real-life context (Eggen and Kauchak, 1994). Effective middle level teachers, in addition to focusing on observable student behavior, also focus on the process and thought patterns students use to arrive at the desired outcome. The teacher will ask students not only to demonstrate certain behavior, but also students will be required to explain the processes required to apply these learnings in the context of authentic, real-life experiences. Given that the modern middle school is built upon the belief that all students can learn and realize success, middle level teachers must use authentic assessment procedures designed to give students a multitude of ways to express the things they have learned.

The Need to Personalize Assessment

The traditional philosophy of assessment has been that all students must be judged against the same criteria as they each perform on exactly the same evaluative task. For example, all students in a history class will take the same test which covers material in a given unit of study, and all students will be given a grade based on the same standards. Typically, these grades were given in such a fashion that each student would receive a score that could easily be compared to the scores of the other students in the class. Current knowledge concerning multiple types of intelligence (Gardner, 1993; Armstrong, 1994) does not support this traditional philosophy of assessment for all students. In fact, the research on multiple intelligences suggests that traditional testing and grading, that too frequently compares student performance on a single type of test, may be detrimental to those students who have had the most difficulty realizing success. Therefore, if the goal of the middle school is to help all students become successful and actualize their potential in an academically relevant curriculum, assessment procedures should offer students a variety of alternative ways to express their learning tailored to the characteristics of the learners involved.

Rotter (1966) reported in a classic study that those students who are more successful in school tend to feel in control of their own successes and failures. Unsuccessful students, on the other hand, tend to attribute their success and failure to forces outside of their own control. Rotter referred to those students who take responsibility for their actions as having an *internal locus of control* while the unsuccessful students who feel out of control are said to have an *external locus of control*. Obviously, locus of control research explains much about the way students perceive assessment. Successful students who have an internal locus of control approach evaluation with the feeling that it is up to them as to whether or not they will perform well or poorly. In other words, students who have an internal locus of control believe they will do well on a test if they prepare for it. Failure, they believe, would occur only if they did not do what they were capable of doing. These students have a personal history of doing well when evaluated; therefore, their self-concepts tend to be strong. The student with an external locus of control approaches assessment from a very different perspective. Such students lack a strong self-concept and have a history spotted with failure. When these students perform poorly, they do not believe they are in control; as a result, they would not think that they had the power to improve. Such students are likely to blame failure on their teachers or the evaluation instruments. This often results in a lack of improvement, more bad work habits, and no improvement in self-concept.

Weiner (1985) pointed out the differences in the way successful students and unsuccessful students approach assessment. Weiner noted that successful students think that they are capable; such students believe that they have high ability and their effort is the determining factor in their success or failure. As a result, if these students receive unfavorable feedback it often tends to motivate them to increase their effort. Unsuccessful students, on the other hand, attribute their success and failure to the ease of the task, luck, or help from others. These students perceive themselves as low in ability; therefore, they rely little on their own effort. Weiner referred to the condition of these unsuccessful students as *learned helplessness*. When being assessed, these unsuccessful students feel helpless; they have no faith in their own ability, and, as a result, they tend not to believe their effort is of any value or will make any difference. Unfavorable feedback to such students can be devastating; failure, to students with a history of failure and a weak self-concept, will lead to continued failure.

It is logical to conclude that an assessment episode for a student with a strong self-concept and history of success is a different experience than the same episode for a student with a history of poor performance and a weak self-concept. Research of scholars such as Rotter and Weiner provide evidence that all students *are not being treated the same* when they sit in the same classroom, receive the same instruction, and are evaluated with the same assessment instrument using identical criteria. If all students are to avoid failure and become lifelong learners, teachers should be aware of each student's strengths and weaknesses.

However, this is not to suggest that ideal assessment should challenge successful students and not challenge unsuccessful students. Ideally, assessment instruments should appropriately challenge all students. It is unforgivable to assess students in a manner that guarantees their failure. At the same time, lowering standards for unsuccessful students so that they can avoid failure will create problems. In order to help students who have a history of failure, teachers must lead these students to believe that their effort is important and that they can experience success. Students who have such histories of failure often withdraw from activities which overly challenge their abilities. For example, such a student might stop doing homework after a series of poor performances. The teacher must work with such students (i.e., students with low self-concepts) in such a way as to lead them to believe that if they try they can be successful. Obviously, teachers will need to give these students interesting assignments within their specific ability range in order that success is possible. Also, these students may need individualized guidance to assure success. Most importantly, the failure cycle must be broken if students who have learned helplessness are going to overcome their feelings of inadequacy and become successful on future assessments (Weiner, 1985).

The reflective teacher approaches the assessment of students with a positive attitude. Students are always seen as capable of learning. Insightful, reflective teachers are aware that students are individuals and must be taught and evaluated as individuals. Students vary in terms of experiential background, self-concept development, willingness to take risks, academic preparation, and overall development in cognitive, social, and physical characteristics. Such diversity can mean only one thing if the middle school is to be manifestly enriching to all students: students must be assessed in terms of their individual potential and progress toward individual educational goals.

Setting Standards of Performance

Middle level teachers must develop realistically high learning standards that will maintain student enthusiasm and promote continuous, life-long learning. Standards, if they are to be realistic, should involve student input. Too frequently, in the past, standards have been set by teachers, administrators, school boards, parents, or other such groups. When individual students are omitted from the development of learning standards, the adult population should not be surprised when many students do not seem to strive for competency or even take seriously the learning goals of the school.

Early cognitive psychologists pointed out the importance of individual goal setting to motivation and learning (Lewin, 1942). A major role of middle school teachers is to know and relate to their students in such a fashion as to assist them in the development of learning goals which are realistic for each individual learner. As teachers work with students to set learning goals, standards for achievement evolve. School officials may set standards in mathematical or foreign language proficiency that all middle level students are supposed to achieve in order to exit a given level of schooling. However, it is unrealistic to assume that all students are going to reach the desired level of ability unless all students believe in the importance of such standards. This is not to argue that there is anything wrong with desiring high levels of competency in all academic content. To the contrary, educators should want their students to achieve maximum levels of competency; anything less would be both harmful and dangerous to the students and to society. However, the point is, students should not feel as though these standards are superimposed on them. Students must believe that the standards for learning come from within them and are owned by them. For example, if a student had a severe learning disability that kept the student from expressing thoughts in writing, it would be likely that failure would occur if that student were to be evaluated solely through standards for written expression. As an accommodation, this student could perhaps use audiotapes or class presentations using visual aids as an avenue to demonstrate the ability to communicate thoughts.

In the past, when standards were developed without concern for individual student diversity, the results were often less than desirable for all students. Often, low-achieving students learned to feel helpless and disenfranchised early in their educational experiences. They learned to perceive themselves as failures and, as a result, often became either withdrawn or rebellious. Regardless, they were almost, without question, labeled in a negative way by their teachers. This approach was also ineffective for the higher-achieving students. Since the stated standards were frequently minimal in order that a majority of students could reach them, the higher-achieving students were too often not challenged and developed poor learning habits. The highest- and lowest-achieving students were the ones who had the most difficulty in this system because all students were being compared to the same standards which frequently were designed to be minimal for a hypothetical average student. *Turning Points: Preparing American Youth for the 21st Century* (Carnegie, 1989) stresses that all middle level students must have an opportunity for success in all facets of the middle level program without regard to achievement levels. This goal may never be realized unless students are aided in the development of realistic learning standards that will serve as criteria to judge if they are making adequate learning progress.

Realistic goals are not unreachable nor too easily achieved. Successful students set goals that are challenging, yet reachable. Unsuccessful students tend to set goals that are either unrealistically difficult to obtain (a built-in excuse for failure) or so easily reached that failure is nearly impossible (Atkinson, 1964). The reflective teacher must help students set standards for performance that will challenge them to grow beyond their current level while, at the same time, assuring the possibility for success. This approach is the only way all students will realize their right to be in schools where they can achieve at high levels of personal academic performance.

Types of Assessment

Hobar (1994a) has identified two basic forms of assessment: traditional assessment and alternative assessment. The teacher who desires to be a reflective scholar in the learning environment must seriously consider the advantages of alternative assessment.

Traditional assessment has frequently taken place through the use of paper and pencil tests which are either standardized or teacher-made. Often, the items on such tests have been written in the multiple-choice, true-false, matching or other similar formats. These test items usually measure cognitive ability to recognize or recall material that has been learned at the knowledge or comprehension levels (i.e., low levels of the cognitive domain). Also, as these test items frequently focus on isolated facts and skills, the assessment experience is often far from being a learning experience. The traditional assessment episode has typically been created by teachers or measurement experts with little or no input from individual students being assessed.

Currently, two new concepts are being discussed in relation to the assessment of student performance: Authentic Assessment and Alternative Assessment. Alternative assessment is a measurement process that is different from traditional testing procedures. Authentic assessment is evaluation using procedures that allow students to be measured while performing in situations as close to real-life application as possible. For example, if a teacher were to evaluate students' ability to measure flat surfaces by giving the students measuring tools and asking them to determine the square footage of the parking lot, this would be an alternative assessment (not a traditional mathematics test) and it would be authentic in nature (real-life application).

Moreover, alternative assessment must measure thought processes that students use to arrive at answers to questions or problems. Students are not just evaluated on what they know or can do; students must be able to explain the processes used to arrive at their responses. For example, if a student were to submit a model as a project to be evaluated, the model alone would not be assessed. The student must also submit (in writing, on audiotape, etc.) a statement that explains in detail why the model was developed in such a way. As a result, alternative assessment measures are likely to be open-ended. That is, students will not all be required to respond in the same manner. Responses will thus be personalized in many cases.

Alternative assessment can take several forms in the middle level classroom: portfolios, performances, exhibits, or other similar techniques (Hobar, 1994b). Such formats involve students more in the actual structuring of the assessment. When this occurs, assessment techniques will be more meaningful for students and will actually be learning experiences in themselves. Jones (1994) noted that alternative assessment places emphasis on process skills such as observing, inferring, experimenting, and interpreting which will increase students' ability to use critical thinking and problem-solving skills.

The portfolio has become a very popular mode of alternative assessment used in many middle level classrooms as a replacement or supplement for teacher-made tests (Case, 1994; Hamm and Adams, 1991). A portfolio is an accumulation of evidence gathered and organized by a student to demonstrate personal competency in some area of study. Each portfolio contains many examples of a student's work, assembled by the student, as a statement of that student's knowledge and skills. The portfolio may contain written products such as essays or journal entries along with other products such as audiotapes and videotapes or the results of original research. The portfolio will contain examples of work completed over time. It is hoped that the work contained in a portfolio assesses several facets of an integrated curriculum with an array of products from real-life settings. Most importantly, the portfolio should include (written or otherwise expressed) evidence that the student can describe the thought processes associated with the production of the evidence in the collection. It is not enough to simply produce a collection of material; students must be able to discuss the cognitive processes used to develop each of the products.

Performances have become a basic model for alternative assessment. In fact, the term "performance-based" is often used in conjunction with alternative assessment. There are many types of performance formats; in all performance assessments, students are to demonstrate the specific behaviors. That is, if the teacher wants to evaluate the student's ability to read, the students will read. The teacher would not use a test of phonics analysis if reading were the desired behavior.

Exhibits are demonstrations of skills, knowledge, and creative endeavors very similar to the projects described by the great progressive educator William H. Kilpatrick (1918). An exhibit takes place when students share the results of their learning endeavors with their classmates and teachers. An exhibit can be the culmination of personal or group inquiry that results in a unique, personal product that has challenged the high-level thinking of the students being evaluated. For example, a student might create a model of the Jamestown Fort as it appeared in 1607. The student could then present the model to the class explaining the details of the model as they relate to life in early colonial America.

Middle level educators are turning more and more to alternative assessment instead of traditional tests for several reasons. Alternative assessment

- helps students think at higher levels,
- is owned by students as well as teachers and school districts,
- is not contrived but reflects authentic, real-life activity,
- allows students to choose how best to demonstrate what they know and can do,
- can be a learning experience in and of itself,
- is an active endeavor which tends to make the experience more engaging and enjoyable for all students, and
- is in conjunction with the modern philosophy of middle level education as explained in such guiding documents as *Turning Points: Preparing American Youth for the 21st Century* (Carnegie, 1989).

It is not productive to assume that all teacher-made tests should be totally eliminated. There are times when teachers need to assess their students to determine if certain factual knowledge has been learned. Just as a farmer would not use dynamite to uproot a weed, a teacher would not use a portfolio assessment to determine if students had memorized the multiplication tables. The purpose of alternative assessment is to go beyond the scope of traditional testing by applying a variety of assessment measures and to offer a more appropriate balance to the teacher's assessment program.

Integrating Instruction and Assessment

It is not unusual to suggest that teachers should instruct their classes in such a way as to elicit high-order thinking from their students. However, in the past, educators often attempted to teach at one level and assess students at another level. Alternative assessment, when used in the middle level classroom, provides teachers an opportunity to mesh instruction and assessment in such a way as to provide continuous, on-going higher order learning.

When teachers use alternative assessment continuously, it is difficult to determine the difference between an instructional episode and an assessment episode. The major difference between authentic assessment and effective instruction is that the teacher will withdraw from the assessment episode and focus on the individual performance and thought processes of each student involved.

The philosophy involved here, once again, is based on cognitive constructivist theory (Watson and Konicek, 1990; Clements and Battista, 1990). Learning is viewed as the creation of knowledge, and performance-based assessment is the continuing development of that creation. Assessment and learning become molded into a continuous experience where students learn and apply knowledge through thoughtful, challenging, real-life experiences. This total process upgrades the quality and significance of learning for all students regardless of their background or developmental level. In short, the singular advantage of alternative assessment over traditional assessment is that alternative, performance-based assessment supports a type of instruction based on current knowledge of effective instruction (Gardner, 1993; Armstrong, 1994).

Assigning Grades

To this point, assessment has been described as a method to gain feedback concerning student learning and teacher instruction. This type of assessment is used to gain information that aids the teacher in making adjustments when students are not making expected progress; this is referred to as "formative evaluation." Also, assessment can be used to assign a value or grade to the quality of work that students have produced. This type of evaluation is generally referred to as "summative evaluation." Summative evaluation is used to give feedback to students (and their parents) concerning the quality of their progress. As explained earlier, this type of feedback is critical to the motivation of students as it relates to how certain feedback affects successful and unsuccessful students.

One of the real concerns about alternative assessment techniques, such as portfolios, is subjectivity and lack of what is usually called "test reliability". Although several researchers have noted technical problems with the use of alternative assessment (Messick, 1992; Gardner, 1993; Shavelson, Gao, and Baxter, 1993), it is obvious that similar problems also existed with teacher-made traditional assessment measures. Cheek (1993) has noted that although such limitations currently exist, there is reason to believe these limitations will be diminished as more research and development is done in the area of alternative assessment of middle level students.

Johnson (1992), Kulm and Malcom (1991), Ostlund (1992), and Romberg (1992) are just some of the assessment experts who have worked with the refinement of alternative assessment measures. In order to quantify performance-based assessment, middle level teachers are encouraged to precisely list all criteria used to assess performances, portfolios, exhibits, and simulations. This precise list of criteria is currently being referred to as a "rubric." Rubrics are used to guide the evaluator as student performance or products are being assessed. However, rubrics are much more. A rubric acts as a guide to students as they learn; a rubric functions as an advance organizer (Ausubel, 1968) to guide students and help them organize and structure their learning experiences. The rubric should be designed to describe the levels of performance desired. If the teacher desires to maintain a traditional grading format (e.g., A, B, C, D), the rubric can describe the level of performance required to achieve each level of the grading scale. Eggen and Kauchak (1994) have noted that one of the most critical factors involved in using alternative assessment is defining the criteria to be used. It is essential that the criteria be described and well defined. Typically, rubrics are formatted similar to checklists or rating scales to accomplish this clarity.

If alternative assessment is to be consistent for all students, rubrics must be written in such detail that there will be no question as to how well the performance has been completed. A sample rubric is presented in Figure 7.1.

Pate, Homestead, and McGinnis (1993) have suggested certain steps teachers should follow when creating a scoring rubric. The teacher or interdisciplinary team:

1. analyzes the learning task listing all important characteristics including such factors as process, content, mechanics, quality of presentation, sources, and neatness, then
2. develops a scale associated with these expectations starting with

Task Description: Research and prepare a report for class presentation on an aspect of Hispanic culture introduced in class. The research is to be completed by viewing or downloading files via World Wide Web sites, available through Netscape or other Web browsers.

Procedures: Discuss your proposed topic with your teacher; begin your Internet search; have your final topic approved by your teacher; have a conference with your teacher when you have identified five sources; have a conference with your teacher when you have written an outline/draft of your paper. When your draft has been discussed with your teacher, prepare the final report and plan your class presentation.

Evaluation: The final project will be evaluated using the following criteria: quality of research, content, expression of ideas, conventions, and presentation.

Scale:

1=Not yet   Some criteria are not met.

2=Fair   All criteria at least partially met.

3=Okay   All criteria minimally met.

4=Good   Most criteria fully met.

5=Great   All criteria fully met.

1 2 3 4 5	Research:	The paper references at least five WWW sites, using the MLA style citation of electronic sources.
1 2 3 4 5	Content:	The written report is informative and accurate.
1 2 3 4 5	Expression of ideas:	The written report introduces and develops the topic and has an appropriate conclusion.
1 2 3 4 5	Conventions:	The written report uses conventional spelling, punctuation and grammar. Drafts presented show effort in editing the final product.
1 2 3 4 5	Presentation:	The class presentation is informative and accurate, organized, and audible.

Figure 7.1. A sample scoring rubric.

the highest level (i.e., "excellence" or the grade of "A") clearly describing criteria for as many levels as are required, and
3. concludes by analyzing each characteristic or criterion to decide which ones are most important and assigning weight to each criterion accordingly.

Further, Pate, Homestead, and McGinnis (1993) have suggested a format that would be appropriate for most middle level classrooms:

	Criteria 1	Criteria 2	Criteria 3	Criteria 4	Score x Weight	Total
Section I					xn	pts
Section II					xn	pts
Section III					xn	pts
Section IV					xn	pts
Section V					xn	pts
Section VI					xn	pts

In the above rubric format, each section to be evaluated is listed at the left. In the column labeled Criteria 1-4, the students' performance is judged on a scale where 4 would be excellent and 1 would be nonexistent. In the next column, the criterion score (e.g., 1, 2, 3, 4) is multiplied by a weight (n) that the teacher has assigned based on the relative importance of the given section. The product (or total) would be the number of points the student earned for that criterion. For example, if this format were used to assess a student's research paper and if Section I involved judging the reference page, the teacher might assign a weight of three. If a student did an excellent job performing this task (i.e., reaching criteria 4), the teacher would multiply the student's score (4) by the weight of the criteria (3) and award the student 12 points for Section I (See Figure 7.2 for further illustration).

The direction of current middle level education is toward creating a school environment that allows all students to achieve at high levels; middle schools should not trap their students in a curriculum that calls for only minimal competency. Rubrics must reflect state, district, school, and teacher expectations; however, standards must be realistic and challenging to individual students. Alternative assessment should give each student the opportunity to exhibit individual talents through avenues that are best for the particular student being assessed. Therefore, rubrics are to be developed individually with some input from the students. Obviously, this does not mean that thirty students would have to have thirty unique rubrics within the same classroom. Many students will perform similar tasks and be evaluated with the same criteria. However, some students will have special strengths or unique weaknesses that will require some personalization in the development of their assessment rubrics.

Self-Evaluation

A major facet of alternative assessment is student self-evaluation. Kritt (1993) noted that self-assessment is necessary if reflection and metacognitive strategies are going to be part of each student's learning experience. The essential aspect of alternative assessment is to provide an opportunity for students to construct a product or demonstrate a performance and reflect upon it. The authenticity of the learning and the assessment is dependent upon the fact that students reflect upon what they have done. This reflection becomes a self-assessment that makes lifelong learning a possibility. The questions that students ask themselves as they reflect upon their work are the most important part of any inquiry. These questions may include: (1) Why did I answer the question that way?, (2) How can I improve my question?, and (3) What did I not understand?.

Teaching students to perform this type of high level thought and analysis is certainly no easy task. Middle level students should be entering more advanced cognitive development to make such introspection possible; yet, this does not mean that self-assessment comes automatically to middle level students. Teachers must structure learning experiences to elicit and guide such self-analysis.

One strategy a teacher can use with middle level students is group analysis of peers or team members to model the thought processes and questioning techniques required. Teachers using this strategy with middle level students are encouraged to propose open-ended questions to the group to insure that students learn to analyze team members' work without the students perceiving the comments to be personal in nature. Students must learn that critiquing a performance is different than making negative comments about the performer. It is hoped that going through this process under the direction of a teacher will lead individuals to go through the same processes internally when reflecting upon their own work.

Powell (1993) recommends that middle school teachers develop rubrics for the students to use when evaluating their own work. Moreover, Powell suggests three different assessment formats: one for teacher evaluation, one for self-evaluation, and one for team evaluation. It is felt that only through these three unique perspectives can the student get a clear picture of personal performance.

If learning is to be continuous and lifelong in nature, students must learn to reflect on their personal growth toward individual goals. When meeting with middle level students, teachers should not refer solely to teacher assessment of the students' work. Teachers must ask questions that lead students to assess themselves and reflect upon future learning goals. Such questions might be: (1) How did you arrive at that answer?, (2) What could you have said that makes your answer more clear?, and (3) What areas did you study the least? If this process is promoted in the middle level classroom, those students who were less successful when traditional assessment procedures were used have a greater opportunity to realize future success and continuous progress toward their true potential.

Developing Alternative Assessments

There have been several models created for the development of alternative assessment tasks. As one might expect, these models vary somewhat according to the academic area and type of performance to be assessed. Teachers who work in the area of teaching students to write have dealt with these concepts for several years (Perrone, 1991).

An interesting model for the development of alternative assessment tasks has been formulated by Hobar (1994b). This model is quite inclusive and is applicable to many alternative formats. Hobar recommends that the tasks be developed cooperatively by a team of teachers in order to receive the most professional input as possible.

1. Begin with the selection of outcomes based on national, state, and local standards.
2. Brainstorm the concepts, skills, processes, and content students are to perform.
3. Brainstorm the real life context in which students will perform desired outcomes.
4. Develop specific problems for the students to solve framed around unstructured prompts. These are the tasks that will be rated at various levels.
5. Review and revise the tasks in terms of content, task characteristics, scoring, fairness and administration which includes special student needs.
6. Develop scoring rubrics to include: a description of each task, possible student responses, and expected levels of performance.
7. Prepare directions for administrating the task. The directions include such concerns as individual directions, group directions, peer review, and use of materials.

This model and others provide important guidelines to teachers who wish to develop alternative assessment tasks for their middle level students. Middle level teachers who are reflective scholars must study a number of such models and extrapolate data to create a model that works in their classroom. Such a model should be under constant review as more data are collected. With that in mind, such a model is presented here for further review.

1. Begin with a diagnosis of the students giving attention to such factors as individual academic preparation, social backgrounds, developmental levels of preparedness, and other considerations concerning student homogeneity and diversity.
2. List desired outcomes for the unit of study. Attention should be given to national, state and local standards as well as the personal goals for the individual students involved. This must focus on the personal aspects of assessment and instruction if students are all to have success in a challenging, dynamic curriculum.

3. Develop the assessment tasks. The following guidelines should be of assistance in developing the actual tasks.

 • Standards should reflect multiple tasks that can be used for their measurement. If the system is to improve upon traditional assessment systems, students must make choices from options. This is the only avenue to true authenticity.

 • The tasks should be personalized to the middle level students being assessed. Students must have input and ownership if alternative assessment is to be successful. Assessment cannot be seen as something teachers do to students.

 • The tasks should resemble real-life experiences that middle level students can relate to their own lives. If learning is to be continuous and meaningful, this authenticity is necessary in instruction and assessment.

 • The assessment tasks must mesh with the instructional tasks. Middle level teachers cannot teach at one level of understanding and measure students' growth at another level. It should, at times, be difficult to observe the classroom and determine if an instructional or an assessment episode is in progress. Assessment, in fact, must be thought as of as a learning experience.

4. Develop procedures for student self-evaluation. This process is too critical to the overall learning environment to allow it to take place without careful planning and organization.

5. Review and revise the tasks that have been developed. Careful attention should be given to gaining feedback from fellow teachers as well as students.

6. Consider the scoring rubrics to be used. Rubrics must define the tasks completely; teachers must also give attention to possible student responses and how they will be scored during both teacher evaluation and self-assessment (see Figure 7.2).

7. Revise the tasks after they have been used. This formative assessment is based on teacher and student review of the processes.

The process of developing effective alternative assessment tasks is not an easy one. The simplest way to develop assessment is to use the same multiple-choice or true or false items year after year. These items are frequently provided by textbook companies and require little insight or effort on the teacher's behalf. The teacher who wants to become an insightful, reflective scholar must understand that time and effort must be dedicated to professional activity.

Criteria to be assessed	Level 1	Level 2	Level 3	Level 4	Score X Weight	Total
I. Reference page with updated books and articles				x	4 x 3	12
II. Proper grammar is used throughout		x			2 x 3	6
III. Purpose is clearly stated in the instruction				x	4 x 2	8
IV. Proper credits given to material referenced				x		8
V. The essay is written using the prescribed format		x			2 x 3	6
VI. The essay is synthesized in the conclusion using original thoughts		x			2 x 5	10

Figure 7.2. Teacher-developed rating scale.

Learning as Continuous Progress

A discussion of assessment cannot be concluded without some reflection on the continuous nature of learning in an effective middle school. George and Alexander (1993), in their keystone investigations into the nature of effective middle level education, have noted that assessment with immediate feedback is the most critical element to the maintenance of continuous progress in learning. A major goal of middle level education (in fact, all education) is to produce students who are high-level thinkers capable of independent problem solving.

In order to insure that learning is continuous throughout the middle level experience and extends to a lifelong endeavor, teachers must develop assessment techniques that encourage continuous progress, not thwart it. In order to encourage such growth, it is important that teachers be aware of their students' entry levels into the curriculum. Students' individual strengths and weaknesses must be noted in order that instruction and assessment focuses on augmenting those strengths while diminishing the weaknesses.

One of the most important concepts to be understood is that assessment opportunities need to focus on the individual students' strengths. Assessment that focuses on weaknesses will do one thing: create failure. This is why options within alternative assessments are critical. Students need to be able to demonstrate what they know through procedures that are effective for them. As Schurr (1993) noted, some students are left-brain and some are right-brain dominated. Left-brain students need to, at times, demonstrate their keen ability to deal well with structure and convergent thought. Right-brain students, at the same time, need opportunities to solve open-ended problems through divergent thought processes.

Continuous progress can only be realized if all students are challenged in a meaningful, realistic learning environment. Mere performance-based assessment is not enough. After all, minimal competency testing, which has negative affects on the continuous progress of many students, grew out of a belief in performance-based objectives. If continuous progress is to be a reality, standards must go beyond the minimal. All students must be challenged to understand the thought processes behind their behaviors at levels which require all students to stretch to their limits. This can only be accomplished by avoiding superimposing someone else's standards on students in ways that are not meaningful to them. In short, all students must be taken from where they are and challenged to be all they can become. This can only take place where instruction and assessment is personalized, authentic, and challenging in a continuous progress format.

Reporting Progress

There are few activities that give middle level teachers more concern than giving and reporting grades. As noted earlier, the reporting of grades can be critical to the continued progress of middle level students. It is one of the teacher's most critcal responsibilities.

Report cards have long been discussed and analyzed in order to determine the best possible format for reporting grades. The best format is going to be the one that communicates most clearly. A report that does not clearly and honestly indicate student progress so that students and parents can understand both strengths and weaknesses has little value.

Since in large part report cards are for parents, any attempt to refine or revise them must include parents. Kenny and Perry (1994) outline a successful plan to move from a traditional to a performance-based report card system. All along the way, parents were involved in revising and refining the instrument, and educators made adjustments in order to maintain parent support. The situation is not complex, no reporting system can be successful if the clients (in this case parents) are displeased.

Guskey (1994) noted that report cards can reflect three types of learning criteria: Product, Process, and Progress. *Product* criteria focus on the quality of work done when students are involved in tests, projects, portfolios, or other such assessment tasks. *Process* criteria emphasize the effort and thought students put forth to achieve a product. *Progress* criteria focus on the amount of personal improvement an individual student has gained as a result of the learning experiences. Wiggins (1994) suggests that a reporting system must be devised to give parents data related to all three of these criteria. Anything less will be less than honest and fair communication.

Obviously, it is difficult to create a letter grading system that adequately communicates a clear representation of a student's status as it relates to product, process, and progress. A less successful student who puts forth a great deal of effort may get a good grade based on process and possibly even progress. However, as Wiggins notes, such a high grade does not communicate how well that student is doing relative to standards for the grade level. Yet, a poor grade does not adequately reflect what that particular student is doing in the classroom. In order to be fair, a less skilled student should not be graded only in comparison to more successful students. Wiggins has noted that to address this issue it is necessary that report cards reflect grades and scores that are based upon production, process, and progress. Some grades would be comparative while others would not. An example of a reporting system such as this is presented in Figure 7.3.

All student grades must be reported in terms of high standards, and, if all students are to learn continuously and meaningfully, students' grades must also be reported in light of their effort and progress toward personal goals. This is a complex task that will require communication and cooperation among educators and parents. As a result, report cards must be developed over time to meet the unique needs of a middle school and the community it serves.

Science

Student:_____

Grade:_____

D........Demonstrated (85 - 100)

I..........Improving (75 - 84)

ND.....Not Demonstrated (0 - 74)

	D	I	ND			D	I	ND
Interprets data collected	__	__	__	Accurately and constantly collects and records data		__	__	__
Effective use of problem-solving skills	__	__	__					
				Uses patterns to explain past, present, and future events		__	__	__
Uses equipment appropriately to collect data	__	__	__					
				Constructs models to represent real-world objects or events		__	__	__
Draws conclusions based on data and observations	__	__	__					
				Does well on science assessments		__	__	__
Effective use of observational skills	__	__	__					
				Communicates effectively using written expressions		__	__	__
Relates science knowledge to real-world situations	__	__	__					
Follows the scientific method	__	__	__					
Communicates effectively using oral expression	__	__	__					
Knowledgeable in science	__	__	__					
Applies appropriate laboratory skills	__	__	__					

Figure 7.3. A report attending to progress, product, and process for middle school science.

Report Card Day at Quest Middle School

Mr. Boone, the principal of Quest Middle School, feels that he should meet with each instructional team during planning sessions on occasion. Recently, he met with the Lobo team made up of Mr. Adams, Ms. Brown, Ms. Jones, and Mr. Watts. As he entered the meeting, he was delighted to hear that the teachers were discussing assessment of the Lobo students.

Ms. Brown was discussing an article she had recently read on assessment and noted how important she felt it was that a variety of methods might be used to assess student performance. Ms. Jones shared that in her methods class at the university, the students had developed portfolios as part of their assessment. She noted that she was anxious to try this technique with middle level students. Mr. Adams indicated that he was concerned that the new authentic styles of assessment would not fully measure basic skills. He added that he still had some students who made simple multiplication errors and stated that, "I feel I still must give paper and pencil tests to be certain that students are learning basic facts." Mr. Watts added that he had students who were also struggling with too many of his students making low grades. He commented, "I go back and reteach the material, and they still too frequently fail my tests."

"Are we considering such factors as multiple intelligence and learning styles when we test? I sometimes feel I teach one way but then test another way," Ms. Brown said.

"I agree with Ms. Brown. If we are going to insure that all students are to be a success, we must be more authentic in our assessment. I really think portfolios might be an answer to our problems," stated Ms. Jones.

"Now, you all know that I want all of the students to realize success. I have read the materials on multiple intelligence and authentic assessment, and it really makes good sense. However, I know if students are not able to master the basic skills of mathematics it will be almost impossible to function in algebra and geometry, much less to go on to higher levels of mathematics. I guess I am getting confused," said Mr. Adams.

Mr. Boone listened to this discussion and smiled. He knew the Lobo team was beginning to think and question themselves about a critical area of instruction. They did not have the answers, but this group of teachers was on the right path. He felt good things were going to happen. Before leaving, he said, "Remember, there is usually more than one answer to such problems. Part of being a reflective practitioner is the ability to adjust your techniques to the needs of a given situation."

Reflection Questions

1. If you were Ms. Brown or Ms. Jones, what might you say to Mr. Adams to help him with his confusion?
2. Mr. Watts has a problem in his classroom. With a colleague, discuss what you think the problem might be and how it may be solved.
3. How might the teachers of the Lobo team personalize assessment in order to address student differences and encourage more student involvement in the process?
4. Ms. Brown was concerned that her teaching and assessment did not mesh. Give an example of how a middle level teacher might teach something the same way it is assessed.

Summary

In the last several years, middle school educators have concluded that best practice research dictates a new perspective on instruction and assessment. This new perspective is a constructivist viewpoint based on research in cognitive psychology. Those middle level educators who work diligently to formulate authentic, performance-based assessment tasks and scoring rubrics have come to realize that instruction must be performance-based and authentic if it is to meet student needs. That is, instruction and assessment must complement one another to the benefit of all learners. With the goal firmly in place that all students learn in a meaningful and challenging way, middle level educators are promoting continuous progress and life-long learning, in part, through the use of alternative assessment and student self-evaluation. As society's obsession with factual memorization and isolated skill learning is replaced with an emphasis on high-order thinking and problem solving, alternative, authentic assessment tasks will replace the popular emphasis on paper and pencil tests of a minimal competencies orientation. Educators, students, and parents must collaborate to develop new paradigms that will allow all to view assessment and grading in ways, up to this time, used infrequently in the American educational system.

REFERENCES

Armstrong, T. (1994). *Multiple intelligences in the classroom.* Alexandria, VA: Association for Supervision and Curriculum Development.

Atkinson, J.W. (1964). *An introduction to motivation.* Princeton, NJ: D. VanNostrand.

Ausubel, D. (1968). *Educational psychology: A cognitive view.* New York: Holt, Rhinehart, and Winston.

Carnegie Council on Adolescent Development. (1989). *Turning points: Preparing American youth for the 21st century.* Washington, D.C.: Carnegie Corporation.

Case, S.H. (1994). "Will mandating portfolios undermine their value?" *Educational Leadership,* 52(2), 46-47.

Cheek, D.W. (1993). "Plain talk about alternative assessment." *Middle School Journal,* Vol. 25-2, pp. 6-10.

Clements, B., & Battista, M. (1990). "Constructivist learning and teaching." *Arithemetic Teacher,* 38, 34-35.

Eggen, P., & Kauchak, D. (1994). *Educational psychology: Classroom connections.* New York: Merrill.

Gardner, H. (1993). *Frames and mind: The theory of multiple intelligences.* New York: Basic Books.

George, P.S., & Alexander, W. (1993). *The exemplary middle school.* Fort Worth, TX: Harcourt Brace.

Guskey, T.R. (1994). "Making the grade: What benefits the student?" *Educational Leadership.* Vol. 52-2, pp. 14-20.

Hamm, M., & Adams, D. (1991). "Portfolio: It's not just for artists anymore." *The Science Teacher,* 55(5), 18-21.

Hobar, N. (1994a). Alternative assessment: Mirroring quality instruction. A workshop for Horry County Schools. Cockeysville, MD: Workforce 2000 Inc.

Hobar, N. (1994b). Alternative assessment: Performance assessment task development. A workshop for Horry County Schools. Cockeysville, MD: Workforce 2000 Inc.

Johnson, P.H. (1992). *Constructive evaluation of literate activity.* New York: Longman.

Jones, M.G. (1994). "Performance-based assessment in middle school science." *Middle School Journal,* Vol. 25-4, pp. 35-38.

Kenny, E., & Perry S. (1994). "Talking with parents about performance-based report cards." *Educational Leadership,* Vol. 52-2, pp 24-27.

Kilpatrick, W.H. (1918). *The project method.* New York: Teachers College, Columbia University.

Kritt, D. (1993). "Authenticity, reflection, and self-evaluation in alternative assessment." *Middle School Journal.,* Vol. 25-2, pp. 43-45.

Kulm, G., & Malcom, S. (Eds.). (1991). *Science assessment in the service of reform.* Washington, D.C.: American Association for the Advancement of Science.

Lewin, K. (1942). Field theory of learning. In N.B. Henry (Ed.), *The psychology of learning. The forty-first yearbook of the National Society for the Study of Education, Part II* (pp. 215-242). Chicago: University of Chicago Press.

Messick, S. (1992). Validity. In M.C. Alkin (Ed.), *Encyclopedia of educational research* (Vol. IV: 1487-1495). New York: Macmillan.

Ostlund, K.L. (1992). *Science process skills: Assessing hands-on student performance.* Menlo Park, CA: Addison-Wesley.

Pate, P.E., Homestead, E., & McGinnis, K. (1993). "Designing rubrics for authentic assessment." *Middle School Journal,* Vol. 25-2, pp. 25-27.

Perrone, V. (1991). *A letter to teachers.* San Francisco: Jossey-Bass.

Powell, J.C. (1993). "What does it mean to have authentic assessment?" *Middle School Journal,* Vol. 25-2, pp. 36-41.

Romberg, T.A. (Ed.). (1992). *Mathematics assessment and evaluation: Imperatives for mathematics educators.* Albany, NY: State University of New York Press.

Rotter, J. (1966). "Generalized expectancies for internal versus external control of reinforcement." *Psychological Monographs,* (No. 609).

Schurr, S. (1993). *The abc's of evaluation: 26 alternative ways to assess student progress.* Columbus, OH: National Middle School Association.

Shavelson, R.J., Gao, X., & Baxter, G.P. (1993). *Sampling variability of performance assessments.* Los Angeles, CA: University of California Center for Research on Evaluation, Standards and Student Testing, Technical Report 361.

Watson, B., & Konicek, R. (1990). "Teaching for conceptual change: Confronting children's experience." *Phi Delta Kappan,* 65, 419-421.

Weiner, B. (1985). *Human motivation.* New York: Springer-Verlag.

Wiggins, G. (1994). Toward better report cards. *Educational Leadership.* Vol. 52-2, pp. 28-37.

Chapter 8

MIDDLE SCHOOLS:
A VIEW OF THE FUTURE

As this text has suggested, considerable change has taken place throughout the history of the middle level movement. And yet, it could well be argued that the most critical period of the development of this important concept is yet to come. While there is little doubt that the middle school has all but replaced the junior high school as the prominent organizational and instructional design in the education of young people between the elementary and high school years, it also could be argued that in some instances, sadly many instances, this change has occurred in name only. The middle school movement stands in a fragile state in terms of its further advancement forward to a next, most significant developmental level.

John C. Lundt (1996), former middle school teacher, administrator, and futurist, has identified a remarkable potential for the middle school in serving the needs of early adolescents and also as a vehicle to spirit and lead change in the entire K–12 curriculum. Lundt notes that in the analysis of the middle school one can observe many similarities between the characteristics of effective middle school educators and futurists themselves. These characteristics serve as the basis and underpinning for the future growth and evolution of the middle school. Figure 8.1 lists those characteristics shared by both futurists and middle level educators.

The exploration and study of these similarities gives rise to an optimism for the future. To be fully realized, this future must be grounded in the middle school philosophy itself which calls for a dynamic and developing rather than static design. Middle schools must represent environments adaptive to the changes in and the needs of early adolescents. They must adapt to changes in technology along with dynamics in the American society itself. The middle school philosophy, as analyzed by Lundt, is focused more on preparing students for the future than maintaining the traditions of the past. This is a major strength of the philosophy.

---

1. Belief in the potential of humanity;

2. Forward-looking, dynamic and programmatic philosophies;

3. Willingness to explore the unknown;

4. Seeing issues as interdisciplinary;

5. Collaborating to solve problems;

6. Focus on a future-oriented skills curriculum;

7. Clear thinking, evaluation, and analysis;

8. Understanding the environment;

9. Accessing information and solving for the unknown;

10. Personal competence through lifelong learning; and

11. Social diversity and global citizenship.

Figure 8.1. Characteristics showed by middle level educators and futurists as conceptualized by Lundt.

However, a total optimism at this time seems impossible. It is the traditions of the past, or perhaps present as well, which cause some concern for the maintenance of momentum in the further development of the middle school concept. An analysis of the future of the middle school must of necessity consider a number of critical elements that potentially work against its continued positive evolution. Approached successfully, the addressing of these elements might well spell the difference between the continuation of a vibrant, exciting, and effective movement in the education of young adolescents or the plateauing of the same. Those critical elements selected for special attention and analysis here are:

1. The Research Base for Understanding the Needs and Characteristics of Early adolescents
2. Middle Level Teacher Preparation and Certification
3. Societal Goals for Student Academic Performance
4. Restructuring the Middle Level School as a Community of Learners
5. Developing a True K–12 Curriculum

The Research Base for Understanding the Needs and Characteristics of Early Adolescents

Perhaps because of the ongoing dynamic change in society itself, the challenges faced by educators at the middle level continue to grow and grow in each passing year. Research on child development or on the development of the transescent learner, while growing steadily as an important body of knowledge, remains in need of greater specificity, depth, and breadth for this information to be of its optimal benefit to the middle school teacher in the classroom. Indeed, information on the learning challenges and learning exceptionalities that middle school youngsters face must be further explored. Too, strategies to link this information to classroom practice remain all too limited and traditional.

Clark and Clark (1994) have described early adolescence as a unique period of life when children begin the complex process of making the transition to adulthood. One might argue, however, that one of the major challenges faced by middle school educators is that many middle school students actually begin this transition to adulthood long before they enter early adolescence. Indeed, a great part of the complex diversity of the middle school is brought on because so many students at so many different developmental levels are all brought together at the same time in the same learning environment. As discussed in Chapter 3, the unique developmental period of the middle school years encompasses physical, emotional, and intellectual development. Early adolescence (which traditionally is considered to include youth from ages 10 to 14) is strongly characterized as a time of diversity and change. Clark and Clark (1994) noted the following:

. . .[T]his change and diversity, which often is not well understood by parents and educators, frequently leads to anxiety and misunderstandings among young adolescents, their peers, and the significant adults who work with them daily. Understanding young adolescents, their developmental needs and characteristics, is of prime importance for middle level educators. (p. 61)

Kramer (1992) adds yet another and perhaps more important dimension to the focus on the characteristics and needs of the early adolescent in bringing attention closer to actual classroom practice itself. This dimension is with respect to how much or how well educators actually apply and utilize what they know. Many would argue not nearly enough. Kramer comments that young adolescents should not be seen as passive recipients of teaching, no matter how uninvolved they may appear to be in the classroom. Students need to think about school and school life. Further, the agreement is quite strong that the perceptions that students hold about school influence both their own achievement as well as the instructional behaviors of teachers. Weinstein (1989) has observed that the differences in how students perceive school may be the missing link between instructional strategies and achievement outcomes. This may explain why some students are more successful in certain specific content areas than in others. Regrettably, this is an area worthy of much greater attention than it now receives from middle level educators and must receive greater attention in the future.

In their attention to the importance of developing an understanding of the early adolescent and developmental needs, Clark and Clark provide a valuable listing of essential characteristics of the middle school which should be present if the school is to be truly responsive to the needs of the early adolescent learner. These characteristics are listed in Figure 8.2 in a checklist format in order to provide a means of reviewing the effectiveness of the middle school. This checklist is of value when evaluating the learning environments of middle schools moving into the twenty-first century.

Clark and Clark conclude by stating that the answer to these questions can be used as a foundation upon which a responsive middle level school can be built. One must give serious consideration as to whether what is known is what needs to be known and whether or not what is known is actually applied by middle level educators. It is likely the case that (1) much more needs to be known than what is known, and (2) middle level educators themselves need to give much greater attention to applying what is known in the classroom and in the school to improve their own instructional practice if middle level education in the future is to meet its maximum potential.

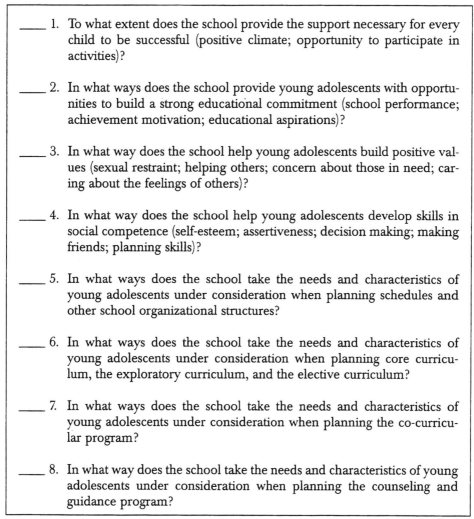

_____ 1. To what extent does the school provide the support necessary for every child to be successful (positive climate; opportunity to participate in activities)?

_____ 2. In what ways does the school provide young adolescents with opportunities to build a strong educational commitment (school performance; achievement motivation; educational aspirations)?

_____ 3. In what way does the school help young adolescents build positive values (sexual restraint; helping others; concern about those in need; caring about the feelings of others)?

_____ 4. In what way does the school help young adolescents develop skills in social competence (self-esteem; assertiveness; decision making; making friends; planning skills)?

_____ 5. In what ways does the school take the needs and characteristics of young adolescents under consideration when planning schedules and other school organizational structures?

_____ 6. In what ways does the school take the needs and characteristics of young adolescents under consideration when planning core curriculum, the exploratory curriculum, and the elective curriculum?

_____ 7. In what ways does the school take the needs and characteristics of young adolescents under consideration when planning the co-curricular program?

_____ 8. In what way does the school take the needs and characteristics of young adolescents under consideration when planning the counseling and guidance program?

Figure 8.2. Checklist to evaluate middle school environments now and in the future based on Clark and Clark (1994).

Middle Level Teacher Preparation and Certification

As discussed in Chapter 1, middle level professionals along with their professional associations have argued for years the need for more specialized preparation for those teachers, and administrators, who work at the middle level. The argument is indeed a powerful one resting on the position that if positive change in middle level education is truly what is desired that this can only come about through the work of talented, committed, and informed middle level educators. While this position may be defensible, Scales (1994) has noted that although middle schools have become the most common and fastest-growing form of school for young adolescents, previous research has shown that only a fifth of middle grades teachers undergo any special preparation for teaching at the middle level. Growth in specialized training for middle grades educators is moving forward at a slow pace at best.

In general, those professionals currently working in middle level schools have arrived there more secondarily than primarily in terms of their initial preparation for a career in teaching early adolescents. Many current middle level teachers have arrived through a secondary education background that has been strongly subject matter focused and desire to work in a school setting where this is emphasized (Bedwell and Hunt, 1997). Many others have arrived through an elementary education background which, by comparison, is often much more student-centered. Many of these educators, like the secondary-trained middle level teachers, desire to relocate to an instructional setting more in line with their initial preparatory work, which is, in this instance, an elementary school. As Erb (1995) has noted, the ideal middle level teacher in the future will provide student-centeredness while, at the same time, providing high levels of content preparation.

Few states across the country actually mandate specialized, initial teacher preparation or certification for those professionals accepting positions in the middle grades. And, though such preparation is offered in some states, the definition of the middle grades seems to differ from state to state. McEwin (1992) has observed the following:

> [A] perennial roadblock to excellence in middle level education is the practice of staffing middle level schools with teachers and other professional personnel who have no special preparation for teaching or working in other ways with young adolescents. Teacher preparation institutions, state departments of education, and the profession itself have largely failed to recognize the importance of designing specific preparation programs for middle level teachers and other professionals who are responsible for the education and welfare of these youth. (p. 369).

McEwin concludes by noting that, because of this, many middle level educators are frankly unprepared for the tasks of understanding, working with, and effectively educating young adolescents.

This strong statement and indictment is worthy of some analysis as it clearly is the educator work force that will, in the future, move the profession forward or hold it back, whichever the case may be. While legislation may be passed and mandates handed down, it is the educator in the school and the classroom who will ultimately make the difference in terms of the quality of learning experiences provided. Indeed, few middle level educators have received initial, specialized preparation for the work that they do. Currently only a few states across the United States require specialized preparation of those receiving initial teaching certificates for the middle grades. Though many states offer what is popularly termed the endorsement in the middle grades, due to the common practice of overlapping grade spans for certificates in many states and the generally limited requirements in place for adding on additional certifying areas, the endorsement provides only a modest step forward for specialized teacher preparation. It is a fair connection to make in tying together the challenges of developing a research base for understanding the needs and characteristics of middle level students discussed previously with the challenges of middle level teacher preparation and certification discussed here. If a body of knowledge associated with understanding the middle level learner is to have its greatest meaning, it can only have this meaning through its application by an informed educator or administrator who sees and understands it for what it is and is committed and dedicated to the improvement of educational practices in the middle grades through its use.

Though one would be hardpressed to state that specialized middle level preparation provides a guarantee of future effective and successful teaching, it might well be argued that the absence of such preparation clearly diminishes this possibility. Allen, Splittgerber, and Manning (1993) have provided a helpful listing of eighteen important qualities and characteristics of effective middle level teachers. Careful attention to this listing will reveal that many of these qualities and characteristics are quite personal rather than being specifically skill-related. In this, the analysis must include the observation that those teachers who are effective in the middle level have certain personal qualities and characteristics that make them especially suitable for successful work with this age population. Whether or not such personal qualities can be taught by one person to another remains a much debated point within the profession. Those qualities which have received specific attention from these authors are listed in Figure 8.3.

1. Positive Self-Concept

2. Warmth

3. Optimism

4. Enthusiasm

5. Flexibility

6. Spontaneity

7. Acceptance of Students

8. Awareness of Developmental Needs

9. Knowledge of Subject Matter

10. Variety of Instructional Activities and Materials

11. Instructional Planning

12. Monitoring of Learning

13. Utilization of Concrete Materials and Focused Learning Strategies

14. Variety of Questions

15. Indirect Teaching

16. "Success-Building" Behavior

17. Diagnosis of Learner Needs and Prescription of Individualized Instruction

18. Listener

Figure 8.3. Important qualities for middle level teachers noted by Allen, Splittgerber and Manning (1993).

This listing of eighteen qualities of effective middle level teachers clearly deserves special attention. Whether gained through specialized preparation experiences or through more general preparation experiences, they represent qualities traditionally associated with teachers who are effective at the middle level. It is worth pointing out, however, that when the discussion of the value of specialized preparation for future teachers at the middle level is discussed and such qualities are included in the discussion, it is invariably the case that the argument is also made for the importance of these qualities being present in teachers at all levels. Whether or not they are best gained through specialized preparation or not remains a much debated point. This ongoing debate notwithstanding, the position is taken here that specialized preparation for middle grades professionals is essential not only to improving practice in classrooms today but in taking the development of the middle level concept forward into the future.

Societal Goals for Student Academic Performance

One of the most significant challenges facing the advancement of the middle school concept is the ongoing lack of uniform agreement as to just what should be accomplished at the middle level in terms of student performance. This lack of agreement clearly poses a major challenge to the implementation, in part or totally, of the middle school philosophy. While middle schools have been in existence for years, the debate continues over the importance of certain goals. For example, what constitutes the best preparation for high school, the best preparation for life after high school, and even the best preparation for next week or next month? Indeed, this debate seems even to be taking place among the present middle grades work force itself often being represented in the separation of views of teachers coming to the middle grades from an elementary education as opposed to a secondary education background.

In his 1997 State of the Union address, President Clinton reinforced the complexities seen in the challenges faced by our American education system. Called for in the address are the following:

1. all children reading by age 8,
2. every 12-year-old able to log on to the Internet, and
3. every 18-year-old able to go to college.

The charge to increase accountability for teacher and student performance presents a serious challenge to middle level schooling and its emphasis on the needs of the whole child, not just those which are academic. One would be hard-pressed to speak out against the worthwhileness of those goals identified in the president's address. And yet, there are children in schools today who may well find achieving these standards a near impossibility and who, individually, possess needs, personal as well as academic, different from those mentioned here. Those youngsters at the middle level, in particular due to the transitional nature of their lives, have specific needs not typically categorized as being academic. Arnold (1997) has noted that:

> Owing to developmental diversity and individual differences, holding high expectations can seldom mean having the same expectations for all students. A developmentally responsive approach to teaching and learning necessarily implies one that is differentiated and personalized, taking into account individual needs, interests, and abilities. (p. 52)

As with the president's remarks in the State of the Union address, it is difficult to argue with the importance of this view as well. While not necessarily at odds with one another, they do suggest differences of perspective as to what should be accomplished under the banner of standards and excellence. These differences must be addressed as the future of the middle school continues to unfold.

From their research in the late 1980s, Alexander and McEwin (1989) identified six desirable characteristics to be found in good middle schools which would be needed to address the needs of the whole child. These characteristics are as follows:

1. an interdisciplinary organization with a flexible day schedule,
2. an adequate guidance program, including a teacher advisory plan,
3. a full-scale exploratory program,
4. curriculum provision for such broad goals and curriculum areas as personal development, continued learning skills, and basic knowledge areas,
5. varied and effective methodology for the age group, and
6. continued orientation and articulation for students, parents, and teachers.

Clearly not one of these characteristics is incompatible with the current accountability movement and continued demand for higher performance standards. Together, however, they do seek to embrace a school design and philosophy that attempts to address much, much more than cognitive gain. In doing this, and in considering the traditional length of school day and school year, choices have to be made with respect to what aspect of the school will receive what level of attention. It is doubtful that all things can be accomplished at equally high levels. The debate must continue as to just what focus education at the middle will take to help ensure student success and sound development at that level which will reinforce a foundation for greater success and positive development thereafter.

Reinforcing this point, George and Alexander (1993) identify ten characteristics of middle schools that they would classify as exemplary. While the presence of these characteristics should not be argued as elements working against high academic achievement, they do help to reinforce the overall complexity of the world of the middle school and the breadth of demands being placed upon it. This list of characteristics could be used as a guide for developing middle schools for the future. Those characteristics selected by George and Alexander are found in Figure 8.4.

Even with heightened debate about a national curriculum, and frequently a national teacher certification system, there will remain disagreement over what can and should be accomplished at the middle school level. Those at the high school level have certain expectations for those students coming to them from the middle grades just as those at the middle level have certain expectations for their own students coming from elementary schools. Teachers frequently receive mixed signals from the world around them as to just where their greatest energies should be placed, the students' personal or academic development, creating an unhealthy situation resulting in students themselves getting mixed signals from teachers, school administrators, parents, and friends. For middle level education to maintain, or in some schools gain, its positive momentum for the future, the question of balance among academic, societal and personal expectations must receive further exploration. In the past, middle level educators have had a tendency to stress some areas to the detriment of others (see Chapter 1). Future progress depends on a clear definition of purpose.

Restructuring the Middle Level School as a Community of Learners

A significant challenge which exists today and will continue into the future is the basic acceptance of the middle school philosophy (or concept) which sees the school as a community of learners brought

1. The primary focus of the middle school should be on the learners in these schools, usually about ages 10 - 14 and having the many unique needs and interests of early adolescents.

2. Middle school planning should recognize as fully as possible historical factors in the development of this school and level, and its rationale and desired characteristics.

3. The middle school curriculum should include provision for three basic domains or areas: personal development, continued learning skills, and basic knowledge areas.

4. Current information from theory, practice, and research as to instructional methodology should be utilized fully in every middle school and classroom.

5. The middle school should provide an adequate guidance program, with special attention to types and plans of teacher-based guidance.

6. An interdisciplinary team organization is characteristic of an effective middle school.

7. Exemplary middle schools can and should utilize appropriate means of grouping students.

8. Flexible scheduling and various types of space utilization should be planned for each school for its maximum effectiveness.

9. Schools should be evaluated on the extent to which they attain goals related to the needs of the students who are their clients.

10. Sound leadership is essential. Schools take on the characteristics of their leaders.

Figure 8.4. Ten characteristics of exemplary middle schools to guide future development as proposed by George and Alexander.

together to meet the needs of early adolescents. Unlike the primary and elementary levels that focus more on the learner as an individual and the high school level which seems to have historically had its focus on the communication of subject matter, the middle school holds a very special philosophy that depends on, and even encourages, individuals working together for the good of the whole as well as the good of the individual. Sue Swaim (1996), executive director of the National

Middle School Association, has identified the following six character-istics as a foundation that should be in place for the development of sound middle school programming:

1. educators committed to young adolescents,
2. a shared vision,
3. high expectations for all,
4. an adult advocate for every student,
5. family and community partnerships, and
6. a positive school climate.

The middle school concept truly has broad characteristics and appli-cations.

Allen, Splittgerber, and Manning (1993) note that the middle school, at its best, is a school that designs its curriculum, instruction, organization, and support services to respond to the unique develop-mental needs of young adolescents. The school builds from a foun-dation of student-centeredness that places learners first and enables them to feel safe, secure and successful while providing a balanced curriculum that prepares students to function effectively in society both as young adolescents and later as adults. The middle school, in its totality, is generally expected to be all things to all students, friend to the lonely while, at the same time, providing an intellectual chal-lenge to all students to reach their personal capabilities.

Without question the middle school is challenged from both ends of the school continuum as well as the society at large. It is expected to receive young learners from the elementary grades and successful-ly assist them in the transition from a childhood setting where teach-ers traditionally take great responsibility for a student's learning and personal welfare, work with them for approximately three years, and send them on to the high school setting where learning remains typi-cally subject matter focused with students being expected to accept major responsibility for their own learning. The in-between years, the middle school years, face the tremendous challenge of assisting early adolescents in seeing themselves as worthy, capable, and respected individuals while, at the same time, developing their cognitive skills in traditional school subjects. To date this has proven to be quite a sig-nificant challenge and one, regrettably, that remains little appreciated and under supported.

Many middle school observers see the middle school from the outside in as a grand experiment attempting to embrace the best of elementary education in terms of its focus on child nurturing and the best of high school education in terms of its attention to excellence in subject matter mastery. Such observers likely would conclude that both populations, those at the elementary level and those at the high school level, are unsatisfied with the results that they are seeing. This dissatisfaction in large part rests with the inability, up to this point, for those in the middle to successfully communicate their philosophy, perhaps mission, to these other levels of education. It also should be noted that those outside of the education profession too have difficulty at times in accepting the complex role assumed by the modern middle school. Until this communication can be completed successfully, or at least improved greatly, and until there is much broader support than there is at present from both educator and parent groups, the challenges facing the future of middle grades education will only continue to increase and expand in their complexity. Given the ever-increasing pressure to raise academic standards, most often measured through standardized tests, the middle school presently faces an enormous challenge to retain its focus on a community of learners pursuing both personal and intellectual development.

Developing a True K–12 Curriculum

The challenge of developing a true K–12 curriculum has clear implications for the future of middle school education, and, yet, it is argued here that presently there is not such a curriculum in place. This is in spite of the fact that the phrasing "K–12 curriculum" is a commonly used one. While this is the case, it is more arguable that the American education system is in reality characterized by a series of curriculum sets. Curricula typically has too often been defined as building-level curricula rather than as a designed scope and sequence flowing from grade level to grade level (i.e., grade K to grade 12). Presently it is more commonly and accurately the case that the schooling system is defined by a primary grades, an elementary grades, a middle grades and a high school grades curriculum, rather than a K-12 curriculum.

The result of the absence of a K–12 curriculum is no more devastating for the middle school than for any other school level in the continuum. As this text focuses on the middle grades, however, it is this level that will receive attention here. The absence of a true K–12 curriculum takes its toll on teachers, administrators, parents, as well as the students themselves. The absence of such a curriculum results in a disjointed system of education lacking in the most sound articulation and communication possible from level to level. In a more common vernacular, it is the case that the right hand does not always know what the left hand is doing. With the hands not interlocking as well as they might, and must, the students in the middle are those who suffer the most from this situation.

In exploring curriculum development, articulation is a key principle that must be embraced and which is too frequently lacking in most K–12 curriculum designs. It is naturally the case that certain primary schools send their students to certain elementary schools who in turn send their students to certain middle level schools. In the end these certain middle level schools send their "graduates" on to certain high schools thus completing the K–12 continuum of grade level progression. Throughout the evolution of this continuum, however, one will find little significant and sustained interaction between the faculties of each of the individual schools involved and little more from their administrators. In the end, the curriculum offered along the continuum is far more school-based than interlocking, building from one level to the next in both its design and rigor. This is truly a sad commentary as it is the young learner, progressing from school curriculum to school curriculum, who is faced with inconsistencies, challenges where incomplete preparation has taken place, and a sustained environment of uncertainty requiring unnecessary anxiety and frustration in adjusting from unfamiliar setting to unfamiliar setting. The end result of all of this is frequently a young learner performing below capacity but also coping with inner doubt and a lack of motivation. While the reality of this lack of a K–12 curriculum as previously noted is likely no more harmful at the middle level than at any other, it is felt especially hard in the middle as so much significant change has taken place at this level over the last fifty years and as the middle years are so significant to young learners. The threat to the future of middle level education because of this is both real and powerful. Those working in the middle face a significant challenge to develop more successful interlocking components with both those at the elementary and high school settings.

Content Trends for the Future

Given the concerns identified about finding a balance between affective and cognitive components of the curriculum, middle level teachers will face changes in the scope, sequence, and format of the curriculum. As discussed earlier, demands on the school to develop a curriculum that satisfies the academic, societal, and developmental needs of students are significant. Moreover, these demands may be harder to predict than they were in the past. For example, students now face a much more uncertain future as three-fourths of the population in the twenty-first century will be producing goods and offering services not now in existence (Shepherd and Ragan, 1992). Because of this, all educators will need to be even more flexible and adaptable to societal change and demands on school curriculum than ever before.

In an address to middle level teacher educators in South Carolina, Lounsbury (1996) discussed what he predicted to be the major content trends for middle level schools in the decades to come. Figure 8.5 lists these trends.

•   Integrated curricula
•   Authentic assessment
•   Concern for life skills
•   Service learning and community involvement
•   Character education
•   Technological training

Figure 8.5. Lounsbury's trends guiding the development of future middle level curriculum.

Curriculum integration will allow more constructive learning. Integrated curriculum alone, however, does not guarantee excellence. First, the integrated curriculum cannot be effective unless all students, regardless of ability or style of learning, are challenged to reach their optimal level of learning. Second, as discussed earlier, the curriculum must also have adequate vertical organization; that is, the content must be developed over time (e.g., K–12) so that appropriate content can be presented from a simple format to a more complex one (Horn, 1997).

Assessment (as discussed in Chapter 7) is changing and is likely to continue to change to more authentic methods of measurement. In the future, middle school students will be evaluated more through the use of such devices as journals, portfolios, and grading rubrics which emphasize self-evaluation and reflection (Lounsbury, 1996). Again, the emphasis is upon becoming more realistically related to the way middle level students learn, not upon becoming less challenging.

Life skills are procedural skills and are not taught as isolated facts. These are lifelong skills which will allow students to live productively in the future. For example, the skills associated with data gathering, problem solving, reasoning, information processing, and interpersonal relations are life skills of the future. Schools must change in the way these skills are conceptualized; schools were designed for the industrial age, have passed through the information age, and have entered the technological age.

The separation of school and community life hopefully will lessen in the future. Since the days of the early American Progressive movement and even before, insightful educators have understood the importance of expanding the school to include the community in the learning environment (Dewey, 1902). It is the nature of middle level students to have community concern. The job of educators is to make certain that community service learning is tied to the goals and objectives of the academic program. (See Chapter 4 for a detailed discussion of the relationships between the school and community.)

Schools in the future clearly cannot afford to be morally neutral. Changes in society due to the technological age and other influences have made it possible for students to receive a wide variety of very confusing and difficult to process information. Middle level students who are searching for answers about themselves and life in general will need more help and guidance than most students if they are to become happy, productive citizens. Unfortunately, it is extremely difficult to agree on what should be taught and how it should be presented when reflecting on morals and character education in the middle school curriculum (Kohn, 1997; Doyle, 1997).

Throughout this book, the critical need for students to become computer literate and confident in their use of technology has been stressed. This will be even more critical in the decades to come. Students will need to learn how to critically reflect on and interpret the vast amounts of new information that will be provided to them. Students of the future must come to a point where they see computers and other technological advancements as tools for learning much like earlier students saw, for example, books, periodicals, or atlases.

If the middle level reform movement is to prosper in the future, strong leadership (especially from superintendents) will be necessary (Lipsitz, Mizell, Jackson, and Austin, 1997). Too frequently, school systems have had leadership which changed too often and seldom has had a sound philosophical and operational understanding of middle level education. The problems in leadership seem to be highly related to a lack of intensity and focus which has diminished the impact of middle level reform in many school districts.

If the middle level movement is to progress in the future, reform cannot be guided by guesswork and emotion. Future decisions must be based on sound data collection, especially through longitudinal studies such as the Middle Start Initiative which was begun in 1993 by the Kellogg Foundation (Austin, 1997).

Summary

In this chapter, a view of the future of middle level education has been presented which, while optimistic, recognizes some of the possible dangers that could impede the progress of student-centered middle schools. Before the onset of the technology age, a clear understanding of our past and present laid an adequate foundation for predicting the future. Today, those predictions are more difficult to make; however, selected concepts and perspectives, often quite global in nature through necessity, on the direction middle schools are apt to take in the decades to come have been identified. One thing seems certain, the future of our country, actually the entire world, hinges upon the ability of educators to provide high-quality education to tomorrow's youth. While much can be done to improve American education at all levels, the current focus on the future development of education at the middle level gives rise to optimism as the student-centered emphasis, at the heart of the middle level philosophy, guides this development into the future.

REFERENCES

Alexander, W.M., & McEwin, C.K. (1989). *Schools in the middle: Status and progress.* Columbus, Ohio: National Middle School Association.

Allen, H.A., Splittgerber, F.L., & Manning, M. L. (1993). *Teaching and learning in the middle level school.* New York: Macmillan Publishing Company.

Arnold, J. (1997). "High expectations for all: Perspective and practice." *Middle School Journal* 28, (3) 51-53.

Austin, L.M. (1997). "The middle start initiative." *Kappan,* 78, (7) 530-531.

Bedwell, L. & Hunt, G. (1997). "Perception of a middle level field experience by pre-service high school teachers." *The High School Journal,* 80, (3) 210-214.

Clark, S. N., & Clark, D. C. (1994). *Restoring the middle level school.* Albany, New York: State University of New York Press.

Dewey, J. (1902). *The child and the curriculum.* Chicago: The University of Chicago Press.

Doyle, D.P. (1997). "Education and character: A conservative view." *Kappan,* 78, (6) 429-439.

Erb, T. (1995). "It's academics, stupid! If you care enough." *Middle School Journal,* 27, (1) 2.

George, P., & Alexander, W. (1993). *The exemplary middle school.* New York: Harcourt Brace College Publishers.

Horn, R.V. (1997). "Bad ideas: Technology integration and job-entry skills." *Kappan,* 78, (5) 417-418.

Kohn, A. (1997). "How not to teach values: A critical look at character education." *Kappan,* 78, (6) 440-443.

Kramer, L.R. (1992). "Young adolescents' perceptions of school." In J.L. Irvin (Ed.), *Transforming middle level education* (pp. 28-45). Boston: Allyn and Bacon.

Lipsitz, J., Mizell, M.H., Jackson, A.W., & Austin, L.M. (1997). "Speaking with one voice: A manifesto for middle-grades reform." Kappan, 78, (7) 533-540.

Lounsbury, J. (1996, October). *Major trends in education and their implications for teacher education.* Paper presented at the meeting of Southeastern Association of Teacher Educators, Charleston, South Carolina.

Lundt, J.C. (1996). "Curriculum for the future: A futurist looks at middle school." *Middle School Journal,* 27, (5) 29-34.

McEwin, C.K. (1992). "Middle Level Teacher Preparation and Certification." In *Transforming middle level education: Perspectives and possibilities* by Judith L. Irvin (Ed.). Needham Heights, MA: Allyn and Bacon.

Scales, P. (1994) "Strengthening middle grade teacher preparation programs." *Middle School Journal,* 26, (1) 59-65.

Shepherd, G.D., & Ragan, W.B. (1992). *Modern elementary curriculum.* New York: Harcourt Brace Jovanovich.

Swaim, S. (1996). "Developing and implementing a 'Shared Vision." *Middle School Journal,* 28, (1) 54-57.

Weinstein, R.S. (1989). "Perceptions of classroom processes and student motivation: Children's views of self-fulfilling prophecies." In *Transforming middle level education: Perspectives and possibilities* by Judith L. Irvin (Ed.). Needham Heights, MA: Allyn and Bacon.

INDEX